SOCIAL PERSPECTIVES ON MOBILITY

Social Perspectives on Mobility

Edited by

THYRA UTH THOMSEN
Copenhagen Business School, Denmark

LISE DREWES NIELSEN
Roskilde University, Denmark

HENRIK GUDMUNDSSON
National Environmental Research Institute, Denmark

ASHGATE

Published by
Ashgate Publishing Limited
Gower House
Croft Road
Aldershot
Hampshire GU11 3HR
England

Ashgate Publishing Company
Suite 420
101 Cherry Street
Burlington, VT05401-4405
USA

Ashgate website: http://www.ashgate.com

British Library Cataloguing in Publication Data
Social perspectives on mobility. - (Transport and society)
    1.Transportation - Social aspects 2.Transportation -
    Government policy
    I.Thomsen, Thyra Uth II. Nielsen, Lise Drewes
    III.Gudmundsson, Henrik
    388

Library of Congress Cataloging-in-Publication Data
Social perspectives on mobility / edited by Thyra Uth Thomsen, Lise Drewes Nielsen, and Henrik Gudmundsson.
        p. cm. -- (Transport and society)
    Includes bibliographical references and index.
    ISBN 0-7546-4456-1
    1. Transportation--Social aspects--Research. 2. Transportation--Research--Scandinavia. I. Thomsen, Thyra Uth. II. Nielsen, Lise Drewes. III. Gudmundsson, Henrik. IV. Series.

    HE192.5.S63 2005
    303.48'32--dc22

2005003555

ISBN 0 7546 4456 1

Printed and bound in Great Britain by MPG Books Ltd, Bodmin, Cornwall

Contents

PART III: MOBILITY AS A POLICY THEME

List of Contributors

Maria Figueroa is a PhD Student at the Department of Environment, Technology and Social Studies, Roskilde University. She holds two M.Sc.s in City and Regional Planning and Energy and Resources from University of California at Berkeley. Her interests include questions concerning mobility, democracy environmental planning and the formation of public spheres. Her work experience lies in the area of transport, energy and environment in developing countries.

Malene Freudendal-Pedersen holds an M.Sc. in Environmental Planning from Roskilde University, where she is also currently writing her doctoral thesis that examines the role of the public transport system in modern, everyday life. The research is theoretically focused on space, time, individuality and ambivalences and examines the strong relations between mobility and modernity. Her interests are to develop ideas on how to combine understandings of mobility with public participation in planning processes.

Henrik Gudmundsson is Senior Researcher at the National Environmental Research Institute of Denmark. He holds an M.Sc. in Environmental Planning from Roskilde University, and a PhD in Sustainable Mobility from the Copenhagen Business School. His research area is mobility, sustainability and environmental policy. His key research interest concerns the construction and use of performance indicators in transport and environment policy making.

Leif Gjesing Hansen is Associate Professor at Aalborg University in Denmark. He holds an M.Soc.Sc. in Geography and Public Planning from Roskilde University, and a PhD in Freight Transport and Regional Development from the Copenhagen Business School. His research area covers mobility, freight transport and regional development. His key research interest concerns relationships between new traffic infrastructures and changes in mobility patterns of individual companies and whole regions.

Anne Jensen holds an M.Sc. in Environmental Planning from Roskilde University, where she is also currently writing her doctoral thesis which analyses how the institutionalisation of certain perceptions of mobility in European transport policy has influenced the governing approaches of the EU within transport. Her research engagement is furthered by a keen interest in environmental issues and social constructivist policy analysis.

Per Homann Jespersen is Associate Professor in planning at Roskilde University. He has a background in chemical engineering, production planning and technology assessment. His present research areas are freight transport, transport policy and planning, as well as the methodology and practice of transdisciplinary research.

Lise Drewes Nielsen is Professor at Department of Environment, Technology and Social Studies, Roskilde University and has a background in sociology. Her field of research is transport and mobility, especially the development of sustainable (ecological and social) systems of transport in relations to mobility in modern life. Another research interest is the relations between mobility, modernity and planning. The research is theoretically focused on flexibility, flow, space, time and power relations from a sociological, geographical and politological perspective. She has extensive experience in empirical research using qualitative methods and action research.

Claus Hedegaard Sørensen is Senior Research Political Scientist at Institute of Transport Economics, Norway. He holds a Master of Political Science and Public Administration from Aalborg University, Denmark, and a PhD in Environmental Policy Integration in Transport from Roskilde University, Denmark. His research area is institutional and organisational conditions, NPM-reforms, decision-making and implementation in the transport sector.

Thyra Uth Thomsen is Associate Professor at Copenhagen Business School. She holds an M.Sc. in Marketing and a PhD in Consumer Behavior from the Aarhus School of Business. Her transport related research is concerned with both adults' and children's consumption of mobility and travel mode choice. Her key research interests are symbolic consumption, self-perception, and identity construction.

Acknowledgements

The authors wish to thank Andrew Crabtree for proofreading the volume. Moreover, the authors wish to thank for the financial support provided by the former Danish Transport Council to several of the individual research projects that have made this volume possible. Finally, the editors wish to thank the following who have commented on individual chapters of the book, as indicated in the acknowledgements to each chapter: Jørgen Ole Bærenholdt, Bo Elling, Randi Hjorthol, Ole B. Jensen, Peter Jones, Hanne Warming Nielsen, Ole Jess Olsen, Inger-Anne Ravlum, Jens Stærdahl, Petri Tapio, Craig Townsend and Erik Werlauff.

Acknowledgements

Introduction

Mobility Research –
A Growing Field of Social Enquiry

Lise Drewes Nielsen, Henrik Gudmundsson and
Thyra Uth Thomsen

Modernity is heavily dependent on transport to link individuals, corporations and communities to global arenas of networks and flows. People and goods travel over longer distances and with higher frequency than before. Motion, movement and mobility have become integrated parts of late modern identity, practice and thought. A state of *FLUX* can be sensed everywhere.

Meanwhile, post-war policy strategies to 'predict and provide' for transport growth as well as post-oil shock strategies to 'predict and prevent' it have largely failed. Even 'advanced' Scandinavian welfare states like Denmark have been unable to effectively control it and match demand and supply. Nevertheless, pressures to intervene against transport inefficiencies, unsustainability, and induced social exclusion are constantly renewed, from below (consumers, citizens), as well as from above (United Nations, European Union).

At the beginning of a new millennium we therefore face a challenge to find new ways to understand the complex causal web in which transport is embedded. A starting point for this task is to recognise mobility as a precondition for modern social life as well as a derived product of it. Mobility and transport systems must be understood and apprehended in this context, rather than assumed or wished away.

Transport and mobility represent rich areas for exploration and experimentation, in terms of new policies, practices, research methods and knowledge claims. Oscillating between a focus on 'transport' and 'mobility' provides just one lever to scrutinise this important driver of social change within a wide range of different social contexts, ranging from children's day care to the palaces of European power brokers.

This volume presents contemporary social science research perspectives on transport and mobility from an interdisciplinary group of nine Danish transport researchers to an international audience of scholars, students, planners and activists. The book represents a collective output of the FLUX transport research group, which is situated at the Department of Environment, Technology and Social Studies, Roskilde University, Denmark. The volume does not suggest a new unifying perspective on transport and mobility. At this point there is, rather, a need to go beyond singular rationalities and draw new inspiration to transport research from contemporary sociology, human geography and political science, as well as from actor-oriented behavioural studies and empirical research. Ultimately, the aim of this approach is not only to improve the understanding of transport and mobility but also to help demonstrate the potential of cross-disciplinary mobility research as a full-blown field of social enquiry.

The nine contributions in the volume address three broad themes divided into three different parts of the anthology. The following will give a brief overview of the different parts and their specific research contributions.

Part I: Mobility as Constructed Social Reality

The first part focuses on the social construction of reality and its implications for transport and mobility. Individuals construct notions of mobility in their everyday lives and practice. These notions actively contribute to justifying and maintaining specific patterns of travel choice and behaviour. Research contributions in this section empirically demonstrate how this takes place for such key issues as modal choice, traffic safety and children's mobility patterns. Beyond that, the research also evokes theoretical concepts of late modernity like reflexivity and deconstruction in order to explore avenues for potential disturbance and change to current patterns.

In chapter one, Thomsen investigates parent's social construction of safety and its implications on children's independent mobility. In Denmark, like in other European countries, children's independent mobility is diminishing. Instead, children are increasingly ferried around by car. One of the most commonly stated reasons for this tendency is adults' concern with traffic safety. Interestingly, though, children's traffic risk measured by numbers of accidents has decreased throughout the last decades. The aim of this chapter is to make sense of this counter factual span by examining how adults construct the safety of children in traffic. Based in the social constructivist paradigm, the analysis incorporates risk theory and in-depth interviews with parents who are adult gatekeepers of children's independent movement. In conclusion, Thomsen demonstrates how existing perceptions of children's traffic risks can be approached for the good of children's independent mobility.

In chapter two Freudendal-Pedersen introduces the term 'structural stories' and applies it to the analysis of individual mobility. 'Structural stories' is a concept used to cover the arguments people commonly use to legitimise their actions and decisions. Freudendal-Pedersen provides examples of such tales and illuminates them by drawing on theories about modernity and mobility. The analysis shows that addressing the transport user's structural stories explicitly may reveal cracks in the surface and open mobility for reflexiveness at the individual level. The structural story can therefore help to open doors and question the apparent obviousness of present mobility patterns. This may be seen as a manifestation of 'reflexive mobility' at the individual level, which some scholars have proposed as a precondition for changing actual mobility e.g. in a more environmentally friendly direction.

In the third and final chapter of the first part Drewes Nielsen takes us deeper into the concept of reflexive mobility. Her point of departure is the assumption that science plays a role as a change agent in relation to the development of transport and transport systems. Transport is an integrated part of the economic, technological and political system of the postmodern capitalist society, and, as such, it embodies relations of power and suppression linked to the social and to nature. Transport is also an integrated part of everyday experiences in terms of personal mobility, global production, and consumption. In this chapter Drewes Nielsen poses the question of whether it is possible to develop a concept of reflexive mobility in order to contribute to critically investigate deliberate and conscious changes in the transport system as opposed to 'blind growth'. What type of scientific questions does such a perspective pose and what sorts of empirical fields and methodologies does it apply to? These questions are discussed against the background of the author's long-standing work within different dimensions of transport research and her extensive experience with critical and action oriented social research.

Part II: Mobility as Spatial Co-ordination and Transgression

The second part of the anthology looks upon mobility from the perspectives of spatial coordination and transgression of borders. The transportation of goods and passengers is a cornerstone in the international economy. Through increasing globalisation of the social division of labour within companies and between regions, the need to co-ordinate flows of commodities and passengers across borders has become a key task for transport operators and policymakers. This second part of the anthology provides fresh evidence on what new interregional and national infrastructure links may mean for freight transport flows and the restructuring of industrial production systems and it also presents an innovative methodological arena for participant oriented investigations into freight transport system development.

In Chapter four Hansen investigates the impacts of major traffic infrastructures on firms' organisation of logistics and transport. The research is based on an analysis of impacts following from the opening of fixed links across the straits of the Great Belt and Oresund in Denmark. The opening of the fixed links in 1997 and 2000 was eagerly anticipated in both Denmark and Sweden with great prospects of radical changes in traffic and transport patterns, regional development, changes in firms' organisation, trading patterns etc. The scenarios were manifold and even contradictory. On the one hand, the fixed links were expected to increase traffic flows due to the elimination of 'friction' caused by the ferries. On the other hand, the expectations reflected a desire to improve planning, coordination and consolidation of freight transport, which would not necessarily produce an increase in traffic flows. Hansen investigates the effects on firms' organisation following from the opening of the fixed links. On top of illuminating the case at hand, the findings also contribute to a more general discussion on how new major traffic infrastructures affect transport logistical systems in terms of fundamental structural changes and increases in physical mobility.

Chapter five has a methodological focus. Jespersen and Drewes Nielsen describe how freight transport actors have become actively integrated in the production of knowledge by means of so called 'future workshop' methodology. The future workshop can be seen as a realisation of a new way to produce knowledge in the context of application, which transgresses disciplinary as well as organisational boundaries. It seeks to integrate knowledge production with creation of strategies for change. In a number of cases the authors have conducted future workshops with stakeholders from the freight transport sector, and in this chapter results and experience from this work are presented. In each future workshop a number of 20-30 participants met to discuss a pre-selected theme for a full day. The discussions were organised into three phases, each conducted under a strict set of rules. In the *critique* phase, the theme is seen from a problem-oriented angle, whereas the *utopian vision* phase focuses on constructively establishing ideal goals. Finally, the *realisation* phase seeks to transform these goals into viable strategies and possibly programs for transformation. Depending on the actors' involvement, by means of this methodology a high degree of social accountability and reflexivity can be obtained.

Part III: Mobility as a Policy Theme

The third part confronts mobility as a direct challenge for policy making. Transport policies are in a process of radical change. Regulations have been abandoned, markets liberalised and long-standing national monopolies have been broken up. Meanwhile, congestion threatens to choke the arteries of what was supposed to be a dynamic European economy while citizens in some cases mobilise against new destructive infrastructure projects. The contributions in this section explore recent developments in transport policy at national and European levels, including how notions of mobility, efficiency and sustainability, and they also open up new avenues for negotiating its core rationales as well as its modes of organisation and implementation.

In chapter six Gudmundsson dissects the concept of mobility to make it operational for the monitoring of 'Mobility Policies'. Recent transport policies have signified a shift to embrace the notion of mobility: 'Sustainable Mobility' (and not just free flows) is the official aim of the European Common Transport Policy; and 'Mobility that creates real value' (and not just more mobility) is the vision of the Danish Ministry of Transport. But what are the implications of this 'mobility turn' and can 'mobility policies' really deliver what they claim? To answer this question, mobility needs to be defined and the performance of 'mobility policies' needs to be monitored. With this in mind, four dimensions are discussed: Mobility as potential movement as well as realised movement, mobility as dependent on tendency (the capacity to move) as well as potency (the need to move), mobility as a qualitative notion (in terms of e.g. speed, reliability, safety) and finally, mobility as internally and externally sustainable. By addressing these dimensions Gudmundsson aims to force a clarification of what a mobility policy should deliver, rather than just more traffic and transport.

Mobility as a policy theme is also the focus of chapter seven. In contrast to Gudmundsson's realist view, Jensen adopts a social constructivist approach to policy analysis. The theme is the development of a common European transport policy since the 1957 Treaty of Rome with a special attention to the most recent phase since 1992. From the vantage point of new institutional analysis, Jensen argues that the cognitive dimension of a transport policy plays a key role. Meaning and knowledge frame, enable and limit the actual transport policy-making. This is analysed by way of three so-called institutional orders, a descriptive, a narrative and an argumentative order respectively. In the case of mobility, Jensen demonstrates how the concept has served to justify the establishment of transport as a legitimate policy issue at the European level, with a key role to provide cognitive linkages to other key policy areas like the formation of the internal market and the cohesion of the Union. One significant implication is that mobility as a goal in itself cannot be questioned, not even by the environmental policy aims present in the common transport policy. Also, this conceptualisation has – strongly supported by connotations of 'freedom' inscribed in mobility – further contributed to consolidate the very political integration of the Community.

Chapter eight investigates to what extent and in what way conditions for decision-making and coordination in the area of transport have changed. Hedegaard Sørensen takes a closer look at corporatisation and division in the Danish railway sector, with a special focus on the largest railway operator in Denmark (DSB). Three themes are discussed: Autonomy, logic of action, and coordination. Parallel to developments in other countries, an organisational revolution has taken place in the Danish transport sector. Corporatisation, division and tendering have become widespread. From a theoretical point of view one could expect that this revolution would create a new way of making decisions and coordination in the field. Hence, decision-making through network management and negotiations should be widespread. One could also expect a lack of coordination. The analysis shows that the process of coordination is more difficult compared to earlier, and at lower organisational levels networks seem to be an important mechanism of coordination. Contrary to expectations, so far the autonomy of DSB has not increased, and so far DSB's logic of action has not changed. The concepts of New Public Management clearly change the railway sector in Denmark. However, for the time being, the consequences of these changes should not be exaggerated.

Finally, Figueroa in chapter nine addresses the topic of democracy and automobility paying specific attention to battles against motorways. The main questions concern how we can understand civil society protesting against motorways and what we can learn from them. The analysis presents insights from one particular road battle case in the town of Silkeborg, in Denmark. The case exemplifies how an active public sphere has the potential to help improve democratic practices in transport decision-making. The protest groups make specific demands to the administrative apparatus for more democracy, for consideration of other transport modes in decision, and for compliance with environmental regulations. The administrative apparatus is forced to respond to these demands. This exemplifies how protests against new motorway building are becoming a more sophisticated and prominent form of political contestation beyond narrow self-interested 'not in my backyard' and environmental critique. The protest, however, focuses on the system 'motorways' and not on the individual responsibility of car users. In this way, the protests also reflect a perception of ambivalence towards automobility as a goal of modern society. The significance of civil society protesting motorways as an evolving practice of political dissent is thus highlighted in this essay.

As this description of the volume illustrates, the authors touch upon various aspects of transport, mobility and policy. All of the authors have felt a need to explore what the 'lived world' of mobility looks like and how it works, not least to be better equipped to understand possible interventions in it. The final section of the book is an attempt to reflect on the authors' subsequent discussions of how these explorations intertwine with issues of *sustainability*. Sustainability has been considered by members of the FLUX group as one of the most important 'social perspectives on mobility' around, but to remain alive and productive this notion has to be constantly revisited in view of what we learn. Therefore, as an epilogue to the volume, the meaning and usefulness of the concept of sustainability to social inquiries on mobility are re-addressed in an attempt to maintain a shared, critical research agenda.

All in all, this volume covers several different social perspectives on mobility, which combined enrich the understanding and the debate on mobility in late modernity. Although different in paradigmatic scope, the contributions share some common ground in their application of social inquiry, critical perspectives, and qualitative methods. Also, as should be evident, the authors seek to transgress the often dichotomic realist-constructivist divide in spite of the embedded epistemological differences. We share an understanding of 'mobility' that goes beyond physical movements and networks to encompass also potentials, institutions, stories and other intangible but nevertheless highly consequential social constructions.

The book serves the double purpose of communicating distinct but complementary research approaches from the FLUX group to the global research community and to support teaching of advanced students in transport and mobility. Also, the book aims to provide input to policy oriented and participatory research exploring the future.

PART I
MOBILITY AS CONSTRUCTED
SOCIAL REALITY

Chapter 1

Parents' Construction of Traffic Safety: Children's Independent Mobility at Risk?

Thyra Uth Thomsen

Introduction

Denmark is sometimes presented as a country where children can move around freely (Hillman, 1999). This is not altogether true. Even though Danish children enjoy a certain degree of independent movement, they are increasingly chauffeured by car. Six to ten year-olds have doubled their car trips and reduced their walking trips by 40 per cent during the last two decades. At the same time eleven to fifteen year-olds have tripled their car trips. (Jensen and Hummer, 2002). The situation in Denmark has come to resemble the situation in other European countries, e.g. the UK (EU 2000; O'Brien et al., 2000). The question remains, though, whether or not this is a problem. The following line of reasoning does not seek to support any normative ideal that children's independent mobility is inherently good, nor does it hold that escorting or ferrying children is inherently bad. Even so, the confinement of children's mobility may have consequences for children's health, safety, equality, development and quality of life (Hillmann et al., 1990; Hillmann, 1993; Thomsen, 2004; Fotel and Thomsen, 2004; Christensen and O'Brien, 2003; Freund and Martin, 1993). While some of these consequences may be intended, such as increasing the safety of the chauffeured child, others are unintended, as is the case when chauffeuring children by car results in increased traffic risks on children that go by bicycle. Other unintended consequences are the increased health risks that follow from the immobilization of children's bodies.

Thus, the choice of children's travel mode and especially their increased automobilization is buried in huge dilemmas. On this basis, it may seem peculiar that children are increasingly taken by car. In Denmark, the increase in children's automobilization is attributed to the following factors (Jensen and Hummer, 2002):

- 5-15 per cent is due to a rise in car ownership
- 5-15 per cent is due to local school closures
- 25-30 per cent is due to a lower average age among school children

The remaining 40-65 per cent of the increase is unaccounted for and attributed to changed perceptions and attitudes. Parents seem to be less positive towards cycling; possibly because of increased car traffic, road safety campaigns and the media all of which have heightened parents' concern with children's independent mobility (Jensen and Hummer, 2002). This hypothesis is supported by other empirical research (Olsen, 2003; Fotel and Thomsen, 2004). Parents' concern with children's road safety is one of the major reasons for taking their children by car if they can. This phenomenon is also documented in other European countries such as Norway and the UK (Fyhri, 2002; Bradshaw and Jones, 2000). This research shows how the fear of traffic accidents on the child's trip to school is statistically linked to chauffeuring them by car.

It may therefore seem puzzling to note that the number of children involved in traffic accidents has decreased during the last decades as illustrated below.

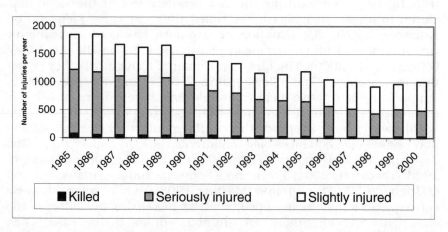

Figure 1.1   Number of children age 6-16 involved in traffic accidents

Source: Jensen and Hummer (2002).

The number of seriously injured children in particular shows a significant decrease. If the number of accidents is an adequate measure of traffic risks, this means that statistically traffic safety has increased, while perceived traffic safety seems to have decreased. In the following, I will expand on this and offer one possible way of making sense of this paradox. The theoretical framework presented builds on social constructivist theory (Berger and Luckmann, 1966; Schwandt, 1994; Gergen, 1997; Thomsen, 2001) and academic discourses about the nature of risk (Giddens, 1991/1998; Luhmann, 1991; Beck, 1992; Rasborg, 2002; Roberts et al., 1995).

The Deconstruction of the Paradox

One way of making sense of the paradox outlined above may be to assume that parents' fears actually lead to an increase in their children's safety in the traffic. Thus, parents' worries about their children's safety could urge them to an increased restriction, monitoring or accompaniment of their children, reducing the possibility for children to get harmed in the traffic. This tendency is a well-known feature of the late modern society (Fotel and Thomsen, 2004; Davis and Jones, 1996) – not only as far as traffic is concerned but also in other aspects of children's lives (Qvortrup, 1994; Dencik and Schultz Jørgensen, 1999; Lyon, 2001). Valentine (1996) even claims that today's public space is produced as adult space. Still, the increased monitoring of children's mobility cannot account for the entire decrease in children's traffic injuries (Jensen and Hummer, 2002: chapter 5) and thus is not sufficient to account for the paradox in question.

Another way of making sense of the paradox is to assume that the number of injuries reflected in accident statistics is not an adequate measure of children's traffic risks. Based on their case study of an urban community in the UK, Roberts et al. (1995) argue that injury statistics are insufficient as they neglect important injury data, such as near miss accidents and accidents that are treated at home and thus not included in injury statistics. Even though Roberts et al. investigate parental safety concerns at large, instead of focusing on mobility, their point is applicable to this discussion. If the extent of parental worries are in fact a product of children's risk experiences on the street, then they should be compared to the overall number of risky situations that children have been in – including near miss situations and accidents that are not recorded by the police or a hospital, because they are not reported and treated at home. Still, even if the number of accidents reflected in Figure 1.1 is a low estimate of the real number of accidents, it is safe to assume that this does not change the overall trend reflected by the figure. Thus, this rather important point also fails to account for the paradox in question.

An alternative way of making sense of the paradox is to build on the assumption that parental worries are complex social phenomena, which cannot be reduced to a simple mirror of child accidents. In the following, this alternative hypothesis is developed within an interpretive, social constructivist framework (Denzin and Lincoln, 1994; Thomsen, 2001; Berger and Luckmann, 1966). Interpretive sciences and social constructivist theory are dedicated to the investigation of social reality (Schwandt, 1994). Social reality consists of what individuals perceive to be real. Within this framework, any statistical account of traffic injuries is only relevant insofar as it affects a parent's interpretation of their children's traffic risks. Moreover, the way it is interpreted may differ from parent to parent. According to this constructivist framework, the individual takes active part in constructing the social reality he or she lives in and that every single person chooses and interprets the webs of knowledge that constitute social life. Injury statistics are merely one aspect of social knowledge, which may or may not be taken into account in a parent's conception of risk. Thus, there is no direct causal relationship between worries and accidents. Instead, accidents may be viewed as just one of multiple sources of parental worries. In the following, three other possible sources of parental worries are presented; namely public information, the mobility environment at large and personal history. They will be the focal point of the following investigation and may be illustrated as in Figure 1.2.

It illustrates how parental concern can be viewed as a product of parent's interpretation of traffic risks based on public information (i.e. injury statistics and safety campaigns), the mobility environment (i.e. traffic density and infrastructure) and personal history (i.e. experience with traffic accidents and the child's behaviour). It is important to note, however, that there are many more sources of parental concern, illustrated by the arrow between the middle circle and the surrounding symbolic universe. The arrow indicates that a parent's interpretation of the three focal points is bound up with other spheres of the parent's social reality e.g., a parent's understanding of what a *good parent* should be like. If – in his view – a good parent must protect his child, then this can affect his interpretation of traffic risks since they become the parent's responsibility. If, on the other hand, a good parent is seen as someone who lets his child run freely, then he will probably deal with traffic risks in a different way. Thus, parents' choice of children's travel mode reflects on parents themselves, and hence mobility choices can become a matter of personal significance (Thomsen, 2001). In spite of the fact that parental worries have

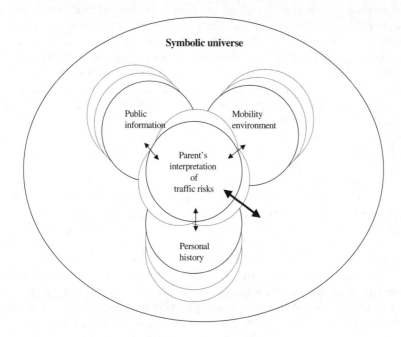

Figure 1.2   Selected sources of parental concern with children's traffic risks

many sources, in the following I will expand on the three illustrated in Figure 1.2, with a special focus on personal history.

According to Roberts et al.'s (1995) case study on parental concern with children's safety, public information and the mobility environment influence parental worries. Roberts et al. (1995) approach the nature of risk from the perspective of policy making. They are concerned with the fact that policy within this area focuses on high profile dangers, i.e. child abuse, at the expense of the most common dangers that children face – injuries at home and in the street which account for 47 per cent of all causes of death amongst people aged one to 19 in the UK in 1990 (Roberts et al., 1995: p 3). According to Roberts et al. "whereas policies on child abuse are predicated on the assumption that the child is innocent, there is a very strongly child-blaming or child-responsible culture in relation to child accidents" (Roberts et al., 1995: p 16). They substantiate their assertion by illustrating how the government takes responsibility in child abuse cases by removing the child from the home, while primarily relying on educating children and parents about traffic accident avoidance instead of altering the mobility environment, thus implying that these traffic accidents are the responsibility of the families. Roberts et al. (1995: p 8) pose a thought-provoking question: "Why do we remove children from *dangerous families* but tolerate *dangerous places*?" According to Roberts et al., parents bear the entire responsibility for child accidents both at home and in the street, but are not involved in the way governmental money is spent on injury prevention. In an attempt to even out this imbalance, Roberts et al. seek to investigate parent's views on children's injuries at home and in the street to see if local knowledge is an appropriate input into policy making within this area.

Their findings suggest that injury statistics are poorly linked with parental worries since they do not include accidents treated at home and near miss situations. Also, these findings imply that it is not necessarily the average number of child injuries that counts, but the parent's experiences with dangerous situations in his/her surroundings. An accident does not necessarily have to take place – the threat itself can feed into parent's worries. Thus, it is not only public information about injuries or personal experience of injuries that matter; parents' understanding of the number of accident risks built into the local environment itself is of paramount importance to their construction of accident risks (Roberts et al., 1995: p 61).

All in all, it should be clear by now how traffic risks measured by the number of traffic injuries can fall while parents' worries about traffic dangers increase. Within the social constructivist framework outlined here, there does not have to be a paradoxical relationship between these two trends. Parental worries can be viewed as much more complex social phenomena which have many other sources than those displayed in injury statistics. Hence, it makes sense that parental fears are increasing in spite of a decrease in the number of children involved in road accidents. While this paradox may lead to deeming parents' worries exaggerated, I approach it from a different perspective.

Apart from a matter of personal interpretation, risk is also said to be a central feature of contemporary society – also termed the risk society (Beck, 1992). In the risk society, we are doomed to reflexivity and thus to an increasing awareness of risk. Our awareness of risk is linked with but not necessarily equivalent to the risk itself. According to the constructivist approach to the theory of risk, the amount of dangers we face depends on our risk perception (Luhmann, 1991). Using Luhmann's understanding of risk (Kneer and Nassehi, 1997), this would essentially mean that if parents believe traffic to be very dangerous, then they, in fact, face all of these dangers. From a constructivist view, risks do not necessarily exist as such; they are constructed and thus they are a matter of perspective – within a phenomenological approach, it is a matter of *personal* perspective. Within this framework, it is the individual's perception of risk, rather than a mechanical response to statistics about road safety, that guides parents' protective measures.

In the following, I will turn the focus away from injury statistics and mobility environment and elaborate on personal perspectives on traffic risk to illustrate how they are linked to the lower part of Figure 1.2, that is personal history. The analysis will be based on empirical findings from a study based on in-depth interviews with eight parents of children aged 10-12.

The Nature of Traffic Dangers

Within the theoretical framework outlined above, risk can be viewed as being dependent on the position from which it is observed. In the following, I will present a few of these positions – namely several parents' constructions of the traffic dangers their children face.

In order to gain insights about these constructions, eight in-depth interviews with parents of children aged ten to twelve were undertaken. This interview form is a relevant and necessary method for building up the individual's own account of social issues (Kvale, 1996). The selection of the interviewees was based on families who faced varying traffic conditions, in order to gain as many differing views on the topic as possible (see Thomsen, 2004 for further methodological reflections). Thus, parents in both urban and rural areas, with children of different sexes, different home-school distances and different travel behaviour were interviewed. The sample consists of the following eight parents:

Table 1.1 Interviewees

Area	Interviewee	School-home dist. (kms)	No. of family cars	Child's use of travel mode (home-school)*			
				bicycle	walking	car	school bus
urban	Camilla's mother	3.5	2	•		•••	
	Tina's mother	0.1	0	•	•••		
	Martin's mother	2	1	•••	•••	•••	
	Norman's mother	0.4	2		•••	•	
rural	Karen's mother	4	3	•••		•••	•
	Sarah's father	3	2	••		•••	•
	Ole's mother	1.5	2	•••		•••	
	Larry's mother	4	1	•		••	•••

* blank = never, • = seldom, •• = from time to time, ••• = often

The analysis evokes relevant themes that emerge from a phenomenological reading and meaning condensation of the interview texts (Thomsen, 2001; Kvale, 1996; Denzin and Lincoln, 1994). Through a reciprocal, hermeneutic approach to theory and empirical findings (Denzin and Lincoln, 1994), I elaborate on those themes that seem especially helpful in broadening our understanding of parents' construction of traffic dangers. The following is not a comprehensive list of the forms that, according to parents, traffic dangers can take. The aim of the analysis is rather to build a productive hypothesis to help increase our understanding of socially constructed fears that prevent parents from letting their children move around freely.

Let me comment on some central terms of the analysis before I engage in presenting the results: In spite of the vast body of theory about risk, in this chapter the terms risk and danger – and their consequences in the shape of worries, fears and safety concerns – have so far been used in their everyday sense. In order to tease out some differences between parents' views on the dangers that traffic poses to their children, I will introduce some theoretical conceptions of a few central terms throughout the course of the following analysis. The concepts introduced primarily originate from Luhmann's (1991) and Beck's (1992) writings on risk theory, in spite of the fact that their theoretical frameworks are different from each other and different from the one at hand. Even though they both have certain constructivist features, Luhmann's and Beck's approaches are rather structural, whereas the framework presented in this chapter focuses heavily on the individual's contribution to the construction of risk. Thus, the following analysis is inspired by some of Luhmann's and Beck's central terms but not consistent with their overall theoretical framework.

Luhmann (1991) distinguishes between risks and dangers. Whereas a man who decides to race his car takes risks, the child affected by the consequences of this risk-taking behaviour is faced with its danger. Thus risks are closely linked with decision-making. Consequently, you could argue, parents who let their children move independently face dangers, since they have no control of the decisions made by their own children or by the other traffic users. An interesting implication of this distinction is that whereas risks are calculable and linked to knowledge, dangers are, in principle, unlimited and linked to uncertainty. Thus, parents are exposed to an infinite number of dangers when they let their child move around freely, depending on their own fears, knowledge, and hopes. The question is what these fears are targeted at. Not only have parents different views on what *danger* is, but they also have different views on *traffic*. In the following we will learn how some parents refer to traffic dangers as dangers following from automobility. Others think of traffic dangers as *mobility dangers*, which follow from *moving around out there* instead of being at home. Thus, facing traffic becomes analogous with facing automobility, mobility, unprotectedness, and so on. Research shows that parents' fears are multiple; targeted at heavy traffic, traffic accidents and children's traffic competence, as well as abduction, stranger danger and estranged parents (Joshi and MacLean, 1995; Valentine and McKendrick, 1997; Valentine, 1996; Jones et al., 2000; Blakely, 1994).

On top of knowing what parents' fears are targeted at, it is important to gain insight into some of the dynamics that underlie the formation of parental fears and their compulsion to use protective measures. Two dynamics fostering different risk perceptions are conspicuous in the material and will be presented in the following.

How Is the Construction of Traffic Danger Connected to Parents' Perception of Safety?

A thorough reading of the interviews led me to hypothesise that parents' perception of traffic danger and protective measures against it is connected to parents' perception of safety. Parents perceive the possibility of avoiding traffic risks, and thus to achieve safety, in fairly different ways. Some parents view the traffic risks their children face as unavoidable and a natural part of life. Other parents seek to minimize the dangers of traffic in several different ways, e.g. through monitoring and accompanying the child, through intensive traffic training, through rules and restrictions of the child's independent movement (Fotel and Thomsen, 2004). According to Luhmann (1990), safety does not exist – it is a fantasy and a desire more than a possibility. Thus, parents may be chasing a dream when they try to protect their children from traffic. Instead risk, uncertainty, dangers and fears may be viewed as an existential, unavoidable part of life in modernity (Beck, 1992; Luhmann, 1991; Giddens, 1990). The question is how a person handles these risks. The mother of a twelve-year-old girl gives an interesting account.

"I think it is important to talk about parents' attitudes towards what they allow their children to do. I think we have become enormously afraid of daring to let our kids go out. A lot of children are driven to school even though they really don't live that far away. We have allowed our children to cross streets from an early age. Of course they have to know traffic regulations, but apart from that, I think it is parents' attitudes that have to change. Children become much better traffic users by getting an early start. Maybe it's because we live in the countryside and that is a dangerous place to live. They have to learn that you shouldn't touch the electric fence, otherwise you would get electric shocks all the time. Don't go see the pig when it has small piglets, cause then you get eaten or bitten. All the things they have to do and have to know – that's just the way it is. Just like traffic regulations. You have to comply with them otherwise things can go wrong. Children can also be hurt in a car. Life is dangerous!" (Karen's mother)

Karen's mother lets her daughter ride her bicycle to school even though they live four kilometres away from it. It is interesting to note how the mother describes danger as an unavoidable part of life. In her view, the best way to meet danger seems to be to accept it, to face it and to live with it – literally. According to her, by living with danger instead of avoiding it, you learn about it and thus you learn to handle it. Other parents seem to believe that they can influence their children's traffic safety through different measures like protecting them, accompanying them, instructing them, driving them, and so forth (Fotel and Thomsen, 2004). Norman's mother reports:

"Norman and I have had – and still have – a completely fixed pattern when we cycle together. We cycle next to each other. Norman on my right hand side. He learned that from the very beginning and we can even do a left turn together, while he stays on my right hand side." (Norman's mother)

These protective measures against the dangers of traffic make no sense to Karen's mother, though. From her point of view, danger is *natural* and – just as Luhmann reasons – safety is thus a utopia[1]. Still, she acknowledges the importance of rules, regulations and experience in coping with danger. Her trust relies on the confidence she has in the expert systems (Giddens 1991; Beck 1992). Karen's mother believes in traffic regulations and trusts other traffic users to comply with them, something that Beck might call risk ignorance, whereas it is a perfectly valid risk assessment within the framework at hand, where risk depends on the position from which it is viewed. In accordance with this, other parents fear that this may not be the case and that even though their own children act according to traffic regulations they could still get hurt. Even though this risk assessment is just as valid as Karen's mother's

---

[1] Within this framework, traffic safety and traffic dangers are both viewed as social constructions. They are two sides of the same phenomenon and will be treated as such in the following.

view, it may lead to counter effective measures, that is parents instructing their children to act in contravention of traffic regulations in order to avoid dangers from other traffic users disobeying traffic law:

> "The funny thing is, since she wanted to walk to school on her own and because they said that the safest route to school is to cross at the pedestrian crossing down the road, we tried to walk that way together. But then a car came from behind and tore right across. That's what they do, they just turn. And then I said: we don't do this. We will cross over there. That is safer even though there is no pedestrian crossing. I have been trying to tell my children that a pedestrian crossing does not mean that they will stop." (Tina's mother)

It is easy to see that Tina's mother does not believe in the expert system of traffic regulations to the same extent as Karen's mother. Her children are instructed to behave in accordance with area specific traffic rules created by their mother rather than traffic regulations in general.

You could argue that seeking to achieve traffic safety for their children – the way Tina's and Norman's mothers do – is to try to fight uncertainty and to increase safety through control. According to Beck (1992) and Giddens (1998), this must be regarded as a traditional way of approaching risks, since modern risks are not calculable and cannot be insured against. In a more constructivist view on risk, on the other hand, any strategy parents apply to feel safer can also lead to the reduction of risks, since safety, just like risk, is a way of observing a given phenomenon (Rasborg, 2002). As long as parents perceive that they can reduce the traffic dangers their children have to meet they might try to do so. Thus, I argue, parents' response to risk may be dependent on their perception of risk and safety either as a given fact beyond their control or as a social phenomenon, which they have control and influence over.

How Is the Construction of Traffic Danger Connected to Parents' Own Childhood Experiences?

The theory of knowledge is built on the assumption that in order to perceive anything you must be able to distinguish it from something else. If everything were the same colour, blue, you wouldn't be able to perceive blue as a colour since there would be nothing different from it to help you recognise it. Thus, knowledge is based on contrast. This rather simple line of reasoning is important if we are to comprehend parents' construction of the traffic dangers that their children face. Parents may perceive traffic as dangerous by using their own childhood experiences as a frame of reference. Thus, parents may find traffic more dangerous now than it was before, when they themselves were children. From this point of view, it makes sense that children sometimes do not perceive traffic as being dangerous while their parents do (Thomsen, 2004; Olsen, 2003). They have different frames of reference.

"From the time when I was a child and until now – car density and traffic safety have changed tremendously. In some ways, it was completely different back then. Our children have never experienced anything else, so to them it may seem natural that there is so much traffic, but it must make them scared that something might happen, and they have seen accidents, people falling from their bicycles and things like that. When I was a child you didn't think that way. Adults and society at large have become much more conscious about cycling safety and about children's movement on the streets. I don't think you devoted yourself to it in the same way 30 years ago, as you do today. This, of course, has been a gradual development throughout the last 30 years due to the increase in traffic. There are many more cars on the streets, right! In the old days not every family had a car. Today most have two cars. Statistically our fleet of cars has just grown ... almost 45 per cent. I would think, right?" (Camilla's mother)

Camilla's mother points to the fact that today's children may have a different view of traffic dangers than their parents since they have never faced traffic in any other form than it has today. Heavy traffic seems natural to them; in other words they have reified a socially constructed phenomenon into being an unchangeable part of reality (Berger and Luckmann, 1966), and thus can be much more accepting of it than their parents. Interviews with children do indeed show such tendencies (Thomsen, 2004).

But it is not just the perception of traffic danger that has changed. According to Ole's mother, it is the view concerning children per se that has changed. She has experienced how children are increasingly perceived as something you have to take good care of, as if they could otherwise break:

"I grew up in a residential neighbourhood. So I was completely free; I could go and cycle wherever I wanted to and I started very early to go by bus and train by myself. I remember going to the dentist by bus on my own when I was ten. I had a much larger radius than my kids have today. But there was much less traffic, that's how I try to justify it. Also maybe there was not as much focus on children as there is today. We really want to roll them in cotton wool and monitor them 24 hours a day. The children I played with almost all had mothers that didn't work. They were housewives and the level of service was not that high. The service level is lower when you're a housewife – that's how it is – children are just not as interesting. Whereas, if you have been away from them all day you really want to be all over them when you're finally together." (Ole's mother)

It is interesting to note how Ole's mother links the increasing focus on children to parental absence during the day. The question then arises if increasing parental fears are linked to decreasing insight into their children's lives altogether. This could make sense since lack of knowledge increases uncertainty (Beck, 1992) and thus opens a Pandora's box of possible risk. Therefore, a meaningful hypothesis would be that parental traffic worries are just one way in which this uncertainty – due to an increased absence from their children – manifests itself. Perhaps this is also the reason why driving them has special appeal to many parents. While driving their children is in fact more dangerous than letting them walk (Granville, 2002), it gives parents a chance to be with their children and thus decrease their overall uncertainty.

While some parents disclose a reluctant acceptance of the changes they observe from their own childhood experience until now, other parents express their frustration. For instance, Sarah's father gives this painful account of how he is torn between his own memories and his present fears.

"It is irritating to take the children by car. It's also a matter of principle: to make them independent. That's how I was at that age – I lived on a bicycle. If I had to walk four metres I took my bike. There wasn't as much traffic as now. Everything was completely different. Nobody was driven anywhere, by and large. Maybe for an evening party some of the girls were driven, but everyone else went by bicycle. I also think that times have changed. Not that many families had two cars back then. The father usually had the car. A lot of people didn't have a car at all. You weren't just ferried around. It was a pain, but I think it was very good for us. My wife is scared that a car might hit our children, and of course so am I, but I also know what it was like to be a child and to feel like you owned the world because you were mobile." (Sarah's father)

This frustration can also be traced in other parents' accounts of their children's mobility. Larry's mother states that:

"Parents are generally more anxious today, with darkness, violence, the street and everything. And the consequence is that the children are ferried around by us – that's a pity. It is such a lovely freedom to ride your bike and get the wind in your hair." (Larry's mother)

Thus, parents can be ambivalent as to how they should cope with wanting their children to thrive on the advantages of independent mobility without having to face the dangers they perceive to be linked to it (Fotel and Thomsen, 2004).

Besides being tied to childhood experiences, the construction of traffic danger can be a matter of prior experience. It is important to note, however, that there is no simple causal one to one relationship between an experience and your perception of traffic danger. For instance, Ole and his mother have been involved in a traffic accident. Still, his mother does not relate to this experience when she gives her account of traffic danger. Other parents though, express how their view on traffic dangers is formed by past experiences. For instance, Camilla's mother explains how she finds Denmark a safe place for cycling in comparison to her prior experiences when her family lived in Belgium:

> "In Belgium it is very, very dangerous to cycle on public streets, because traffic is enormously heavy. In Belgium she wasn't allowed to go anywhere by bicycle, but when you come back to Denmark, well, here traffic safety is safe, right! In Denmark, you have always been able to cycle, and there are always bicycles on the streets. She hasn't been allowed to cycle to school on her own, yet. She often cycles to the local grocery store to do some shopping. That is no problem. But I still have this fear of traffic in me from back then." (Camilla's mother)

It is interesting to note how Camilla's mother on the one hand finds Denmark much safer for cycling than Belgium, while on the other hand she carries the fears of traffic per se with her in spite of the spatial change. Thus, how you assess traffic danger can be a matter of how you interpret personal experience – you may judge something as safe in comparison to your experience of something less safe or you may carry your uneasiness with traffic with you.

Summary and Concluding Reflections

In the above, I have offered a way to make sense of the seemingly paradoxical relationship between increasing parental fears and children's increasing road safety. Partly due to parental concern, children are increasingly taken by car, while traffic risks measured by the number of recorded injuries have decreased more than the increased chauffeuring of children can account for.

The increased chauffeuring of children can pose threats both to children who are not taken by car and to the chauffeured children themselves – the first due to an increase in traffic volume and the latter due to a decrease in bodily movement. Also, children's independent movement per se is at stake. Therefore, an investigation into the sources of parental concern with traffic safety is an important research subject. In order to do so, I draw on theories about the social construction of reality and risk. I argue that parents' protective measures – rather than being mechanically adjusted to statistics about road safety – may be guided by parents' individual risk perception. Within the outlined social constructivist framework, this risk perception can be viewed as complex social phenomenon, which has many other sources than mere injury statistics. Of the numerous possible sources of parental worries with children's traffic safety, three of paramount importance are investigated; that is public information, the mobility environment and personal history.

On top of presenting these sources of parents' worries, insight into some of the dynamics that underlie the formation of parental fears and the compulsion to use protective measures have been presented. Based on eight in-depth interviews with parents, two different dynamics were investigated: The first is how the construction of traffic danger is linked to parents' perception of safety. Parent's accounts differ with regard to how they cope with their children's traffic risks or seek to increase their children's safety. To some parents, safety is a utopia and risks are a fact of life. To other parents, safety is worth pursuing and risks must be minimized. Thus parents' construction of safety reflects on their understanding of risks and the measures that are taken accordingly. The second dynamic that was investigated is how a parent's construction of traffic danger is connected to childhood experiences. The way children and traffic were perceived some decades ago prove to be important frames of reference in some of the parent's views on the traffic risks that children face today.

All in all, the theoretical framework and empirical analysis illustrate how parental fears can be viewed as a complex social construction and subject to personal interpretation, rather than as being a mirror of child injuries. It is important to note, however, that even though parental fears of traffic dangers are presented as socially constructed phenomena in the above, they may be just as real, natural and forceful for parental life as having to eat. My intention is not to diminish or ridicule parental fears of traffic dangers and the resulting actions towards their children's mobility. On the contrary, as noted earlier within the applied paradigm, social constructions are said to be the kind of reality that people face and act on in everyday life.

Still, it is an important finding. If the curtailment of children's mobility is based on socially constructed fears, it will be useless to meet these fears with traditional traffic safety campaigns. If parents are told how to protect their children through helmet usage this could even increase parents' perception of risk. Instead, it is of paramount importance to see through the mechanisms that underlie the social construction of traffic danger and to confront them. Engaging in a dialogue with parents about the differences between their own and their children's upbringings and competences could be one promising approach. Also, it could prove beneficial to engage in a dialogue about safety as a social value and the consequences, which the pursuit of safety has for the children. In essence, if parental worries are socially constructed and safety can be viewed as a utopia, these concepts can be deconstructed and become objects of critical reflection, which allows for a negotiation of parents' safety needs and children's need for freedom.

Acknowledgements

The author wishes to thank Hanne Warming Nielsen, Lise Drewes Nielsen, Leif Gjesing Hansen and Claus Hedegaard Sørensen for their comments on early drafts of the chapter. Also, the author wishes to express her gratitude to Lin Jaafar for language revisions.

References

Beck, U. (1992), *Risk Society. Towards a new Modernity*, Sage, London.
Berger, P. L. and Luckmann, T. (1966), *The social construction of reality: A treatise in the sociology of knowledge*, Doubleday, New York.
Blakeley, K. (1994) 'Parents' conceptions of social dangers to children in the urban environment', *Children's Environments*, 11, pp 16-25.
Bradshaw, R. and Jones, P. (2000), *The Family and the School Run: What would make a real difference*, AA Foundation for Road Safety Research, Great Britain.
Christensen, P. and O'Brien, M. (eds) (2003), *Children in the City: Home, neighborhood and community*, Routledge Falmers, London.
Davis, A. and Jones, L. (1996), 'Children in the urban environment: an issue for the new public health agenda', *Health & Place*, vol.2, 2, pp 107-113.
Dencik, L. and Schultz Jørgensen, P. (1999), 'Introduktion', in L. Dencik og P. Schultz Jørgensen (eds) *Børn og familie i det postmoderne samfund*. [Children and family in the postmodern society], Hans Reitzels Forlag, Copenhagen.
Denzin, N. K. and Lincoln, Y. S. (eds) (1994), *Handbook of Qualitative Research*, Sage Publications, London.
EU (2002), *Kids on the move*, Environment Directorate-General. Office for official publications of the European Communities, Luxembourg.
Fotel, T. N. and Thomsen, T. (2004), 'The Surveillance of Children's Mobility', *Surveillance & Society* 1 (4), pp 535-554.
Freund, P. and Martin, G. (1993), *The ecology of the automobile*, Black Rose Books Ltd, New York.
Fyhri, A. (2002), *Barns reiser til skolen. En spørreundersøkelse om*

reisevaner og trafikksikkerhet på skoleveien [Children's travel to school. A survey about transportmode and safety], Report 616, Transportøkonomisk Institut, Norway.

Gergen, K. J. (1997), *Realities and relationships: soundings in social construction*, Harvard University Press, Cambridge.

Giddens, A. (1990), *The consequences of modernity*, Polity Press, Cambridge.

Giddens, A. (1991), *Modernity and Self-Identity. Self and Society in the Late Modern Age*, Polity Press, Cambridge.

Giddens, A. (1998), 'Risk Society: the Context of British Politics', in J. Franklin (ed.), *The Politics of Risk Society*, Polity Press, Cambridge, pp 23-34.

Granville S., Laird, A., Barber, M. and Rait, F. (2002), *Why do parents drive their children to school?* Scottish Executive Central Research Unit, Edinburgh.

Hillman, M. (1999), *The impact of transport policy on children's development*, Safe Routes to Schools project seminar on 29th May, Canterbury.

Hillman, M. (ed.) (1993), *Children, Transport and the Quality of Life*, Policy Studies Institute, London.

Hillman, M. et al. (1990), *One False Move: A Study of Children's Independent Mobility*, Policy Studies Institute, London.

Jensen, S. U. and C.H. Hummer (2002), *Sikre Skoleveje: en undersøgelse af børns trafiksikkerhed og transportvaner* [Safe routes to school: an investigation of children's traffic safety and transport habits], Danmarks Transportforskning, Lyngby, Denmark.

Jones, L., Davis, A. and Eyers, T. (2000), 'Young people, transport and risk: comparing access and independent mobility in urban, suburban and rural environments', *Health Education Journal*, 59, pp 315-328.

Joshi, M. S. and MacLean, M. (1995), 'Parental attitudes to children's journeys to school', *World Transport Policy and Practice*, vol.1 (4), pp 29-26.

Kneer, G. and Nassehi, A. (1997), *Niklas Luhmann – introduktion til teorien om sociale systemer* [Niklas Luhmann – introduction to the theory of social systems], Hans Reitzels Forlag, Copenhagen, pp 172-183.

Kvale, S. (1996), *Inter Views – An introduction to qualitative research interviewing*, Sage, Thousand Oaks.

Luhmann, N. (1990), 'Risiko und Gefahr' [Risk and danger], *Soziologische Aufklärung 5. Konstruktivistische Perspektiven*, Westdeutscher Verlag, Opladen, pp 131-169.

Luhmann, N. (1991), *Soziologie des Risikos* [The sociology of risk], De Gruyter, Berlin.

Lyon, D. (2001), *Surveillance society. Monitoring everyday life*, Issues in Society, Open University Press, Buckingham.

McKendrick, J. H. (2000), 'The geography of children. An annotated bibliography', *Childhood* 7(3), pp 359-387.

O'Brien, M. et al. (2000), 'Children's independent spatial mobility in the urban public realm', *Childhood*, Vol. 7, no. 3, pp 257-277.

Olsen, T. V. (2003), *Hvorfor kører forældre deres børn til skole i bil?* [Why do parents drive their children to school?], Thesis, Aalborg University, Denmark.

Qvortrup, J. (1994), *Børn halv pris. Nordisk barndom i samfundsperspektiv* [Children half price. Nordic childhood in a social perspective], Sydjysk Universitetsforlag, Esbjerg, Denmark.

Rasborg, K. (2002), 'Beyond the risk society', paper presented at Nordisk Sociologkongres, Reykjavik, August 15-17, 2002.

Roberts, H. et al. (1995), *Children at risk? Safety as a social value*, Open University Press, Buckingham.

Schwandt, T. A. (1994), 'Constructivist, interpretivist approaches to human inquiry', in Denzin, N. K. and Lincoln, Y. S. (eds) (1994), *Handbook of Qualitative Research*, Sage Publications, London, pp 118-137.

Thomsen, T. U. (2001), *Persontransportens betydning for individet i et identitetsperspektiv – med fokus på transportmiddelvalg* [What does mobility mean to the traveller? – An identity perspective on mode choice], PhD thesis, The Aarhus School of Business, Department of Marketing, Denmark.

Thomsen, T. U. (2004), 'Children – automobility's immobilized others?' *Transport Reviews* 24(5), pp 515-532.

Valentine, G. (1996), 'Children should be seen and not heard: The production and transgression of adults' public space', *Urban Geography*, 17(3), pp 205-220.

Valentine, G. and McKendrick, J. (1997), 'Children's Outdoor Play: Exploring Parental Concerns About Children's Safety and the Changing nature of Childhood.' *Geoforum*, Vol. 28(2), pp 219-235.

Chapter 2

Structural Stories, Mobility and (Un)freedom

Malene Freudendal-Pedersen

"One gets a hell of a lot of freedom when one has a car". (Man, one car)

"Telling people not to drive their car is like if one told everybody not to have sex, one does it anyway". (Man, two cars)

Introduction

Over the past decade, a growing interest in unearthing the sociological mechanisms that underlie the way in which we choose to transport ourselves has developed. This chapter will touch upon some of the essential themes of late modern society and describe how they are interwoven with the kind of mobility one chooses. I wish to highlight some ideas and stories about the car and the public transport system that are accepted as 'common knowledge' and 'common truth' and as such guide transport behaviour. This will be done by presenting the term 'structural stories', these can be found in all areas of life, but here they are related to mobility, a theme that was developed as a part of my Master's thesis (Freudendal-Pedersen, Hartmann-Petersen and Roslind, 2002).

When I started research into transport, the concept of structural stories was not part of the plan, but when working with in depth interviews concerning mobility, the structural stories emerged from the material (Freudendal-Pedersen, Hartmann-Petersen and Roslind, 1999; 2000; 2002), and it became obvious that these stories were an essential part of how individuals understood and explained their mobility in everyday life. In wanting to understand and analyze the individual's actions in relation to mobility, the 'structural stories' played an important role. It was not possible to find any theoretical conceptualization that could contain the structural stories; the only possibility was to deconstruct them to see what they contained. I developed them together with two fellow students on the basis of 25 in-depth interviews and two focus group interviews. This means that the structural stories are based on empirical data that I have since placed in a theoretical framework. There will probably be a large variation in the use of structural stories between different groups of people, when conceptions of risks, attitudes towards the environment and the relation to the experts systems will vary among different social groups. This will also be visible in how the feature of modernity such as individualization and time pressure influences different lives. However it is my belief that one can find these structural stories in all of these different layers of the society. A large number of them will be expressed differently among different groups but then again some will have a universal character and will appear across social boundaries.

I take a moderate social constructivist approach to my research; I start from the belief that the material world has an influence on how we as individuals construct the social (Berger and Luckmann, 1996; Burr, 1995; Sayer, 2000). Ontologically, this means that knowledge is constructed in an interaction between the individual and society, between actors and structures, and it is in this process that the structural stories are formed and become common truths. Giddens (1984 and 1991) defines structures as embedded in the consciousness of the individual, the individual acts on the basis of already existing structures and at the same time the structures get reproduced when the individual acts. According to his concept of structuration, structures do not exist as an outer frame but only in praxis and in human memory. The structural stories are so-called because they are closely linked to Giddens' understanding of structures.

This leads us to the definition of what a *structural story* is and what it contains: *A structural story contains the arguments people commonly use to legitimize their actions and decisions. The individual view and expresses structural stories as universal truths, agreed upon by all. A structural story is used to explain the way we act and the choices we make when exercising our daily routines. It is a guide to certain actions that, at the same time, emancipate us from responsibility.*

The key to comprehending structural stories is understanding the conditions under which late modern societies mould their foundation and understanding the mechanisms of control that maintain the generally accepted validity of the structural stories. The structural stories form the basis that determines how the individual views certain problems and their solutions. The social practice of the individual produces and reproduces these structural stories, when they contribute to the maintenance of society's need for high mobility. Structural stories work as a kind of automatic explanation that expresses a certain standard in society. The stories are often marked by references to a person as 'one' instead of the more personal 'I'. An example of a structural story could be "when one has children one needs a car" or "one can not relay on the public transport system, there are always delays". Everyday life is filled with a series of competing discourses, all of which have great significance for the increasing need for mobility. The structural stories discussed here are the outcome of these diverse discourses. In this way, structural stories can serve as a logical, short, explanation for one's choices, which most people accept without further ado. It is essential to understand the way the structural stories are interwoven with the cultural notion of mobility and late modernity with essential characteristics as reflexivity and individualization.

Some structural stories are more extreme than others. The following example expresses an idea about society that I often found; this man just has a very straightforward and metaphoric way explain his reasons:

> "We are subordinated to some mechanisms, this goes for the car, the computer and technology - we can't say no to them. In some ways they force themselves through and shape our society. Cities and togetherness are formed by cars. One must not fool oneself into believing this is under democratic control, we have as much influence as the potatoes had on whether they wanted to become widespread in west Europe. Cars are not something that man has, they are a socio-cultural unit which has man – cars have a life of their own". (Man, two cars)

In this example, the man says "One must not fool oneself into believing this is under democratic control". What he is saying is that we as individuals have no influence over the development of society, we are suppressed into a framework where our actions are unimportant. This resigned attitude in relation to the individuals' influence on society is something I often met especially in relation to environmental issues. Another more common example is the next quotation, which appears in the story about how a normal everyday passes:

> "We are dependent on two cars. It is actually impossible for the public transport system to comply with a schedule because of all the traffic. That is why one can't trust the public transport system, so I prioritize my car". (Man, two cars)

Here the more commonly "one can't trust the public transport system" is expressed; this statement will be met with sympathy in most circles. These quotations appear as structural stories when the individual refers to "one can not" or "one must not" as an explanation that is conceived as a common truth that everybody agrees on. This is an ongoing process because the structural story on mobility is a story about how modern society shapes the individual and vice versa. It is a story about what the good life contains and about the ambivalences and risks the individual lives with in everyday life. Through the structural stories, I found a way to understand how late modern rationality is shaped and on the basis of what.

Structural Stories' Foundation in Late Modernity

The generation of structural stories on mobility is closely connected to the characteristic of late modern everyday life. Individualization, separation of time and space, the notion of risks and the ambivalences that follow are some of the important ingredients in the formation of the structural stories on mobility. The characteristic of late modern life as described in the following does not necessarily describe how every individual live their everyday life, many people do not live an individualized life where they pack a large number of activities into their everyday life while they, at the same time, worry about the risks they take and feel ambivalent about what they do not do. But most people live a life where some of these characteristics of late modern life play an important role and in some parts of their life they use the structural stories to comply with the pressure of handling everyday life in a adequate matter. In describing structural stories' foundation in late modern life I tell the extreme version when it, in a more efficient way, highlights the conception of structural stories.

Everyday Life and Individualization

Today, mobility is an essential part of nearly all lifestyles (Giddens, 1991). As today's lifestyles include elements scattered over large geographical areas, mobility provides the means for achieving a modern lifestyle. The nature of a certain lifestyle is reflected upon to a much higher degree though, than the use of mobility to achieve these lifestyles. This is due to the late-modern individual's preoccupation with exercising choice of lifestyle to create an identity (Giddens, 1991). Choosing a lifestyle is also important in avoiding everyday life becoming too incalculable, because when you choose a particular lifestyle where some choices are already given, it emancipates you from a number of choices (Giddens, 1991). A lifestyle involves a cluster of habits and orientations and thereby defines a number of the routine actions that individuals undertake in their everyday lives. Choosing a lifestyle gives the individual a continuing sense of ontological security, while at the same time it contains a certain unity that connects the large number of options that appear in our everyday life (Giddens, 1991). Every day, the late modern individual is a part of a large number of lifestyles. The workplace can demand one kind of lifestyle, which is perhaps very different from the attitude signalled among friends. What is important is to be ready to seek new opportunities, as increasing opportunities are an import part of an everyday life (Giddens, 1991; Beckmann, 2001). A necessary provision is mobility; the more mobile the individual is, the more possibilities are available. Important in this context is that mobility is becoming the vital link between these elements of lifestyle making it impossible to exclude some and include others, and to bridge the distance between lifestyles (Urry, 2000).

Closely related to choice of lifestyle is the organization of everyday life. Here the family assumes a central role, in that it is largely the nature of the family's everyday life that determines each of the member's transportation habits. Many factors, including the home, workplace, day-care and school location, not to mention recreational and social activities, have an influence on the families' need for mobility. Unique for late modern individuals is that fitting in all of the above elements and activities into one's life is, in fact, possible (Giddens, 1991; Beck, 1992). Organizing and planning everyday life has thus come to generate increased mobility, as we pack more and more into it. Today it seems that the act of reaching all the components that define our everyday life is becoming more important than the components themselves. The following example of a family coping with a large number of activities in everyday life is a story I often heard when interviewing families:

> "Monday I have exercises, Wednesday my husband has squash and Thursday my son has football and swimming, on Friday and in the weekends there are the football matches so everything has to be very well planned". (Woman, two cars)

It is also important to note that the sports club chosen for the family's activities is not the local sports club but the "best sports club" even though it is an hour away by car. In late modern life, there is a tendency to seek out new groups and activities to participate in; this is partly a consequence of the fading importance of tradition. The individual is no longer restrained by tradition, place, social relationships and activities, the modern individual has developed a need to seek out new and different social interactions:

> "They have 1½ hour of transport each way, they have to catch the train every morning at 6.30, but it is without a doubt the best school so there is nothing to do about it. It was worse when they were younger (6-9 years old)". (Man, one car)

In contrast to earlier modern life, these new communities are selected in spite of the longer distance, rather than on the basis of physical proximity alone (Giddens, 1991). In that manner, mobility is also about the construction of "the good life", what it contains, how to get it, and at what cost. In the same way you can say that everyday life is so planned and compressed that there is no spare time to use on mobility, which is why an important characteristic of mobility is to overcome space as quickly as possible.

Social relations are often independent of time and space, as a consequence of technological innovations especially in the ICT area (Giddens, 1990). This separation of time and space has a great impact on production and global flows of goods, and it also has a great impact on the way the individuals choose to organize their everyday life (Giddens, 1991). Time then becomes an abstract category that is used to organize the crossing of different spaces, which the individual is a part of in everyday life (Zeitler, 1998; Urry, 2000). Late modern life is marked by provisionality (Bauman, 2000), to be mobile becomes important; to be on your way to something else. When mobility is of such great significance in everyday life, and in constructing the "good life" it becomes troubling if the individual has to look at the downsides and risks connected to mobility and consider them while planning their everyday lives. Therefore, they construct the structural story, when it deliberates the individual for the ambivalences that follows in choosing certain actions over others.

Risks and Ambivalences

The risks and the coherent ambivalences we live with in our everyday life are of great significance in developing the structural stories. Living with a large number of risks is an integrated part of late modern life and is closely connected to the separation of time and space where the social relations are lifted out of the local connections and are rearticulated cross boundless time-space areas - what Giddens describes as disembedding (Giddens, 1991). The trust of the individual relies on the confidence he or she has in the expert systems that play an important role in the relationships the individual has in everyday life. When interviewing, mistrust in the expert system is something one often meets:

> "All this about the CO_2 problem is something the researchers have invented to get more money". (Man, two cars)

This kind of statement is linked to the trust the individual has to the expert system. The individual makes everyday life choices and opinions based on the knowledge of the expert systems and they choose to trust the experts they find most likeable. An individual cannot on his or her own have full knowledge of the extent of the environmental problems and consequences, and, therefore, has to decide which experts he/she trusts (Beck ,1992). In this selection of knowledge, the individual often chooses knowledge that does not interfere with everyday life and frees them of responsibility, often the reasoning will be based on a structural story. These kinds of structural stories can be supported and expressed by different kinds of studies presented in different medias, for example a newspaper article such as the one this person refers to:

> "I read the other day that if a large numbers of motorists stopped [driving their cars], the pollution from CO_2 would only be reduced by 0.3 per cent". (Woman, two cars)

The woman read this article and remembers it and relies on it because it supports the routines of her everyday life. One of the reasons for this displacement of responsibility can be found in the representation of the environmental problems in the media. The media is often the basis on which the re-evaluation of knowledge is communicated to individuals, where the presentation often matters more than the news itself. Furthermore, histories and subjects, which in reality have nothing in common except that they are newsworthy, often get juxtaposed in their presentation (Giddens, 1991). It becomes everyday that often tragic events become, in a dramatic way, a part of the everyday consciousness. All this causes'basic insecurity about the truth of the new knowledge. The individual cannot know for sure that new knowledge will not be revised. This insecurity means that ambivalence becomes an invertible consequence of modern life (Bauman, 1991; Smart, 1999). When individuals make a decision, they choose something instead of something else, in that choice the individual is very much aware of the risks a certain decision implies (Beck, 1992). To be able to handle everyday life and the risks it implies, one has to ignore some of those risks (Beck, 1992). In this context a structural story like the following appears:

"We consider the environment to the extent society makes it possible".
(Man, one car)

This explanation about how society limits the individual's
possibilities for action and structures the way it is possible to act is
very common in most aspects of life. This is a good example of a
structural story, when the structural stories contain the arguments
people commonly use to legitimize their actions and decisions.
When the individual uses a structural story they themselves believe
that they are expressing a universal truth, agreed upon by all.
Therefore the structural story helps to eliminate the perception of
risks in everyday life when they contain a structure "everybody"
accepts as a fact. The structural stories often work as a crutch for
the ambivalences, because the structural stories become the
explanation that legitimizes the ambivalences, so that the options
disappear. Having ambivalences is an inevitable part of life and they
are also an explanation as to why the structural stories are mostly
not questioned. In some ways the structural stories are a way to
legitimize the ambivalences, and the individual learn to live with the
ambivalences by the structural stories.

Reflexive Mobility and Structural Stories

It is one thing to uncover the structural story; the question then
becomes how to use them in regulating, in an environmentally
friendly way, the growing mobility. An answer could be to use such
stories in promoting reflexive mobility that is a voice that has grown
in response to the connection between mobility and late modernity.
The term reflexive mobility includes the individual's reflexivity in
connection with everyday life into the everyday life
mobility/transportation. In the following section I wish to highlight
the connection between mobility and late modernity, and then
present structural stories as a tool in the reflexive mobility
research.

Mobility and Modernity

The interconnection between mobility and modernity arises from
the idea that late modernity is closely connected to and dependent
on mobility when they encourage each other in a reciprocal process
(Harvey, 1989; Giddens, 1990; Urry, 2000; Beckmann, 2000),
because modernity both demands and facilitates mobility. Living a
late modern life demands a certain level of mobility. The individual

has to be able to get from one place to another fast, to be flexible and ready to move in a second, and most importantly have the possibility of mobility so that the idea of all the potentials embedded in everyday life does not get clouded. Mobility and modernity are a part of a dialectical relationship where there is a mutual dependence and constitution. Urry (2000) expresses this radically in saying that "the social as society" is replaced by "the social as mobility". In the social theorizing about late modern societies mobility has become the central category. "Modern society is a society on the move" (Lash and Urry 1994, p.252), and mobility is "responsible for altering how people appear to experience the modern world" (Lash and Urry 1994, p.256). This means that the starting point for understanding modernity has changed when the social from the mobility perspectives is being constituted through movement (Nielsen and Oldrup 2001).

Possibilities related to mobility are characterized by being able to do whatever you want, whenever you want, as often as you want. Essential in understanding mobility is therefore not alone the definite distance covered, but even more the potentials for movement (Gudmundsson, 2000; Høyer, 2000) – when it is in the potentials the possibilities lie. In this way, it is the potential which is closely connected with late modern life, and it is also in the light of the potentials that one has to understand how mobility is the starting point for maintaining late modern everyday life. Beckman expresses the relation of mobility to traffic as follows "traffic, in opposition to mobility, is 'realised movement in concrete geographical space'; traffic is 'materialised' mobility" (Beckmann, 2001, p.31).

Reflexive Mobility

Some kinds of mobility create environmental problems, this is especially the case with automobility, and it becomes important to consider possible ways of changing the use of different kinds of mobility. To comply with this need, the term reflexive mobility has emerged (Beckman, 2001). Reflexive mobility originates from Beck's (1994) definition of reflexivity where the individual in his or her actions incorporates the risks based on the knowledge one has. This means that with reflexive mobility, transport, which is primarily a question of getting from A-B, is not only replaced by mobility, which also covers the potential for transport, but also includes the meaning and notions of the reflexive individual. Beckmann (2001) explains that "With reflexive automobilisation we witness the decline of the one dimensional vehicle-oriented, view

and the rise of a number of multi-dimensional mobility views"
(Beckmann, 2001, p.131). Instead of only focusing on traditional
technological problem solving, other angles, for example the
organization of everyday life, are considered. In this way, reflexive
mobility becomes a tool "...for action and policymaking in the field
of transportation and mobility" (Beckmann 2001, p.106).

Reflexive mobility also contains somewhat of a 'vision' for future
mobilities, it carries the potential to reform everyday mobility not
only to be about automobility and thereby minimize some of the
risks the car is carrying. In working with reflexive mobility, the aim
becomes to mobilize the transport user's reflection on patterns of
mobilization - get them to reflect critically on how their mobility
patterns are connected to the everyday life they wish to lead. This
has to be done in policymaking on the mobility area. In this
manner, the unfolding of the structural stories, their background,
and their connection to the conception of the good life become very
important. The structural stories reveal areas of everyday life which
are filled with so many ambivalences that the individual has to use
a structural story to avoid the discomfort and difficulty of being
ambivalent. Finding a different angle than the covered transport
can be very important in the area of regulating mobility, when direct
regulation like increasing gasoline prices, road pricing, higher levies
on car purchases are almost impossible to implement, because it is
difficult to find a politician which would suggest these strategies
when he would know that many individuals would perceive this as
an act against them in person and the loss of votes would probably
be huge.

> "Raising the price on gasoline I would perceive as harassment against
> the people who choose to transport themselves, a harassment against
> those who choose to be active instead of using the public transportation
> system. I would perceive it as a suggestion from the socialists against
> those who act on their own. I would definitely perceive it as a political
> move, not to protect the environment". (Man, one car)

What this quotation clearly marks is that the challenge becomes
to find the right access to reflexive mobility and there are, in fact, a
number of places this reflexivity could emerge from. The health
angles could be pursued such as emphasizing the negative impacts
of pollution and the lack of physical activity, the time-space
compression and the shortage of time in everyday life, the risk
perspective etc, all important entrances to challenging mobility in
everyday life. Reflexivity is already a part of different choices of
lifestyles, and it raises a moral question which the individual and
the decision makers have to confront, and as a consequence the

individual engages in life politics which are the politics of the lifestyles (Giddens, 1991).

Life politics is a politic where, in late modern life, the individual reflexively makes choices on the basis of an abundance of information and experiences that he or she builds up. For some reason being reflexive about mobility does not play an important part in this life policy making. The structural stories can help us in finding the doorways through which the themes of mobility and health, time or risk perspectives of the life politics can go.

Community and Freedom as an Institutional Supporter

There are some institutional and symbolic characteristics that support the structural stories on mobility and thereby constitute barriers for reflexive mobility. One of the things closely connected to mobility is the concept of freedom, and a structural story that follows this is that "one gets more freedom when one has got a car". When carrying out interviews, especially with car users, freedom is the buzzword one hears repeatedly:

> "It is a world of difference because you have the freedom to drive a car. One has the freedom to drive wherever one wants whenever one wants and is not forced to wait for the public transport system". (Man, two cars)

This confirms the notion that when you are mobile (especially automobile), you are no longer confined to a specific area but are, instead, able to move around as it suits you. This is at least the utopia of the concept of freedom. There is a reality side to the possibilities of freedom, freedom is not possible for all at the same time - as Bauman says "To be free means to be allowed and to be able to keep others unfree" (Baumann, 1988, p.45). Being free, thus, means that somebody else has to be suppressed and the feeling of freedom originates from the possibility to act on one's own intensions (Bauman, 1988). Freedom is also characterized by the possibility of buying what you want and freedom is thereby marked by its intimate relation with capitalism (Bauman, 1988). This was very well expressed by a woman:

> "To me the car is freedom; I have the money to choose the freedom I have. A few years ago I did not have the same amount of money, so I was forced to use trains and buses". (Woman, one car)

You have the freedom to buy whatever you want. You can plan and organize your everyday life with the kind of products you feel comply best with your kind of lifestyle. Advertising for a specific product and emphasizing a specific symbolic significance or power becomes very important in capitalist society, because it is primarily the symbolic power of the merchandise that makes the individual buy the specific product (Bauman, 1988). This is why commercials often use numbers in their advertising. In commercials, it becomes very important to put a number on how many other individuals have chosen this specific product as their solution (Bauman, 1988).

"The paramount function of the argument-through-numbers is not however to imbue certainty of the kind induced with the help of scientific authority. Percentages and majorities are quoted as symbols of social approval; they deputize for the once so powerful, now weakened or missing communal support negotiated in the past through face-to-face interaction". (Bauman 1988, p.65)

This means that when the individual, in trying to create the lifestyle which contains the right symbols, has to use all the right kind of products, frequent the right kind of places, and know the right kind of people, all of this is important in sending the right message about who you are. This has become much easier today because of capitalist societies' marked methods, today most attitudes can be bought and can therefore be gained if you have the money to pay for them. The providers of symbolically charged objects are being increasingly centralized when capitalism in many ways is becoming increasingly monopolized (Bauman, 1988). This is also why the car in many ways has a head start over the public transport system. The car and its symbols are bound to a sector which spends a great deal of money to convince people that the kind of lifestyle they want to live is not possible without this important symbol. In 2002, the budget used on car commercials in Denmark alone was 305 million Danish crowns. The only sector that spent more was the telecommunication sector (Fredslund, 2003).

The symbols and the possibilities the car contains are more visible in opposition to something else, such as the public transport system. A good example of this is a new commercial for the car Daewoo Nubira. A brand new silver lined car is parked across some old railroad tracks overgrown with grass. The message is: *a new barrier for the public transport system has arrived*. The public transport system is handicapped when the company that runs this system (the state) does not have equal power of budget. Selling the public transport system as an important symbol of the right lifestyle will never have the same budget as the car industry. Baumann (1988) expresses this in connecting the power of symbol to the power of freedom and the interconnection between freedom and capital.

> "Goods and services which are not mediated by the free market (so-called 'public services', ...like...public transport...which are unlikely to be sold at a profit, or by their very nature are unfit for selling to individual costumers) tend to fall in quality and loose in attractiveness in both relative and absolute terms. Unlike the goods and services merchandised by the market, they tend to discourage their prospective consumers; to their utility values negative symbolic values are attached (stigma falling upon those who are obliged to consume them), so that they appear as a liability in the symbolic rivalry serviced by consumption. The overall shoddiness of public goods and their low grading in the hierarchy of positional symbols tend to encourage everybody who can afford it to 'by themselves out' of the dependence of public services, and into the consumer market". (Bauman 1988, pp.69-70)

Based on the structural stories I hear when interviewing and the impression I get when I read the papers, I argue that the public transport system has a far more negative reputation than it deserves. I believe this is, among other things, closely linked to the symbolic value of these transport systems. The symbolic and institutional characteristics of the public transport system and the automobile are an important part of why the individual constructs and accepts the structural stories on mobility. This is because accepting and constructing structural stories is linked to leading a life with a bearable number of ambivalences by choosing lifestyles these lifestyle choices are guided by the symbolic power of different products.

The Car Driver and the Public Transit Passenger

The idea of using the structural stories as a part of reflexive mobility is also to turn around some of the general accepted notions that exist about these different kinds of mobility. To end this chapter, I wish to do exactly that, to try to illuminate some of the entrances from which one can deconstruct the fixed notion about different kinds of mobility. I do this to find the cracks in modern life where there is a possibility to come up with new approaches to the structural story.

It is argued by some that the late modern, individualized society produces individualized transportation needs which only the car can satisfy, but Beck (1996) supplements this by saying that the individualization of the risk society liberates the individual from structures which earlier framed their social being. In this light, living in a modern individualized society means that the traveller can not just use one specific transport mode like the car, but is obliged to ask himself which specific mode of transport he chooses for a specific situation. The car in late modern society is often symbolized by freedom and a liberation from local structures because people are no longer confined to their local area, instead they have a large number of possibilities for moving on to other local societies. Beckmann (2001) states that when the car has liberated us from some structures, it has at the same time imposed some new ones on us when the "mobile individual is re-embedded into a new structure, reintegrated into standardised automotive ways of living. This standardisation is nowhere else more visible than in the periodically recurring traffic jam" (Beckmann 2001, p.49).

One could argue that the public transport user is freer and more individualized than the car driver. The public transport user is like the car driver suppressed into certain systems of transportation, but in the process of moving from A to B, the public transport user has time on his hands that he can use in a way he finds most suitable or pleasant, while moving he is not forced to be alerted to different structures and systems which automobility demands. Most car drivers know this, but still they use a structural story to explain why they don't. The following quotations show that these men know that it is not always rational to use the car for all the trips they make, but they still end up with a structural story to explain why they uses the car every time:

> "Sometimes when I have to travel across the country, it is obviously the smartest thing to do to take the train. It is much more comfortable to sit down in nice surroundings, especially if you go by 1st class. One can use the public transport system reasonably, but a rush hour train is not what one dreams about". (Man, two cars)

> "Driving a car to work is in reality very messy because when driving 5 kilometres the motor doesn't get warm and there are trains and busses right to the door. But it is faster and more convenient and sometimes I have to bring my laptop". (Man, one car)

In our individualized society, where the individual has to create different lifestyles which comply with the symbols that individuals wants to show (Giddens, 1991, Beck, 1992), time is valued as being more and more precious. In daily routines, at work, attending the right cultural event, attending the right football club time is in short supply. The activities of a family today are spread over a larger geographical area. Instead of slowing down and gaining more time from new faster technologies, the family crams more activities into everyday life. Having time on your hands becomes an important signal on which kind of everyday life the individual has. The traffic jam for the car driver becomes a time thief that does not comply very well with the signal of freedom the car driver wishes to send.

The driver controls and the passengers are being controlled, this is something you will hear many car drivers express; they are in control because they decide when to do what. The public transit passenger on the other hand has to fit in to an already fixed pattern together with a number of other passengers. But on the other hand, today's car driver is not as in control and free of traffic systems controlled by other as often perceived. Beckmann (2001) points out that "to perform our daily activities as car-drivers, we have to plan our trips just as much as the public transit passenger" (p.36).

One can say that there is a flip side to automobility, it gives us possibilities but on the other hand it puts tight restraints on our mobility and today everyday life is moulded into a structure that forces people to keep moving. Thus it is possible to question and deconstruct the common knowledge the structural stories consist of. One way of doing this is to confront the arguments shared with counterarguments.

Conclusions

Individuals' mobility patterns are based on a number of conscious and unconscious choices. This is because of the choices of lifestyles and the following fragmentation of everyday life activities in time and space. The mobility pattern the individual chooses is however not only a derived effect of modern life, but is also a necessary provision for modernity because there exists a mutual dependence and constitution between mobility and modernity. A modern everyday life is characterized no longer by a connection to territorial anchored communities, but in a much higher degree of our mobility between a number of different communities. The selection between these different communities is done on the basis of a large number of symbols that make the foundation for the lifestyles the individual chooses. By accepting the connection between mobility and modernity, it opens up a possibility to act on the basis of mobility perceived as a necessity and not an environmental problematic phenomenon that has to be limited. The mobility of late modernity must in a much higher degree be liberated from its close connection to automobility by making other forms of more environmentally friendly mobilities visible. This is where reflexive mobility plays an important role because it offers an action-oriented perspective for changing the present development where the individuals organize their everyday life by increasing automobility. In many countries mobility management is playing an increasingly part of regulating mobility. It contains several initiatives where different measures to changing attitudes are mixed. This is here the structural stories can offer an important analytical angle because they reveals the cracks in everyday life where it is possible to plant a new story on the logical and common knowledge about "what one does". Furthermore increasingly use of the reflexive mobility and the structural stories as an important part of policymaking when promoting new ideas to be used in mobility management can play an important role in a future not drowning in automobiles.

Acknowledgements

I would like to thank my good friends and colleagues Katrine Hartmann-Petersen and Kenneth Roslind with whom I worked in an inspiring and constructive atmosphere for more than three years. It was in this teamwork the Structural Stories emerged and became an important player in understanding mobility. I would also like to thank members of the FLUX group for constructive criticism and inputs especially Lise Drewes Nielsen and Thyra Uth Thomsen for valuable critique of earlier drafts. Furthermore, has Research Manager Randi Hjorthol's (Institute of Transport Economics, Oslo, Norway) sharp and insightful criticism been very helpful. I have also received encouragement and critical comments when an early version of this paper was presented at Environmental Psychology at The Graduate Center of City University of New York. The generous financial support of the Danish State Railways S-Trains is gratefully acknowledged.

References

Bauman, Z. (1988), *Freedom,* Open University Press, Stratford.
Bauman, Z. (1991), *Modernity and Ambivalence,* Cornell University Press, Ithaca, New York.
Bauman, Z. (2000), *Liquid modernity,* Polity Press, Cambridge.
Beck, U. (1992), *Risk society: towards a new modernity,* Sage, London.
Beck, U. (1996), *Reinvention of politics – rethinking modernity in the global social order,* Polity Press, Cambridge.
Beck, U., Giddens, A. and Lash, S. (1994), *Reflexive Modernization - politics, tradition and aesthetics in the modern social order,* Polity Press, Cambridge.
Beckmann, J. (2000), 'Automobilisering som mobilitetsparadigme –

refleksioner over biler, bilister og deres spatiotemporaliteter' [Auto mobilization as mobility paradigm – reflections on car drivers and their spatial temporalities], *Dansk Sociologi [Danish Sociology]*, nr. 1/11. Årg. København.

Beckmann, J. (2001), *Risky mobility – the filtering of automobility's unintended consequences*, Sociologisk Institut, Københavns Universitet, København.

Berger, P. L. and Luckmann, T. (1966), *The social construction of reality: A treatise in the sociology of knowledge*, Doubleday, New York.

Burr, V. (1995), *An Introduction to Social Constructionism*, Routledge, London.

Fredslund, A. (2003), Reklamer for personbiler i stigning [Commercials for cars in growth]. Gallup Adfacts/TNS Media Intelligence http://www.gallup.dk/page.aspx?pageid=554 (date 22.9.03).

Freudendal-Pedersen, M., Hartmann-Petersen, K. and Roslind, K. (1999), *Virksomhedens Trafikale Ansvar [The traffic responsibility of the company]*, Roskilde University.

Freudendal-Pedersen, M., Hartmann-Petersen, K. and Roslind, K. (2000), *Mobilitet i hverdagen – taler vi nok om det? [Mobility in everyday life – do we talk enough about it]*, Roskilde University.

Freudendal-Pedersen, M., Hartmann-Petersen, K. and Roslind, K. (2002), *Strukturelle fortællinger om mobilitet [Structural stories on mobility]*, Roskilde University.

Giddens, A. (1984), *The Constitution of Society*, The University of California Press, California.

Giddens, A. (1990), *The consequences of modernity*, Stanford University Press, Stanford, California.

Giddens, A. (1991), *Modernity and Self-Identity*, Polity Press, Cambridge.

Gudmundsson, H. (2000), *Mobilitet og bæredygtighed – strategier, mål og institutioner i reguleringen af persontransport, [Mobility and sustainability]*, PhD thesis, Copenhagen Business School, Copenhagen.

Harvey, D. (1989), *The condition of postmodernity*, Basil Blackwell, Oxford.

Høyer, K. G. (2000), *Sustainable Mobility – the Concept and its Implications*, PhD thesis, Department of Environment, Technology and Social Studies, Roskilde University.

Lash, S. and Urry, J. (1994), *Economies of signs and space*, Sage, London.

Nielsen, L.D. and Oldrup, H.H. (2001), *Mobility and Transport – An Anthology*, Notat nr. 01. 03, Danish Transport Council, Copenhagen.

Sayer, A. (2000), *Realism and social science*, Sage, London.

Smart, B. (1999), *Facing Modernity – Ambivalence, Reflexivity and Morality*, Sage, London.

Urry, J. (2000), *Sociology Beyond Societies – mobilities for the twenty-first century*, Routledge, London.

Zeitler, U. (1998), *Mobilitet og Moral – aspekter af en transportetik [Mobility and morals – aspects of a transport ethics]*, Notat nr. 98/05, Danish Transport Council, Copenhagen.

Chapter 3

Reflexive Mobility – A Critical and Action Oriented Perspective on Transport Research

Lise Drewes Nielsen

Introduction

In spring 2003, a PhD course entitled 'Future Sustainable Transport' was held for European students working in the field of transport studies. During a lecture I asked them to make a list of priorities relating to their main aims in studying transport. The main theme was clear: to develop knowledge so as to support changes in the transport system in a more acceptable and sustainable direction, both in societal as well as environmental terms. Of course, it was also to produce good science within their disciplines, a main aim of a PhD thesis. But making changes in the field of transport was their main concern.

This convinced me that the discussion of the relationship between theory and the fields of inquiry must reflect a philosophy of science that includes the concepts and ontology of critical and action oriented research. This chapter is an attempt to outline some of the main features of critical and action oriented transport research. It is based on my own experience in undertaking empirically based transport research.

This chapter is also an attempt to follow the line of transport research which have evolved over the last few decades pushing it in a societal or sociological direction. Transport research has traditionally been dominated by the natural sciences, the technical sciences, and engineering and quantitative based economics. During the last decade, a sociologically oriented perspective has evolved inspired by soft science. Transport research has no discipline of its own. It is a field of the application of research inspired by traditional disciplines. It has also been developed through multidisciplinary studies. Often we will find research closely related to empirical field studies, but now and then a discussion of the philosophy of science within the fields is undertaken (Næss and Jensen, 2002).

The main purpose of this chapter is to establish criteria for critical and action oriented social science within transport research. To do this it is important to work through three specific questions. 1) Given a social science perspective, what constitutes the relationship between transport and society, and what are the main issues, characteristics and results? 2) Can a concept of reflexive mobility contribute to critical transport research? 3) How can we establish a new empirical focus in action oriented critical transport research?

Metaphors of Mobility

Connections between society, action and values are often expressed in terms of metaphors. Metaphors are expressed through pictures and are often used in periods or fields containing unsafe and insecure paths of development. They can provide an understanding of the driving forces and relations between the industrial societies' development and the development of transport. Transport research is often founded on an empirical reality, where all individuals have personal experiences and well known images and symbols which can be reflected in metaphors. Metaphors of modern life are often built on metaphors related to transport.

During the last few years, metaphors that relate mobility and the societal have evolved. Three of them are to be mentioned here, selected to represent the views and perspectives which are important for the rest of the chapter.

Time-space compression. David Harvey (1990) analysed production and distribution in late capitalism and conceptualised them in terms of intense phases of time and space compression. This has become a famous metaphor used to illustrate the shrinking globe. The concept of time use for travelling compared to distance is a very good indicator of the diminishing of distance on the globe. Harvey introduced the concepts in a normative and critical analysis of the capitalistic economy and its tendencies to expand production systems throughout the global economy.

Liquid modernity. Bauman (2000) introduced the metaphor of liquid modernity as the characteristic of modern society. His purpose is to describe how institutions, relations and habits have melted from their traditional forms and are becoming liquid. The liquid is moving through time and space and is not related to a specific context. Institutions, relations and habits are only contemporary and constantly on the move. Bauman's metaphor is closely connected to his understanding of movement and mobility. Although Bauman's analyses are not related to an understanding of transport as such, there is an underlying understanding that the transport system and the development of automobility support and integrate the melting forces in liquid modernity. Bauman's analyses include a critique of late modernity. He argues that the liquid must become solid in the future. But the processes that will force this development are not clear. Bauman's metaphor includes a critique of the modern societies' liquidity.

From clock-time to instantaneous time. The focus on time has produced several metaphors relating to time which have been introduced by Urry (2000) and Hylland Eriksen (2001). They argue that post modern societies have changed from clock time developed in relation to the time scheduling of transport technologies such as trains, busses, flights and ferries to instantaneous time, where the technology of automobility and information technology change our views on time towards flexibility and individuality and with independencies of shared or public organised patterns of mobility.

These three examples of metaphors show how mobility and its relationship to economic, technological and cultural development form the basis for understanding developments in late modern society. Mobility is a part of the formation of consciousness, identity and the understanding of development. Social relations are produced and reproduced through movements. If we want to change the movements, we need to understand the underlying relations these movements are parts of, whether they are a part of the capitalist system, a liquid modernity or changes in time, as the three selected metaphors in their own right illustrate. The metaphors are not specifically related to transport research, but the concepts they use: time and space compression as well as time and going liquid are all concepts related to movement, mobility and transport. They all give pictures and images of mobility related to the societal and create relationships between understandings of post modern society and its relations to patterns of mobility (Urry, 2000).

Against this background, two main perspectives on transport deriving from modern transport research will be presented: one taking its departure in studies of the relations between the structural development of the society and its consequences for transport; the other taking its departure in the sociological understanding of the connection between modernity and mobility. I shall argue that these two perspectives are necessary but not sufficient for the development of reflexive transport research. Something must be added.

The Economy-Ecology Mobility Research

Critical transport research has often related to the philosophy of science along the same lines as Harvey's metaphor of time and space compression in capitalist society. In capitalist production and distribution, the transport systems' tasks are to fulfil the demands of the capitalist system. The development of technology seems to fulfil these demands in a convincing way and the political system supports these demands in establishing the necessary infrastructure to support the growth of automobility.

As a transport researcher focussing on freight transport, I have gained great insight into how time, space and speed have developed during the last decades (Drewes Nielsen, Jespersen, Petersen and Hansen, 2003; Petersen and Drewes Nielsen, 2004). The global division of labour and the globalised economy demand growth in the transport system in terms of volume and speed, which the productivity of the transport system has made possible. At the same time, transport prices have decreased when compared to the prices of other products. Indeed, transport costs often count for as little as 5-8 per cent of a product's value. Transport is also cheap because the external costs in terms of investments in infrastructure and environmental expenditures are not included in the price of transport, and because of efficiency in the transport system. This is why transport is a basic element of the global economy, in the European market and in inland distribution. Distance and time have been compressed and the possibilities of creating mobility in the production system are a precondition for building up global and local production and distribution systems. It can be said that the transport system has gained great victories, because it has diminished the friction present in the global production and distribution systems. It is a necessary technological and organisational precondition for the modern global economy.

The growth in transport is closely connected to economic growth, and the relationship is an accumulative one. Transport growth is greater than economic growth. Automobility and the number of cars, the number of kilometres driven, and the number of flights are all growing; consequently there are demands for new and enormous investments in transport infrastructure. The physical space used for transport is also growing and expanding in the cities, as they are required on behalf of other social activities (Graham and Marvin, 2001). The main problem with transport seen from an environmental perspective is the growth curves concerning transport activities, because the environmental gains from technology and security are swallowed up by the growth in the sector.

The EU White Paper (2001) argues that future activities within transport should have the ambition of decoupling the transport curves from the curves in economy, which means lower transport growth than economic growth. But because of the development hitherto, it will demand radical changes in all aspects of transport to break the acceleration in the transport curve. The relation between the economy and transport is that the decoupling between transport and economy is a reality but in the opposite direction. At the concrete level, only a few actors in the field of transport, from scientists, to business people to politicians, believe that this decoupling will take place in the near future. It is thought of as unrealistic, even if it is stated that it will take place in almost all more or less official scenarios (OECD, 2000).

If sustainable development is defined as the ability to balance the relation between human activities and nature and ensure that future generations have the same possibilities as do contemporary generations, the conclusion is clear: the transport system is not sustainable. And if we define rhetoric as 'exaggeration in fluency', you will find empty rhetoric in the attempts to couple sustainability and transport.

At the European level, we have seen recent tendencies to eliminate the discussion of sustainability and given this, we might face a period of no official link between sustainability and transport (EU White Paper, 2001). Even if until now the connection between sustainability and transport has been unclear, it is also evident that the focus on sustainability has forced some directions of building up knowledge and experience with the development and changes of the transport system in other directions than the clear market driven forces, which is now the main agenda in the European and national transport policy. The problems with sustainability in the transport sector have been a driving force in arguing for changes in the transport systems in the direction of ecological modernisation (Hajer, 1995). The worry that the growth in the sector has produced has been translated to a normative, more acceptable, need for changes in order to produce more sustainable transport. After the diminished focus on sustainability, arguments for changing the transport system mentioned above might be found anyway, but now not in the case of sustainability, but because of future fuel scarcity and high prices on fuel.

Critical science within transport research (called economy-ecology mobility research) has followed the debates outlined above, and argued that the ongoing problems with sustainability in the transport sector steadily has to be documented in order to produce knowledge about the relationship in order to convince the public to change the transport system in more sustainable directions. A special part of this research has been environmental research focussed on the damage transport and the growing demand of mobility cause in relation to nature, humans, environment, health and safety. The critical action oriented transport research which concentrates on this area faces however several dilemmas. On the one hand, a major part of transport research focuses on measuring and documenting what is wrong with the close connection between transport, economic growth and the environment, in order to prove the need for changes. But the discussion at the political level is strongly connected to the belief that transport is a precondition for economic growth and that the regulation of or reduction in transport in order to improve sustainable development is a threat to the economy. Thus, often, at a political level, the findings of research into sustainable transport are seen as being useless.

On the other hand, the dilemma is that actors involved in transport (including individuals) seem to be aware of all the risks transport entails in relation to nature, health, and security, and nevertheless demand even faster and more flexible (automobile) transport systems and seems to exclude the knowledge delivered from research, when it comes to decisions and actions within transport. Critical transport research thus faces big problems if the purpose is to change mobility patterns. The philosophy of science linked to this economy-ecology mobility research has been based on traditional disciplines and methodologies: Indicators, interviews, modelling and statistics.

The Social Modernity Mobility Research

The social modernity mobility research focuses on relations between modern society and transport and represents another perspective than that of the economy-ecology mobility research. The development of some areas of transport research in a sociological direction and vice versa, has brought the issue of the relationships between transport and behaviour, actors and social relations onto the agenda. In connection with this, the research connects the understanding of 'transport' with the concept of mobility.

Transport has traditionally been defined as movement from A to B, but the definition has been shown to be too narrow an approach from a sociological perspective in transport research. In order to broaden the concept of transport, the concept of mobility was introduced. Mobility is a well-known sociological concept, related to class, social activity and movement. In transport research, it was introduced as the social aspects of movement (physical and virtual). Mobility refers to both actual and potential movements, and includes corporal, objective and virtual movements. Mobility can refer to movements of persons, information, communication and images (Urry, 2000; Gudmundsson, 2000; Kaufmann, 2002).

The concept of mobility reflects tendencies in post modern society related to concepts such as the fluid society, flow society, network society, etc (Bauman, 2000; Castells, 2000; Graham and Marvin, 2001). Mobility is seen as a precondition for understanding movement in post-modern society and especially understanding how social structures are produced and reproduced through mobility. It means that it is the movement and the social relations formed through movement, which is the point of departure for research and not the localised structures themselves.

In this way, the concept of mobility focuses on the social processes around movement, and creates a challenge for modern social sciences. This can be expressed as follows: "Where the societal often is thought of as being related to structure, to the solid and stable, in the mobility perspective the societal is thought of as being constituted through movement. This means that we must rethink the social and environmental in new and other ways" (Drewes Nielsen and Oldrup, 2001).

Several researchers have, in recent years, described characteristics of modernity, post modernity and late modernity. Few have however related this to mobility. John Urry delivered an exception with his book *Sociology Beyond Society* (2000). He separates mobility into corporal mobility (personal mobility), object mobility (freight transport) and virtual mobility (information) and imaginary mobility (TV and media). His point is that different forms of mobility expand in modern life and together they constitute the structures behind the social. In these movements and their relationships, social life is created, produced and reproduced. He also provides some concepts for analysing the flows of mobility.

Another inspiration in the analyses of mobility is Virilio's book *Speed and Politics* (1986). His point of departure is the concept of speed, the logic of which is determined by the development of technology. New technology will accelerate speed of which the development of transport technologies is an excellent example. The driving force is technology and the societal is subordinated and encompassed in it. Towns are transformed through technology and are formed to fit the technologies of speed. Automobility and its transport systems have transformed cities. Virilio has a normative, critical and pessimistic view on accelerating speed, but points out that the acceleration will meet its own limits resulting in its opposite: silence. Society, in its eagerness to develop speed, will turn to the opposite condition of silence.

Transport research has, as is the case with Urry and Virilio, often analysed the correlation between mobility, the system of transport and its technologies. The transport systems are analysed, on the one hand, as technological constructions and on the other hand as the preconditions for new patterns of mobility. The relation between technology and society is a complicated mix of social and technologically founded routines and patterns. Automobility is a good example; it is studied both as a technological construction but also as a technology with great potential for creating new social patterns, new demands for mobility, and accelerating speed. Automobility has influenced possibilities and demands for transport in modern life as a mix between lifestyles, behaviour and technological possibilities. In these ways, transport research often has a strong focus on technology (automobility with trains, cars and flights) too, as is the case with other research areas with a strong technological dominance.

The publication of Urry's book in 2000 and his interpretation of relations between mobility and modernity created a new platform for transport research, even though Urry does not engage in transport research as such. The focus was not to analyse mobility as a result of the structural changes in society, but the understanding of mobility as represented in social science. The roots of mobility are to be found in modern life. Mobility as such was the point of departure and was to be understood as an integrated part of modern life and of the societal. Accessibility and mobility create identity and relationships. The philosophy of science consistent with Urry's work (the social modernist mobility research) is based on new interpretative research: discourse analysis, interviewing, qualitative research etc. It is quite the opposite of the type of transport research (the economy-ecology mobility research) and its accompanying philosophy of science which was outlined above.

Parts of the mobility-modernity transport research might be questioned as critical research. Often, its eagerness to explain how and why mobility is so closely related to modernity has weakened its relationships to the critique of both mobility and modernity. An overstated focus on super-mobilities, on car studies, on time pressures in modern life and on family patterns linked to automobile life has proved these intentions. In some cases, the research has been in support of the automobile society and taken its existence for granted out of necessity. Conclusions like modern life is busy and it is impossible to live without a car makes a generalising mistake and leaves modern life experiences without a car invisible. However, as a consequence of the generalising mistake and perhaps the research design, the research fails, also in its critical orientation (if ever intended) towards the changes of the automobile transport system.

Some studies have focussed on the dilemma that mobility also produces immobility and inequality (Beckman, 2001a). Mobility patterns create possibilities of immobility for the actors without access to automobility. Others have focussed on the dilemmas of everyday life where the link to the automobility life styles creates reflections of the possibilities of other lifestyles. Only a few studies have however focussed on people in the systems of auto immobility in spite of the fact that 25 per cent of EU inhabitants are without daily access to cars.

Reflexive Mobility – A New Concept

The above arguments lay the ground for the next sections of this chapter: Is it possible to create a new platform for critical mobility research that takes for granted both the nexus of the structural and technological changes in society and transport, and the nexus of mobility and modernity, but adds a critical focus on its relationship? Is it possible for mobility research to contribute to the changes in the transport system needed in order to solve the unacceptable damage that the system creates to the immobilised, to nature, health, and safety and to the societal?

Ulrich Beck formulated one version of the concept of reflexivity in which reflection contains the knowledge about risks and unintended consequences (Beck, 1986; Beck, Giddens and Lash, 1994). Concerning transport, it means that the reflection on transport (persons, organisations and political decisions) also includes the consequences of transport decisions. It can be described as follows: "The term reflexive mobility captures those mobilities that are self-critical. In other words, mobilities that take a more critical stance towards their own unintended consequences" (Beckmann, 2001b; Beckmann, 2002). Beckmann illustrates this with an example of car sharing, where car sharing can be understood as a reflexive approach to the self produced capacity problem of the private car in many urban areas. 'Reflexive mobility' is able to imply ambivalences in modern life (here car use, capacity problems and car-sharing) and might open up possibilities for new ways of understanding the essence of both mobility and the transformation of mobility.

Mobility is an integrated part of reflexive modernisation. The use of travelling and the use of automobility to support mobility are results of reflexive modernisation, of choices and actions. The question is, however, in which way reflexive mobility can include a development that decouples the relationship between modernity and mobility, as expressed by increases in speed, distance, automobility, damage to nature and damage to the societal (Beckmann 2002).

The relationship between mobility and modernity and the metaphors of reflexive mobility contain much ambivalence and contrasts. Firstly it is a question of mobility and immobility; secondly it is a question of mobility and movement decoupled or liberated from the most unacceptable consequences of automobility; thirdly it is a question of mobility decoupled from the acceleration of time and speed and from individualisation; and fourthly a question of mobility decoupled from its differentiation along classes, gender and ethnicity.

Several studies have proved that modernity and automobility are closely linked. The wishes and longings for access are an integrated part of modern life, where families and social ties are formed across greater and greater distances. Mobility and accessibility represent something good and valuable.

The problem is however that when all these aspects of individual behaviour and wishes are summed up and integrated into the transport systems based on automobility something is missing. Much scientific research has proved at the aggregated level that transport in the era of automobility is unsustainable, ineffective, counterproductive and unacceptable; this is in spite of the fact that much scientific research has also stated the opposite. Can a concept of reflexive mobility include these discrepancies? Can transport research?

Two concepts of reflexive mobility might contribute to meeting the above challenge: the concept of reflexive ecomobility and the concept of reflexive shared mobility.

Reflexive Ecomobility

The negative consequences of transport activities have been at the basis of the main research questions in the endless stream of transport research of the Brundtland Era. The documentation is evident; the relationship between the transport system and nature is one of imbalance.

In the search for a critical social transport research and the understanding of the relations between the era of automobility and late modernity, a tendency has developed to over socialise mobility to understand and explain how automobility exploits social relations, institutions and behaviour. It means that mobility is often loosened from its materiality.

In line with the argument presented earlier in the chapter, it seems clear that the two research perspectives have difficulties in meeting. They have different philosophies of science and purposes with their science. But where the ecological-economy inspired research seems to be dominated by structure and consequence thinking as a precondition for change, the mobility-modernity studies are not interested in the ecologically and materialistically founded aspects of mobility.

The consequences of this are clear, if the intention is to include ecological aspects in transport research, new ways of thinking are required. The ecological perspectives need to be included as a platform representing the societal and the preconditions for changes in the transport system. If not, ecology will be excluded as a societal category, left behind as something unintended and forgotten in research. The problems with the risks of automobility are not included and are not delivered as the narratives from one generation of researchers to another. It is also not included in many metaphors.

A concept of reflexive mobility will have to include a concept of sustainability. For this purpose, the concept of ecomobility, mobility that creates less social and environmental damage on the surroundings, ought to be included and developed in transport research. It is not a pattern of mobility which goes back to pre-modern times, but a pattern of mobility which tries to transform modern mobility in the direction of ecomobility.

One point here is the obligation on social researchers to give ecomobility a special space in the understanding of mobility around social research and integrate it into their work by relating it to a concept of reflexive mobility.

Reflexive Shared Mobility

Individualisation is an integrated part of modernisation. As individuals, we face the closure of institutions, and as individuals, we are forced to create new relationships and identities. Mobility is the power we have to build these new relationships. It is a privatised part of modernity to create your own pattern, but also a tendency to individualise the consequences of the chosen patterns (Bauman, 2000).

The processes of individualisation are almost a study of the era of automobility in the industrialised world. Both automobility and individualisation are integrated parts of every day life stories based on stable routines and actions with little or no incentives to change.

Changes in automobility are rarely on the agenda and knowledge of risks around transport activities is also seldom aired.

The tendencies to individualise transport are supported by the development of the transport system. Every demand on individualised transport has a high priority in the political system. The individualised argument is deeply rooted in statements made in discussions concerning transport, and it seems as though it is a personal right to demand automobility, whether personal mobility or mobility of goods. The right to access at the right time and the right to buy fresh goods from all over the world are deeply rooted in every day demands affecting mobility.

The individualised arguments for or rights to transport are often used without taking the consequences of the transport system, in relation to e.g. the environment, health and safety, into account. The demands and rights for access are often also the main political arguments behind decisions for greater infrastructure investments and for the support to automobility.

The question here is whether we can develop a concept of shared responsible mobility taking its departure in the understanding of collective preferences beside or may be above the individualised. Is it possible to introduce socially shared reflection on mobility? To develop a concept of mobility, which always includes both an individualised and a shared perspective? (Beckman, 2001b).

The Cracks in the Seamlessly Growing Mobility

The concept of reflexive mobility ought to be elaborated in relation to decisions concerning transport at all levels: everyday, political, expert (municipalities, government, etc). The concept is however also related to science and research.

This chapter has argued that research studying the relation between economic structure and transport (economy-ecology mobility research) is weak at improving changes in mobility patterns. The chapter has also argued that the research studying relations between mobility and modernity (the social modernity mobility research) often does not include a normative and change oriented perspective. I have tried to suggest some normative concepts for understanding and give the direction of changes in mobility patterns. But I have not, until now, presented any solutions as to how these concepts can be included in research design when it comes to the empirical field. I will elaborate on this.

The understanding of the relations that exist between mobility, modernity and actors has brought new knowledge of the profound relationships that exist between them, and also the knowledge that modern identity is deeply routed in mobility, movement and travelling, and in the technologies that follow with automobility. On the other hand, the mobility patterns are not socially and ecologically acceptable in the long run.

The specification of normativity in scientific work is an obligation for all researchers. This is also the case within transport research. Transport research is often based on empirical interpretation. The researchers' selection of empirical fields of study in the design of the research projects is part of the responsibility of scientists. During the last decade, social science has become more aware of the responsibility of researchers in designing scientific analyses in the relationship between theory and empirical fields. A profound discussion about these responsibilities is, however, often demanded within social science and also often stated in critique coming from outside the field (Nowotny, Scott and Gibbons, 2001). The normativity in the selection of theory, design and empirical field is also an issue in transport research. If we add intentions of change in mobility patterns, it is obvious that normativity is most important.

In transport research the challenge is to describe activities and categories that break the accumulative relation between mobility and modernity in new reflexive ways. The question is, however, whether we can find any evidence of this already. This evidence might be the cracks where the changes will evolve making possible developments in other directions. Is it possible that science can contribute to opening the cracks and broadening the perspectives for changes, and develop fruitful categories and concepts to describe and analyze these changes? A scientific programme for transport and mobility research with this focus could include elements such as the following:

A focus on all examples of limiting automobility. Many examples have been suggested of how the physical reduction in automobility has changed mobility patterns. Reduction in the number of cars in the inner cities has changed mobility patterns. Campaigns for car free cities and car free days have demonstrated the possibilities of daily life without cars. Also the development and support of other transport modes like bicycles, public transport and walking have demonstrated interests and possibilities of changes in mobility patterns.

A focus on relations that decouple understandings of close and automatic correlations between mobility and modernity. A part of modernity is also immobility and mobility without automobility. How does modernity evolve for groups without access to automobility? In the field of freight transport is it possible to organize production and distribution systems with less use of transport? How do rail and inland waterway transport develop?

A focus on new ways of organizing production and distribution. Is it possible to change the global market towards more regionally bound production and distribution systems? Is it possible to organize transport in other directions?

A focus on expanding tools for mobility management. The new concept of 'mobility management' involves tools for changing the demand for transport. If the demand changes, the pressure on the transport system will diminish and the decoupling between modernity and mobility take other paths. Companies' transport plans and individual transport plans are providing an ever increasing number of examples of that development.

A focus on the community based right to mobility and access and not the individual. Many examples of shared mobility have shown that it is possible to diminish the individualized rights to transport: car sharing clubs, effective public transport systems, co-driving, etc.

A focus on modern lives released from the speed metaphor. This implies more radical changes in the correlation between modernity and mobility if modern life is to be released from the speed metaphor. Also here we find tendencies breaking the curves of speed. Movements like down shifters, slow city, and slow food are all examples of cracks in the post modern metaphor of speed.

The discussion about speed and time use has been profound in the Scandinavian countries during the last few years (Hylland Eriksen, 2001; Jönsson, 2000). The debate has its departure in the development of modern life as 'a tyranny of time and speed'. More and more people are involved in the discussion in order to find routines for breaking the time tyranny of daily life. Technological development and especially the information- and communication technologies, the consumer oriented lifestyles and work organizations have all supported the time bands in the daily lives. Along these lines, automobility seems a suitable technology that in some narratives of daily lives is included as a necessity. Transport research and the concept of reflexive mobility can easily be combined with understandings of speed and time-use and to the correlation or cracks in post modern life.

The final research questions are: Can we find all these cracks in modernity in order to breakdown and change the development of mobility? Can we find social scientists that support and give voices to reflexive mobility, to new mobility patterns, and to cracks in modernity?

Research into reflexive mobility will also imply a conscious selection of research topics and methodology, where researchers are aware of their role in data production, actor involvement and changes. The growing interest in action research means that it will be included in future mobility research in order to introduce democratic processes of learning to researchers and actors in the field (Drewes Nielsen and Gjesing Hansen, 1997; Drewes Nielsen, Jespersen and Hartmann-Pedersen, 2004).

Conclusions

Reflexive mobility is a new concept in transport research that indicates new challenges for transport and mobility research orientated towards social and critical science. The concept focuses support on normative and modified transport research, from environmental as well as societal perspectives.

Two approaches in transport research within social sciences have been presented in this chapter. One approach presents studies of the relationships between the economic, technological and politically driven system of automobility and the environment called the economy-ecology mobility research. Another approach represents the relationship between modernity and mobility, where everyday life and identity seem locked around automobility or super mobility, called the social-modernity mobility research.

The chapter argues that the above mentioned approaches have delivered profound and indispensable knowledge about transport, movement and mobility. On the other hand, they have not been able to, for various reasons, contribute to changes in mobility patterns.

The need for new concepts and approaches in transport research and society is obvious if the normative change oriented transport research is to be developed. The concept of reflexive mobility in the hands of critical and action oriented researchers might be such a concept. Reflexive mobility means that the reflection on transport (persons, organisations, political decisions etc) also includes the consequences of transport decisions and includes the risks and the unintended consequences. The concept and its use in empirical research might stimulate movements towards future sustainable transport and mobility. The topics of reflexive mobility inquiries could be: the means of reduction in automobility, new production and distribution systems, new shared mobility patterns away from individualized transport systems, new mobility management with less demand for transport and new directions of speed reduction with demands on slower movements and more time for social activities.

The responsibility for the use of concepts and the formulation of research questions is a normative part of research and is captured by the research design created by researchers. Science also plays a role as a change agent in relation to the development of transport and transport systems. Transport is an integrated part of the economic, technological and political system of the post modern capitalist society. Transport is also an integrated part of everyday experiences in the form of personal mobility and globalised production and consumption. Transport includes relationships of power and suppression linked to the social and natural environments and transport. Transport systems have undergone continuous changes.

This chapter poses the question of whether it is possible from a critical social science approach to influence these changes in more sociological and ecological directions and whether the concept of reflexive mobility in the hands of research contributes to these changes in transport, movement and mobility.

Acknowledgements

I want to thank Research Manager Randi Hjorthol, Institute of Transport Economics, Oslo, Norway for her constructive and critical review of the chapter. I also want to thank colleagues at FLUX – Centre for Transport Research at Roskilde University and colleagues at Danish Sociological Conference at Aalborg University in 2003 for comments and proposals to the basic ideas of the chapter. I also want to thank Andrew Crabtree and David Flynn for language revisions.

References

Bauman, Zygmunt (2000), *Liquid Modernity*, Polity Press, Cambridge.
Beck, Ulrich (1986), *Risikosamfundet på vej mod en ny modernitet*, Hans Reitzels Forlag, Copenhagen. [(1999) *World Risk Society*, Polity Press, Cambridge.]
Beck, Ulrich, Giddens, Anthony and Lash, Scott (1994), *Reflexive modernization: politics, tradition and aesthetics in the modern social order*, Polity, Cambridge.
Beckmann, Jörg (2001a), 'Heavy traffic – paradoxes of a modernity mobility nexus', in L. Drewes Nielsen and H. H. Oldrup, (eds), *Mobility and transport – An anthology*. Note no. 01-03, The Danish Transport Council, Copenhagen. www.transportraadet.dk
Beckmann, Jörg (2001b), *Risky mobility: the filtering of automobility's unintended consequences*, PhD dissertation: 20, Department of Sociology, University of Copenhagen.
Beckmann, Jörg (2002), 'Sustainable transport and reflexive mobility. Definitely economically feasible and always socially acceptable', in

European Conference of Ministers of Transport, *International Seminar managing the fundamental Drivers of Transport Demand.*

Castells, Manuel (2000), *The Information Age: Economy, Society, and Culture* (three volumes), Blackwell, Oxford.

Drewes Nielsen, L. and Gjesing Hansen, L. (1997), 'Involving Citizens in Sustainable Development: Scenario Workshop on Sustainable Mobility', *Journal of Advanced Transportation*, Vol. 31, no. 2.

Drewes Nielsen, L. and Oldrup, H. H. (eds) (2001), *Mobility and Transport*, Note no. 01-03, The Danish Transport Council, Copenhagen, www.transportraadet.dk.

Drewes Nielsen, L., Jespersen, P. H. and Hartmann-Pedersen, K. (2004), 'Future Workshops on freight transport – a methodology for actor involvement', *World Transport Politics & Practice.*

Drewes Nielsen, L., Jespersen, P.H., Petersen, T. and Hansen, L.G. (2003), 'Freight transport growth – a theoretical and methodological framework', *European Journal of Operational Research*, Volume 144, Number 2.

EU (2000), *Forecasting and Assessment of New Technologies and Transport Systems and their Impacts on the Environment* (FANTASIE). http://www.etsu.com/fantasie/fantasie.htm

EU (2001): *White Paper. European transport policy for 2010: time to decide.* http://europa.eu.int/comm/energy_transport/en/lb_en.html

Graham, Stephen and Marvin, Simon (2001), *Splintering urbanism: networked infrastructures, technological mobilities and the urban condition*, Routledge, London.

Gudmundsson, Henrik (2000), *Mobilitet og bæredygtighed. Strategier, mål og institutioner i reguleringen af persontransport*, [*Mobility and sustainability*]PhD serie 8:2000, Copenhagen Business School, Samfundslitteratur, Copenhagen.

Hajer, Maarten A. (1995), *The Politics of Environmental Discourse*, Clarendon Press, Oxford.

Harvey, D. (1990), *The condition of postmodernity*, Blackwell, Oxford.

Hylland Eriksen, Thomas (2001), *Øyeblikkets Tyranni: rask og langsom tid i informationssamfundet*, [*The tyranny of time: quick and slow time in the age of information society*], Aschehoug, Oslo.

Jönsson, Bodil (2000), *Ti tanker om tid*, [*Ten thoughts of time*], Rosinante, København.

Kaufmann Vincent (2002), *Re-thinking mobility: contemporary sociology*, Ashgate, London.

Næss, Peter and Jensen, Ole B. (2002), 'Urban Land Use, Mobility and Theory of Science: Exploring the Potential for Critical Realism in Empirical Research', *Journal of Environmental Policy and Planning*, 4:2002.

Nowotny, Helga, Scott, Peter and Gibbons, Michael (2001), *Re-thinking Science: knowledge and the public in an age of uncertainty*, Polity Press, Oxford.

OECD (2000), *EST! Environmentally Sustainable Transport Guidelines.* http://www.oecd.org/department/0,2688,en_2649_34363_1_1_1_1_1,00.html

Petersen, Tina and Drewes Nielsen, Lise, (2004), 'Fresh Salmon from Norway to Japan – A case study of a global supply chain', *World*

Transport Politics and Practice.
Urry, John (2000), *Sociology Beyond Societies – mobilities for the twenty-first century*, Routledge, London.
Virilio Paul (1986), *Speed and Politics*, Semiotext, New York.

PART II
MOBILITY AS SPATIAL
CO-ORDINATION AND
TRANSGRESSION

Chapter 4

Impacts of Infrastructure Investment on Logistics and Transport – Examples from the Fixed Links of the Great Belt and Oresund in Denmark

Leif Gjesing Hansen

Introduction

The opening of the fixed links across the straits of the Great Belt and Oresund within the last six years has, both in Denmark and Sweden, been awaited with great expectations of radical changes in the traffic and transport patterns, regional development, changes in firms' organisation, trading patterns etc. This chapter has been inspired by some of the results of the research project *Infrastructures, transport and the environment – fixed links and the logistical map of Denmark*. The aim of the project was to study what kind of influence these newly established fixed links have on selected types of firms and their organisation of logistics and transport. The research has been funded by the former Danish Transport Council and was carried out by a research team from FLUX – Centre for Transport Research, Roskilde University in Denmark[1].

The expectations as to what influence the fixed links would have, have been many and even contradictory. On the one hand, the worry has been that the fixed links would increase the traffic flows due to the elimination of the 'friction' caused by the ferries. On the other hand, the expectations reflected a desire to improve the planning, coordination and consolidation of freight transport, and

---

[1] In addition to the author, the research team included: Professor Lise Drewes Nielsen, Associated Professor Per Homann Jespersen and Research Assistants Thomas Budde Christensen, Jacob Lundgaard and Ulrik Røhl.

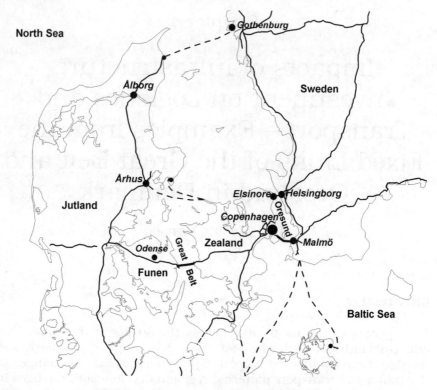

Figure 4.1   The location of the Great Belt and Oresund. The Great Belt link opened for rail traffic in 1997 and for road traffic in 1998. The Oresund link opened for both rail and road traffic in 2000

thereby not necessarily produce an increase in traffic flows. However, there has been a lack of studies on the fixed links effects on firms' organisation of logistics and transport.

These considerations formed the basis for a study among selected examples of firms' within manufacturing, transport and distribution. These examples served as cases focused upon changes in the firms' logistical decision-levels:

- Changes in the firms' localisation
- Changes in the firms' trade relations
- Changes in the firms' organisation of product and transport flows
- Changes in the firms' organisation of transport resources

Previous studies on the logistical effects of the fixed links across the Great Belt and Oresund have mainly focused upon the impacts on manufacturing and service related firms or surveys of industrial sectors (Füssel and Skjøtt-Larsen, 1990; Bjørnland, 1997; Sund and Bælt, 1999). In the present study, the intention has been to look at specific examples of firms and also to include the outermost link in the logistical chain – the transport firms.

In this chapter, it is argued that the most significant impacts of the new fixed links can be identified among transport firms. Hitherto, the effects on the activities among manufacturing and distribution firms included in the study have been limited. The impact on the logistical decision levels such as localisation and organisation of trading relations (supplier and customer links) has been very limited or even absent. A greater impact has been registered on the organisation of material flows and transport resources. A major conclusion that the study makes is, therefore, that freight traffic growth in Denmark seems to be supported by the newly established fixed links, while deeper changes in the firms' logistical organisation have, so far, been absent.

Section two presents an analytical approach that has served as a starting point for the present study and which offers an understanding of the underlying driving forces in a modern or post modern society that tend to affect more specific parameters related to transport and logistics. Section three discusses what kind of significance the actors within the transport sector are attributed in studies of newly established traffic infrastructures' impact on firms' transport and logistics. On the basis of the actor's capabilities to affect the organisation of logistics and transport, the themes investigated in the case studies are sketched out in section four. Section five presents examples from the case studies of firms' possible changes – or lack of them – in their organisation of logistics and transport on the basis of the newly established fixed links of the Great Belt and Oresund straits. Finally, the main conclusions from the study are summarised and discussed in section six.

New Traffic Infrastructures' Effect on Transport and Production Systems

New traffic infrastructures are not isolated phenomena which are established independently of their historical context – political, economic, social etc. Thus, the newly established fixed links can also be seen in the context of underlying structures and tendencies embedded in post-modern society. Post-modern society can be characterised by the *compression of time and space* (Harvey, 1990), which is a state caused by – among other things – the development of new communication and transport technologies, and networks. Communication and transport networks can be perceived as intermediaries of new forms of industrial organisation – both in a literal and conceptual sense. Three main characteristics of the theoretical discourse concerning post-modern society can be related to the conceptualisation of post-modern transport and logistics. The concepts reflect a development in which distance and time are perceived in new ways, and this is a result of the instantaneous connectedness of information, product and transport flows (Beckmann, 1999; Drewes Nielsen and Oldrup, 2001).

The development of transport and information technologies has the consequence that the distance between localities and individuals is perceived to be shrinking. This can be conceptualised as *spatial compression* (Harvey, 1990). Another, closely connected, tendency in post-modern society is *time compression* that similarly is contingent on – among other things - the technological development of transport and communication. The effects are reflected in the way that activities, to a larger extent than previously, are coordinated independently of geographical distances. One can therefore conceptualise this development as a change in the perception of time from 'scheduled time' to 'instantaneous time' (Urry, 2000). The third characteristic of post-modern society, which affects the manifest transport and mobility, is the *flow network*. This characteristic reflects a change in the relations among individuals, organisations, firm's etc. Information and products have a greater tendency to flow continuously among firms than was previously the case, a tendency that has to be understood in connection with the trends of spatial and time compression (Castells, 1997).

These three characteristics or driving forces of post-modern society function as preconditions for the analytical coupling between general societal changes and corresponding changes within logistics and transport. This coupling should not be perceived as a simple cause-effect relationship, where changes on the societal level directly result in changes on the more specific levels of firms, organisations and individuals. The relationships should instead be seen as mutually affecting each other and thereby treating changes in transport and material flows as being capable of affecting the spatial, time and relational structures within society.

Derived Concepts of Transport Logistics

The meta-concepts discussed above are taken from the theoretical discourse concerning post-modern society and cannot, directly, be the subject of an empirical analysis concerned with transport and logistics. In this present study it has therefore been necessary to apply four mediating concepts, which more directly and specifically reflect the transport logistical themes of the three meta-concepts (Drewes Nielsen, Jespersen, Petersen and Hansen, 2003): distance, speed, frequency and time-windows. These concepts have been used to develop an analytical framework based upon themes that often are included in logistical analysis (see e.g. Cooper, Black and Peters, 1994; McKinnon, 1998).

Distance – how far? There is a tendency that firms sell their products and buy their supplies from ever more distant locations. The transport distance of materials often becomes longer when production processes are centralised or when new supplies and markets are expanded worldwide. This spread of activities takes place on local, regional, national and international levels.

Speed – how fast? Demands relating to the speed of delivery of goods have been increased resulting from customer expectations that lead-time should be continuously reduced. Demands results in the use of faster means of transport which affect the customer's choice of transport modes, the ability to optimise load capacity and the environmental impacts of transport.

Frequency – how often? Both manufacturing and retail firms require more frequent deliveries. This demand can, for example, be motivated by the reduction or elimination of internal warehousing. The growth of more frequent deliveries can result in less efficient transport in terms of load capacity and a growth in traffic volumes that – among other things – generate negative environmental impacts.

Time-windows – when? When demands for delivery are heading towards greater precision and smaller time-margins, then it becomes more challenging to plan and coordinate distribution, and utilise transport and human resources efficiently. The demand for tighter delivery schedules is among other things a result of logistical set-ups like just-in-time principles, which require continuous material flows to and from the firms.

The above concepts can be perceived as reflecting underlying tendencies, which affect firms' decision-making relating to their organisation of logistics and transport. New traffic infrastructures can possibly change or enforce the significance of these underlying tendencies concerning the compression of time and space. But, it is worth noting that it could also be the case that the general tendencies within industrial and logistics organisation marginalise the effects of new traffic infrastructures on firms' organisation of transport and logistics.

Social Perspectives on Mobility

The Transport Sector – a Neglected System of Actors?

Freight transport is an activity that is derived from, among other things, firms' decisions concerning the localisation and organisation of production and distribution. Firms are embedded in systems or networks of supplier and customer relations which consist of a flow of raw materials, sub-supplies and end-products. Distance to suppliers and customers, and accessibility between the individual firms in a production system is of central importance. Furthermore,

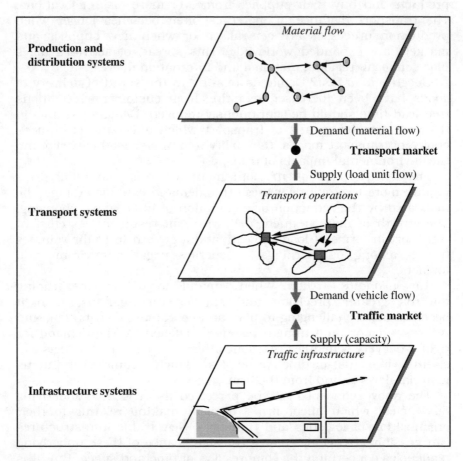

Figure 4.2   Systems of actors and activities, which are central in the relationships among firms' transport and infrastructures

Source: Modified model based on Wandel and Ruijgrok, (1993).

the localisation and quality of the traffic infrastructures are counted as essential factors for how firms and production systems evolve and succeed. However, the freight transport among Danish and European firms is often outsourced to external transport and forwarding firms. In Denmark approximately 70 per cent of the road-based freight transport is organised by haulage and forwarding firms (Bjerregaard et al., 1995; Hansen, 2000). This gives the transport firms a mediating role between, on the one hand, the firms buying transport services and, on the other hand, traffic infrastructures (see Figure 4.2).

Figure 4.2 illustrates a frame of reference for the functional relations among manufacturing/distribution, transport and infrastructure systems. The first layer represents the organisation of production and distribution firms: the logistical organisation of *material flows* between firms in production systems results in a transport demand. The second layer reflects *transport activities* which entail the handling of material flows between shippers, recipients and loading terminals. The transport flows consist of vehicles, trailers, containers etc. These transport flows generate a demand for traffic capacity. The third layer represents *traffic infrastructures*, which establish the supply of traffic capacity for the traffic flows in the form of roads, bridges, tunnels etc.

As shown in the framework presented in Figure 4.2, there is a causal relationship between demand for transport and the corresponding transport services offered. It is also shown explicitly that the traffic infrastructures affect the routes the material flows – between firms and their suppliers and customers – *can* follow. The transport firms are situated in the middle of these two systems and have a capability to affect how the transport of goods *actually* takes place and which routes are *actually* followed. Transport firms thereby represent a more or less central coordinating function for the material flow in production systems – depending on the competencies of the transport firms (Hansen, 2000; Hansen, 2002).

Studies concerning the relationships between new traffic infrastructures and the economic development among firms and regions tend to include effect analyses relating to production and distribution firms only. Results from these studies and analyses have primarily identified a limited effect of traffic infrastructures on firms' organisation and economic development. These studies provide examples from Denmark, the rest of Europe and North America, where the supply of traffic infrastructure in general is of a high quality and dense (Forslund and Karlsson, 1991; Hjalager, 1993; AKF, 1993; Maskell, 1994; McKinnon, 1997; Burmeister and Colletis-Wahl, 1998; SACTRA, 1999). In countries and regions with a generally low accessibility, new traffic infrastructures can, of course, still be identified as main drivers in the economic development of countries, regions and firms (Hoyle and Smith, 1992).

The absence of significant and radical effects of new traffic infrastructures on the economic performance and development of firms might therefore be due to the presence of an already well-functioning traffic infrastructure system. Another plausible explanation might be that studies of effects tend to focus narrowly on manufacturing and service industries. The mediators of the material flows – transport and forwarding firms – are often excluded from this type of study. The relevance of including transport and forwarding firms in such studies can be found in the ongoing tendency within these firms to expand their activities to include third party logistics services for their customers, for example warehousing, packaging, logistical management etc.

Based on the findings and tendencies discussed above, it seems relevant when undertaking studies of effects of new traffic infrastructures to apply a transport logistical chain perspective (Drewes Nielsen, Hansen, Kornum, Nedergaard and Aastrup, 1999). The effects of the newly established fixed links across the Great Belt and Oresund on firms' organisation of transport and logistics may therefore, it is argued here, depend on which types of logistical chains they are part of, and which function they exert in the chain. In the next section, the design of the study is presented, as are the kind of research themes that structured the analysis of the empirical findings.

Research Design and Methodology

Based on empirical findings and experience from previous research projects on freight transport this study applied a transport logistical chain perspective. Six firms from three different positions in logistics and transport chains accepted to take part in an interview-based study of their organisation of logistics and transport of in- and outgoing material flows.

The firms represented activities within manufacturing, distribution and transport:

- Two SMEs within the furniture manufacturing industry (referred to in this chapter as M1 and M2)
- Two large distribution firms within the retailing sector and wholesaling sector of pot plants (referred to in this chapter as D1 and D2)
- Two medium sized road haulage firms (referred to in this chapter as T1 and T2)

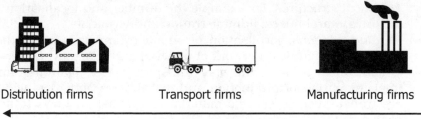

| Distribution firms | Transport firms | Manufacturing firms |

Transport and logistics chain

Figure 4.3   The focus of the study on three different types of firms in a transport and logistics chain perspective: manufacturing, transport and distribution firms

Geographically, the firms are located in different parts of Denmark (Jutland, Funen and Zealand) and they also represented different sizes of firms in terms of number of employees and turnover. The selection criteria of the firms were: To pick examples of different types of functions in transport and logistical chains, and not representative of different branches – see Figure 4.3. It was also the intention to include both firms that were and firms that were not affected by the fixed links. Thus the objective of the study was not only to identify and document changes in the organisation of transport and logistics of these firms, but also to increase the knowledge of *how* this type of traffic infrastructures affects different types of firms in the logistical chain.

Qualitative interviews of managers were used in the six cases to find out how the firm's organised their ingoing and outgoing transport and logistics, and also how far this organisation had undergone major changes within the last five to ten years. In relation to this, we asked the managers what kind of circumstances – including the new fixed links – had caused these organisational changes.

Seen from the individual firm's point of view, decisions concerning actions on transport and logistics can take place on many organisational levels – from the management's decisions to open or close a firm's activities to the driver who makes the route decisions concerning the deliveries. On this basis, Alan McKinnon (1998) has developed a hierarchy of logistical decision-levels that reflects important spaces where decision-making affecting the transport and logistics of firms take place. These are:

- *Logistical structures*: for example the number and localisation of factories, warehouses, administration and terminals.
- *Trading relations*: localisation of suppliers and customers that constitute a manifest network of material and transport flows.
- *Organisation of material and transport flows*: planning and implementation of production and distribution activities, which are transformed to specific material and transport flows to and from a firm.
- *Organisation of transport resources*: for example the use of one's own or external transport modes, route choice, transhipment via terminals and capacity utilisation.

These four levels formed the basis for the themes in the interviews and thereby structured the knowledge that was collected from the six case studies of the selected firms.

The Impact of the Fixed Links on Selected Types of Firms

This section presents examples from the six firms. These examples illustrate effects, or the lack of effects, which have resulted from the new fixed links across the Great Belt and Oresund on the firms' organisation of logistics and transport.

Logistical Structures

The interviews indicate that changes in the firm's physical location of activities (production, warehouses, administration and terminals) are relatively resistant to immediate changes in the accessibility for in- and outgoing transport flows. None of the firms interviewed has been able to identify changes which had taken place during the last five to ten years as a result of the new fixed links in the firm's logistical structures.

Examples of conditions that to a larger extent affect a firm's localisation of their own activities were – among other things – decisions concerning the in- and outsourcing of activities. For the manufacturing firms (within furniture production) that were interviewed, this was exemplified by the issue of production of low or high value furniture to a standardised mass market or order-specific customers. In the latter example, the furniture firm reduced its own physical facilities by out-sourcing activities to dedicated and specialised suppliers. One of the road haulage firms did establish a warehouse which could serve as an intermediate storage and distribution facility for its major customers. These decisions that are related to the firm's physical localisation of its own facilities were affected by factors other than the newly established fixed links.

Nevertheless, it is also necessary to consider the decisions related to logistical structures in a time perspective. This was illustrated in an interview at one of the road hauler firms: "(...) that the future will cause changes on this issue – that is within five to ten years. When future warehouses and logistical centres are to be located, then the existence of the new Oresund link will be taken into consideration. But, because the investments [in new terminals and warehouses] are huge it means that existing facilities are not abandoned in the short run. (...) Zealand is facing a great future as a logistical centre for the Nordic countries, because a large number of consumers and customers can be reached from this region. Similarly, Swedish companies will in the future, to a larger extent, locate in the vicinity of Malmö rather than Gothenburg or Stockholm, because there are better possibilities for transport by ship, lorry and aeroplane" (Interview, T1).

Thus the transport firm points to the fact that time represents a kind of inertia in terms of sunk investments in existing logistical structures. This could result in more significant changes in the long term perspective of the logistical structures through re-locations caused by the new fixed links.

Trading Relations

None of the firms interviewed could identify changes in the location of suppliers and customers as a consequence of the fixed links across the Great Belt and Oresund.

For the two manufacturing firms in the study – M1 and M2 – the choice of suppliers has not been affected by the fixed links, for example in the form of increased accessibility to alternative suppliers. The most important parameters for choice of suppliers for these firms are their competencies and qualifications in relation to the completed furniture product, and transport costs do not play any role in the choice of Danish suppliers. Neither had the customer relations been significantly changed within the last five to ten years as a consequence of the fixed links. Interestingly though, one of the furniture producers did notice that furniture retailers and wholesalers on Zealand – as a consequence of the fixed link across the Great Belt –operated to a larger extent West of the Great Belt than previously. This could indicate that the immediate effects of the fixed links on the logistical chains are felt more significantly in the retail and distribution parts than in the manufacturing parts of the chain.

It was also stated by the two retail and distribution firms that the fixed links had not produced any changes in the location of suppliers and customers. Nevertheless, there were indications that the present location of suppliers and customers could be changed in the near future. At one of the distribution firms – D1 located on Funen – this was primarily due to a possible re-organisation of existing terminals on the island of Funen and in Jutland. This re-organisation will lead to a centralisation of the firm's current distribution activities concerning potted plants from the market gardens in Denmark to customers in Denmark and Europe into one single terminal. This centralisation and thereby possible change in the supplier and customer network was caused by a strategic desire to make a more distinct division of activities within a large companies sub-divisions respectively on Funen and in Jutland.

For D2 located near Greater Copenhagen – a regional division of one of the leading retail companies in Denmark (approximately 40 per cent market share) – the fixed links had not affected the inward bound transport to the warehouses and terminals through changed locations of suppliers or customers. The 'customers' of D2 are the grocery stores of its parent company on Zealand and it has therefore not been affected by the fixed links. The parent company's grocery stores in the Western parts of Denmark (mainly on Funen and in Jutland) are supplied from two regional terminals in Jutland. This regionalisation, into an Eastern and a Western distribution network, is divided by the Great Belt and the fixed link has not affected this division: "The regional terminal at D2 [on Zealand] delivers goods to 400 grocery shops on Zealand. In relation to the fixed link across the Great Belt, we have tested the possibilities of also distributing to our grocery shops on the Eastern part of Funen [on the Western part of the Great Belt], but due to the price of using the [fixed] link, the costs proved to be too high – even though [the parent company] was offered a discount due to the traffic volumes. If the price was lowered considerably, the distribution from the terminal on Zealand to shops on Funen would probably be profitable" (Interview, D2).

In the cases of the two freight haulage firms in the study, it was not possible to identify examples of changes in the location of suppliers or customers as a consequence of the fixed links. However, it is likely that particularly transport firms' supplier and customer relations could be subject to changes, because transport firms often have far more changeable and short-lived relations than manufacturing and distribution firms.

Organisation of Material and Transport Flows

Among the firms interviewed, there was a distinct differentiation in, how directly the new fixed links have affected their organisation of material and transport flows.

The manufacturing firms interviewed had, in general, not experienced any impacts as a result of the fixed links on their organisation of material flows to and from their firms. Other factors played a greater role in how the firms plan and organise their internal and external logistics. At the furniture producing firm M2, one of the most important and critical elements in the logistical planning are the co-ordination between the inward and outward bound material flows. Sofas and chairs are order-produced and the minimisation of the internal storage of finalised furniture is a central strategy. The consequence is that the lead-time – the time it takes from the order is confirmed to actual delivery at a customer – is three to four weeks. But this lead-time is further extended by including the time used for planning the co-ordination of inbound material flows of raw materials and unspecialised components. M2 is therefore obliged to operate with a considerable storage capacity of a variety of standardised components that often require a delivery time far beyond the three to four weeks of the final piece of furniture which is produced. The potential time-savings of the new fixed links in minutes and hours are, in this context, without any significance for the firm.

For the distribution firms, the effects of the fixed links are more significant – although a number of other factors in general are of greater significance for the firms' decision-making on organisation of inward and outward bound material flows.

At D2, the fixed link across the Great Belt had affected the organisation of the transports of fresh goods between the regional terminals of COOP Denmark in particular: "There has been a rise in the number of these transportations and the time saved from the new fixed link across the Great Belt has increased the flexibility in organising these transportations. However, the external road haulage firms still often use the ferry link between East-Jutland and West-Zealand to transport dry goods between the terminals of Greater Copenhagen [on Zealand] and Aalborg [in Jutland]" (Interview, D2).

Other factors have played a far more significant role in generating a growth in the traffic flow of D2 and its parent company than the frequency of internal material and transport flows between regional terminals in the East and West of Denmark referred to above. Examples include new concepts such as 'Fresh Milk', a strategy of milk delivery from farmers to the grocery stores within

24 hours which increases the throughput for milk products, a concept that is beginning to spread to other types of fresh goods. The 'Fresh Milk' strategy is also an attempt to reduce the imports of milk from Germany and the Netherlands, because imported milk cannot be distributed within 24 hours to Danish grocery stores and shops. This distribution concept has lead to an increase in the frequency of deliveries from the regional terminals of D2's parent company to its grocery stores: "[Caused by the volumes] the road haulage firms have to distribute to the stores twice a day (...) even though the terminals storage capacities are big, there is simply no space for it. If all (the grocery stores) have to wait for fresh milk, then it also becomes a space problem for them, because the volumes are so enormous" (Interview, D2). Consequently, the time-pressure that the 'Fresh Milk' concept generates results in a need for more frequent distribution between regional terminals and the grocery stores. This is also due to the fact that the road haulage firms do not want to increase the number of vehicles in order to distribute all the milk in one delivery round, but instead use the same lorries for at least two trips per day: "If they [the transport firms] are forced to use a lot more lorries, which have to run for a shorter period – then they become unhappy and want more compensation for their transport services" (Interview, D2).

The development of increased time-pressure on the organisation of material and transport flows is also a well-known phenomenon at the pot plant wholesaling firm D1 located on Funen. This is partly due to the changed expectations among the customers regarding shorter delivery time, but also partly due to the effect of the fixed link across the Great Belt. The wholesaling firm packs and distributes pot plants from greenhouse gardens on Funen to, mainly, the retailing sector in Denmark. A large part of the deliveries are ordered on the day of delivery. This means that the greenhouse farmers typically receive the orders directly from the retailers between 8 and 11 a.m., thereafter the pot plants are collected and transported to the wholesalers terminal for final packaging. Finally, the consignments of pot plants are distributed to the customers late in the afternoon.

Even though the new fixed links across the Great Belt and Oresund have increased the time-pressure in the logistical chain, it has not had any direct consequences for the organisation of storage and packaging – a core-activity at the wholesaling firm. The impacts have primarily been visible in the transport planning activities: for example the fixed links have broadened the scope for scheduling deliveries due to the improved reliability in crossing the Great Belt and Oresund by bridge/tunnel instead of ferries. Furthermore, the customers of the pot plant wholesaling firm pay attention to the new opportunities: Previously the customers were obliged to order their goods the day before delivery, but this lead-time has been reduced substantially to delivery within the same day of ordering.

For a distributing firm like D1, the fixed link across the Great Belt has had an ambiguous impact on the logistics organisation: On the one hand, the replacement of the ferry link has eliminated a transfer point, which represented an uncertainty in relation to planning of departures and arrivals of deliveries. The ferry timetables functioned as time-windows, which the deliveries from D1 to their customers had to match precisely. On the other hand, the fixed link has amplified the development of new time-windows at other stages of the logistical chain. The transit time from D1 to larger customers on Zealand for instance was reduced by approximately one hour. Due to the short lead-time, the transit time plays a relatively more significant role than at the logistical organisation of the furniture firms referred to above. This results in a more tightly co-ordinated transport and logistical chain that includes more narrow time-windows at the large customers – for example the time margin for delivery that is acceptable at the customer. Typically, this means that if a lorry arrives outside these time-windows, then the haulage firm's or the suppliers (for example D1) are penalised an extra cost by the customer.

Even though the effects of the fixed links among the examples of manufacturing and distribution firms seems limited or non-existent, the effects proved to be more significant at the outermost link of the logistical chain – the freight haulage firms.

At the freight haulage firm T1, near Greater Copenhagen, the transport flows have significantly been affected in terms of increased speed, increased frequency and precision, and through a growth in transported distance. For the haulage firm, the Great Belt link has contributed to a reduction in uncertainty in the planning of transport flows by ensuring better regularity of the trips between Denmark and for example France. A major market for the firm is the transport of airfreight between Copenhagen Airport and other Northern European airports – a transport market where the time factor is of crucial importance. The establishment of the fixed Oresund link has lead to an increase in the firms' departures between a terminal in Malmö (Sweden) and at Copenhagen Airport from three to nine departures. Today, the firm uses smaller lorries due to the fact that the freight volumes have not increased similarly. The reason for the increased frequency is that the firm tries to solve a capacity problem that previously meant that extra-lorries had to be forwarded with rather small consignments: "The reason for increasing the number of departures has been, that previously – when we late in the evening discovered that we needed more loading capacity than four flight-pallets, then we could risk sending the extra flight-pallet with an extra lorry, because it definitely had to be at Copenhagen the following morning. These situations are, today, handled more flexibly by an increase in frequencies" (Interview, T1). However, it has not been possible to avoid a certain number of trips, where the loading factor has been very low: "(...) Approximately three to four times a week the transported volumes are far below the actual loading capacity of our lorries" (Interview, T1). This statement can be seen as an example of a general ongoing process that was already set into motion before the opening of the fixed link across Oresund: The rising demand for frequent transport connections due to the transport customers' expectations of as flexible departures and arrivals of trips as possible. A transport demand which reflects the conceptualisation of just-in-time logistics.

At the second road freight haulage firm in the study, T2 located in the middle of Jutland, the establishment of the fixed Great Belt link has resulted in one less time-window to consider in the daily planning of transport and distribution activities. Thus the establishment of the fixed link has resulted in more flexibly organised transport systems across the Great Belt and trip planning has improved due to the replacement of the ferries: "We can organise the trips without considering the weather conditions as a pre-condition for punctual delivery. And the time-margin, that we have to plan for trips between Funen and Jutland to Copenhagen in order to calculate the exact time for arrival of a consignment, has changed significantly. If we didn't catch a ferry [before the opening of the fixed link], then we had to wait for three quarters to one hour before we could take the next ferry – if this was not over-booked" (Interview, T2).

According to the road freight haulage firm, the establishment of the fixed link has lowered the costs of crossing the Great Belt, but this cost-reduction has been transferred to the transport customers. When the prices for crossing the fixed link were published, the contracts with the largest customers of the road freight haulage firm were re-negotiated – at the demand of the customers. Before the establishment of the Great Belt Link, the ferry cost for road freight haulage was approximately 148 euros. After the opening of the Great Belt Link, the price-level has been lowered to approximately 87 euros.

The road freight haulage firm experienced greater pressure for optimising the utility of the loading capacity before the opening of the fixed link. The high capacity utilisation was primarily reached by consolidating return loads. Today, where costs of crossing the

Great Belt have been reduced, the pressure for a high capacity utilisation has changed.

For the road haulage firm T2, the Great Belt Link has resulted in more frequent trips on some of its routes. The Great Belt Link has also lead to an increased use of express deliveries with short notice and therefore has the haulage firm invested in a number of small lorries and vans. The transit-time has been compressed after the opening of the fixed link across the Great Belt. This seems to be due to a perception among the transport buyers that the transport distance has been reduced by the Great Belt Link and also that the transport costs have been lowered for transport between the East and West of Denmark: "(...) we have felt that [the customers] do not speculate on the costs the same way as before. It is easier to send some goods to Zealand today [from the peninsula of Jutland]. Transport buyers know that there is a different time-horizon. There is another cost-structure" (Interview, T2). It is therefore not only the supply of capacity in the transport system that generates more transport, but also the increased transport demand facilitated by expectations among transport buyers that the transport is managed more frequently, faster and cheaper than before the fixed links were established.

Organisation of Transport Resources

The establishment of the fixed links has affected the way the studied firms organise their transport resources differently. The manufacturing firms did not perceive any changes in the way their in- and outbound transport were organised after the opening of the fixed links. According to the furniture producing firm M1, the Great Belt Link has not generated a greater flexibility in the logistical planning within the firm – even though the transport firms today are not restrained by the fixed schedules of the former ferries. However, the frequent time-schedule of the former ferry link is also given as a reason by the firm as to why there has not been noticed any remarkable change in the transport quality due to the fixed links. The firm has neither experienced a greater pressure for quicker deliveries in the last five to ten years, nor put a greater pressure on their transport providers for faster and cheaper transport services. According to M1, this is mainly due to the firms' high-value products, which serve a market where customers' rank product quality higher than a low lead-time. The total lead-time for producing the furniture products usually amounts to four to six weeks (from receiving the order to being ready for delivery), and therefore the time-saving of one hour from the fixed link across the Great Belt does not play any significant role for the furniture producers' own logistical organisation. The absence of changes in the organisation of in- and outbound transport is probably due to the fact that this firm – like the majority of Danish manufacturing firms – is not directly involved in the coordination and execution of the actual transport. As described above, most manufacturing firms use external transport firms for coordinating and handling their in- and outbound transport and often also logistics activities. The experienced effects of changes in the organisation of transport routes, choice of transport modes, re-loading and consolidation of goods, are often located at the two other types of firms involved in this study – distribution and transport firms. Among these firms the effects on their organisation of transport resources were more significant.

The wholesaling firm D1 expected before the opening of the Oresund link that this link would become the preferred distribution channel to customers in Sweden. The actual transport pattern has so far been very different: "... with the pricing policy so far, it has not been interesting and much too expensive. In short, this means that all goods destined for customers in Helsingborg and further north are still transported via the ferries [Ellsinore-Helsingborg] (...) due to the price of the fixed link. The ferries take 20 minutes and sail very regularly. Previously, there was a lot of waiting-time at the ferries, but this is rare now. There is no incentive to use the fixed link. If you drive from Malmö towards Stockholm, then you have to drive via Helsingborg anyway. It gives you 60 kilometres extra driving for reaching customers north of Helsingborg, if you use the fixed link instead of the ferries" (Interview, D1).

According to the wholesaling firm, a transfer of transports from the ferries to the fixed link will depend on a lowering of the prices. Current rules on resting-time for drivers have also a great influence on the choice of transport channel. Transport to destinations such as Oslo and Stockholm can be reached by using only one driver, because the maximum time limit for driving (10 hours) is not exceeded, when the drivers choose the ferry-link.

Among the road haulage firms in the study, the establishment of the fixed link across Oresund has only had significant influence for distribution and picking-up of goods in the Malmö area. This is especially the case for T1, which among other things transports air cargo between Copenhagen Airport and a freight terminal in Malmö. For both the road haulage firms studied it is not profitable to drive to destinations north of Malmö via the fixed link. Therefore, both firms use the ferries for these destinations.

In general, several of the firms studied pointed to the fact that the fixed Great Belt Link replaced a ferry link in an already existing and heavily used transport corridor between the eastern and western parts of Denmark. Therefore the establishment of this fixed link has not had any significant consequences for the route choice among transport and distribution firms' organisation of transport flows. On the contrary, the fixed Oresund link represents a new corridor for road and rail transport between Denmark and Sweden, since it mainly replaced existing passenger ferries between Copenhagen and Malmö. One could therefore anticipate more dramatic changes in the route choice for transports across Oresund – *from* the existing ferry link *to* the new fixed link. But, this is not the case as indicated in this study and also verified through current statistics on the transport flows across Oresund.

Conclusions

The results of this study should be seen in relation to the expectations concerning whether the new fixed links would generate an increase in traffic due to the elimination of the ferry links, or the fixed links would lead to improvements among firms logistics organisation for coordinating and optimising their transport activities.

The study indicates that the fixed links have supported a dramatic rise in the freight traffic on the roads across the Great Belt and Oresund. Other factors than the fixed links have also had an influence on this growth – for example a general tendency in the firms' organisation of internal and external logistics that reduce the storage capacity at manufacturing firms and thereby increase the demand for frequent in- and outbound transport flows. The fixed links seem to contribute to the growth in the traffic work, but not necessarily to a similar growth in transported goods. The road haulage and distribution firms stressed that the fixed links improved the ability to organise the transport with more frequent deliveries. The transport firms also experienced that transport buyers in general expected greater precision in the pick-up and delivery of consignments after the establishment of the fixed links. On the one hand, and seen from the perspective of the individual transport buyer, this represents a clear improvement in the transport quality. On the other hand, it also makes it difficult for the road haulage firms to coordinate and optimise the capacity utilisation.

The study has contributed with knowledge concerning how the new fixed links across the great Belt and Oresund affect different types of firms' logistical decision-making. The fixed links primarily affect the transport firms and, to a certain extent, distribution firms. On the contrary, the manufacturing firms have not been able to identify any changes in their location of own facilities or location of their suppliers and customers due to the fixed links. Neither have they experienced any changes in their organisation of material flow or transport resources. Instead, other factors were mentioned as being more significant than the time savings and route choices that the new fixed links enabled. The transport and distribution firms stressed that the fixed links enabled more flexible trip planning that is often a core activity for these types of firms. However, these firms also experienced a tendency among their customers to tightening the existing time-windows for picking-up and deliveries due to expectations for faster and more accurate transport. Thus it seems the increased flexibility enabled by the fixed links has ambiguous effects on the ability to organise transport and logistics in an efficient way.

In relation to the above results, the study also clearly reveals that it primarily is the logistical decision-levels closest on the actual and operational organisation of material and transport flows that has been affected by the fixed links. On the contrary, it seems that logistical decisions related to re-location of own firms activities or re-location of suppliers and customers have not been affected by the new fixed links. It is however important to note that a study over a longer period of time could probably show more significant effects of re-location. Factories, storage, terminals etc. represent sunken investments that in a short-term perspective cannot easily be re-located.

Acknowledgements

The author wishes to thank Professor Lise Drewes Nielsen, Associated Professor Per Homann Jespersen and Research Assistants Thomas Budde Christensen, Jacob Lundgaard and Ulrik Røhl for inspiring discussions during the conceptualisation of the line of thinking in this article. Also the colleagues at FLUX – Centre for Transport Research at Roskilde University – have contributed with ideas and comments on earlier drafts of this chapter. The author also wants to thank Andrew Crabtree for language revisions.

References

AKF (1993), *Transportinfrastruktur og regional udvikling – udenlandske undersøgelser* [*Transport infrastructure and regional development – studies abroad*]. The Danish Transport Council, Report nr. 93-06, The Danish Transport Council, Copenhagen.

Beckmann, J. (ed) (1999), *SPEED – A workshop on space, time and mobility*, The Danish Transport Council, Report nr. 99-05, The Danish Transport Council, Copenhagen.

Bjerregaard, E.T.D., Holsbo, A., Andersen, K.B., Kongsted, D. and Kristensen, J.O. (1995), *Virksomhedsstrategi, transportstrategi – En undersøgelse i emballage- og elektronikbranchen* [Business strategy, transport strategy – A study within the industries of packaging and electronics], The Danish Transport Council, Report nr. 95-07, The Danish Transport Council, Copenhagen.

Bjørnland, D. (1997), 'Faste forbindelser', in L. Drewes Nielsen and H. Sornn-Friese, (eds), *Transportvirksomheders relationer – en socioøkonomisk analyse* ['Fixed links' in the publication *Relations of transport firms – a socio-economic study*]. The Danish Transport Council, Report nr. 97-07, The Danish Transport Council, Copenhagen.

Burmeister, A. and Colletis-Wahl, K. (1998), 'Proximity in Networks: The Role of Transport Infrastructure', in A. Reggiani, (ed), *Accessibility, Trade and Locational Behaviour*, Ashgate, Aldershot.

Castells, M. (1997), *The Information Age*, Blackwell, Oxford.

Cooper, J., Black, I. and Peters, M.J. (1994), *European Logistics – Markets, Management and Strategy*, Blackwell Publishers, UK.

Drewes Nielsen, L. and Oldrup, H.H. (eds) (2001), *Mobility and Transport – An Anthology*, The Danish Transport Council, Report, nr. 01-03, The Danish Transport Council, Copenhagen.

Drewes Nielsen, L. and Sornn-Friese, H. (eds) (1997), *Transportvirksomheders relationer – en socioøkonomisk analyse* [Relations of transport firms – a socio-economic study]. The Danish Transport Council, Report nr. 97-07, The Danish Transport Council, Copenhagen.

Drewes Nielsen, L., Hansen, L.G., Kornum, N., Nedergaard, K. and Aastrup, J. (1999), *Godstransport i et kædeperspektiv – erhverv, miljø og planlægning* [Freight transport in a chain perspective – industry, environment and planning]. Working Paper for the Ministry of Environment and Energy, Copenhagen.

Drewes Nielsen, L., Jespersen, P.H., Petersen, T. and Hansen, L.G. (2003), 'Freight transport growth – a theoretical and methodological framework', *European Journal of Operational Research*, 144, p. 295-305.

Forslund, U. and Karlsson, C. (1991), *Infrastrukturens regonala effekter – en genomgång av empiriska studier* [The regional effects of infrastructures – a review of empirical studies]. Industridepartementet (ERU), Ds 1991:55, The Industrial Department, Stockholm.

Füssel, L. and Skjøtt-Larsen, T. (1990), *Logistikplanlægning og infrastruktur* [Logistics planning and infrastructure], The Copenhagen Business School, Copenhagen.

Hansen, L.G. (2000), *Transportvirksomheders organisatoriske fleksibilitet* [The organisational flexibility of transport firms], The Copenhagen Business School, Ph.D.-series nr. 11.2000, The Copenhagen Business School, Copenhagen.

Hansen, L.G. (2002), 'Transportation and Coordination in Clusters', *International Studies of Management and Organization, 2002*, vol. 31, no. 4.

Harvey, D. (1990), *The Condition of Postmodernity*, Blackwell, Oxford.

Hjalager, A.M. (1993), *Transportinfrastruktur og regional udvikling – danske undersøgelser* [*Transport infrastructure and regional development – Danish studies*], The Danish Transport Council, Report nr. 93-07, The Danish Transport Council, Copenhagen.

Hoyle, B.S. and Smith, J. (1992), 'Transport and Development' in B.S. Hoyle and R.D. Knowles (eds), *Modern Transport Geography*, Belhaven Press, London.

Institut for Transportstudier (1997), *Tredje parts logistik i Danmark* [*Third-party logistics in Denmark*]. The Danish Transport Council, nr. 97-06, The Danish Transport Council, Copenhagen.

Maskell, P. (1994), 'Infrastruktur og regional erhvervsmæssig udvikling – med særlig henblik på udviklingen i Danmark', in *Infrastruktur, lokaliseringsegenskaper och produktivitet* ['Infrastructure and regional industrial development – specially the development in Denmark' in *Infrastructure, features of localisation and productivity*], TemaNord, 1994:624, pp. 133-168, The Nordic Government Council, Copenhagen.

McKinnon, A. (1997), 'Logistics, Peripherality and Manufacturing Competitiveness', in B. Fynes, and S. Ennis (eds), *Competing from the Periphery*, The Dryden Press, London.

McKinnon, A. (1998), 'Logistical Restructuring, Freight Traffic Growth and the Environment', in D. Bannister (ed), *Transport Policy and the Environment*, Routledge, London.

SACTRA (the Standing Advisory Committee on Trunk Road Assessment) (1999), *Transport and the Economy*, Department for Transport, Local Government and Regions, London.

Sund & Bælt (1999), *Erhvervslivet og Storebælt – Tilpasning i to hastigheder* [*The industry and the Great Belt – adjustment in two tempi*], Sund & Bælt, Copenhagen.

Urry, J. (2000), *Sociology Beyond Societies: Mobilities for the Twenty-First Century*, Routledge, London.

Chapter 5

Involving Freight Transport Actors in Production of Knowledge – Experience with Future Workshop Methodology

Per Homann Jespersen and Lise Drewes Nielsen

Introduction

The freight transport sector plays a major role in the process of globalisation and accounts for a large and increasing share of the economy and workforce. This growth in turn results in a range of societal problems – externally as environmental and health problems, internally as a number of congestion problems. In spite of this, freight transport has been somewhat neglected in qualitative oriented social sciences such as sociology and socio-economy, and thus a lack of analytical understanding as well as problem solving competences prevail (TNO 1999, Drewes Nielsen et al. 2003).

This chapter presents a methodology where the experience and knowledge of actors in the freight transport sector are included directly in a scientific process in order to develop future and strategic studies.

Future research is often produced as desktop research and presented as the results of scientists' forecasting and scenario building, e.g. EU (2000) and OECD (2000). The validation of the research is taken ex post when the results are presented in reports for discussions in public. The effect of the research on practice is seldom evaluated.

The research presented in this paper has a quite different aim. Taking our inspiration from modern action research, we have in the format of a *future workshop* included freight transport stakeholders in the research process in order to produce knowledge meeting scientific quality criteria and at the same time in a form suitable for improving the problem solving capabilities of the participants.

The Future Workshop

The future workshop concept is linked to the theory of action research, where local actors or stakeholders are involved in the production of future visions, actions and scenario building. The methodology of the workshop is originally developed by Jungk and Müllert (1984), and has been further developed in several contexts in Denmark and Europe.

Researchers and students at Roskilde University have used the methodology in such different areas as industrial sociology, local community studies, urban ecology and business development (Aagaard Nielsen, 2001). Workshops are flexible and can last from a few hours to two days or possibly spread over a period of weeks or months. The workshop is often arranged at places away from people's daily routines in order to create mental and physical free spaces for learning.

This article provides the results from three workshops which were run in 2001-2003. All of the workshops lasted for one day with participants who have an interest in and knowledge about the freight transport sector: from businesses and firms, organisations, government and local municipalities, from planning, consultancy and research. The number of participants in the workshop was between 20 and 30. Each workshop was announced with a specific future oriented theme. Their themes were

* Workshop 1: Future City Logistics in Denmark year 2007 – framework for developing a transport concept (November 2001)
* Workshop 2: Future Rail Freight Transport 2008 – development of concepts (January 2003)
* Workshop 3: Future Freight Transport in Europe 2030 – with focus on environment, economy and regulation (March 2003)

The workshops had different aims. Workshop 1 and 2 both were initial steps in strategy development processes, but whereas the first one focused on consensus building among actors with different interests, workshop 2 was aimed at developing elements of a business strategy. Both of the workshops were parts of a project where consultants and scientists together with actors from business were developing concepts that will help to provide more sustainable transport in the future. The aim of workshop 3 was to create input for the development of qualitative scenarios for the freight transport sector. This workshop was part of a research project where qualitative scenarios are developed in order to form evaluation criteria for modelling within freight transport.

The Future Workshop Methodology

The future workshop has three main characteristics. First, it is an action-oriented approach where stakeholders are involved in the processes of knowledge production and dissemination, change and development. Second, the workshop is facilitated by specific rules of communication in order to create interaction on a common base and eliminate the influence of power relations in the communication between the participants. Third, the workshop is facilitated through specific rules of visualisation and creativity.

The workshop is organized with alternating plenum and group sessions. All statements from the plenum sessions are documented on posters. Also, the groups' works are presented and commented upon by using posters. After the introduction of the workshop theme and a presentation round of the participants in the workshop the first phase of the workshop starts. The future workshop follows a three phase model.

1. Phase of Criticism. The headline of this phase is "*We are consequently negative.*"

This phase starts with a brainstorming session, following three principles:

Figure 5.1   **The brainstorms are organised with rules to allow for a free, non-coercive space of communication**

- all statements are, in a condensed form, written on posters by the two facilitators
- no discussion of statements is allowed
- all statements concerning the theme of the workshop are allowed

After the brainstorming, the participants are asked to vote for the statements, they find most important. The participants normally have three or five votes each. They can vote with all their votes for one single statement or vote for several statements. Votes on statements with similar content are added up.

After the voting, the facilitators count the points and form a list of prioritised themes. The four or five themes with the highest priority are taken as the basis for visualisation groups. After a short period of group work (10 minutes), the groups present their theme (with no use of words) in plenum. The plenum reflects on the visualisation and the comments are written on the posters.

2. Phase of Utopian Vision. The headline of this phase is "*Reality is out of function. We are situated in a perfect world, where everything is possible.*"

This phase starts with a brainstorm session that follows the same three principles as phase 1. Also here four or five themes are selected through a voting process and form the basis for a number of *utopia groups.* These have to develop the utopia and include as many relevant ideas from the brainstorms as possible.

After a longer period of group work, the utopias are presented in plenum and discussed with all participants.

3. Phase of Realisation. The headline of this phase is "*We keep our wishes and dreams, how can they become reality.*"

The realisation phase consists of two parts: First the utopia groups continue their work of bringing the utopia orientations closer to reality. After a longer group work session, the results are presented in plenum and reflected upon. Subsequently, the groups are asked to make agreements to continue the work with the realisations of different plans of action after the workshop. The outputs from the future workshops are:

- A typed protocol of the posters including photos from the workshop is handed out to the participants within two weeks after the workshop. The protocol forms the collective platform for further group work, strategy building, scenario construction, discussion etc. At the same time, it can be used by the individual participant to memorise the context, the ideas and discussions.

Figure 5.2   Through the voting process focus is set on the problems and utopias with the broadest approval

- An analysis of the future workshop done by the research team. The analysis describes the results of the workshop by focusing on the utopias, their foundation in the criticisms and their influence on the scenarios and the future events/actions.
- New knowledge and understanding which can be used in concept development, in general analyses of the sector and in future research and scenario building at the levels of business, industry, organisation and society.
- Shared knowledge and understanding among actors from different organisations, which can be used to produce new strategies.

Results of the workshops

Workshop 1: Consensus Production

The theme of this workshop was: *Future City Logistics in Denmark Year 2007 – Framework for Developing a Transport Concept.* The workshop was initiated in collaboration with a Danish transport company. The company had experienced growing problems with the distribution of freight in the city centres in Denmark. It was aware of future public demand for regulation of transport in the city centres, which would be aimed at diminishing potential conflicts concerning congestion, security and the environment. The participants in the workshop thus represented a broad variety of stakeholders in the sector.

The problems raised in the criticism phase were all founded in the reality of transport problems in the city centres and formulated in statements like: lack of planning, lack of coordination of transport, conflicts between citizens and those employed in transport companies (drivers and warehouse workers) and problems with the narrowing of early morning time windows for unloading of goods to the retailers. The problems had to be addressed by many different players in the field: the municipalities, industry, transport buyers, transport companies and citizens in the cities.

The utopian ideas were related to solving some of these

**Figure 5.3   Visualisations are used for interpretation of the
main problems and to initiate discussion**

problems. The following are two examples selected from the workshop.

Freight buses in cities. The main idea is of a public transport system for freight similar to that for personal transport based on a system of multipurpose vehicles used for personal transport in daytime. The system would be introduced using certification and will employ intelligent logistical systems, which would also include return freight. The capacity use would be high.

City logistics as an integrated part of urban ecology. Transport will be developed as an integrated part of visions of green and compact cities. This development will be based on a profound dialogue among different actors involved with transport: business, shops and citizens. It will reduce the conflicts around transport and develop many new ideas of sustainable city logistic solutions in the city.

The workshop produced many specific ideas, technological and organisational, and discussed a wide range of issues relating to a modern concept of city logistics. The ideas produced in this intensive atmosphere represented accumulated knowledge relating to the concept of city logistics and a listing of initiatives to create future city logistical solutions. It is the participants in the workshop and their collective knowledge and creativity that have produced the ideas, and they represent future concepts, which take future external conditions into account to develop the concept of city logistics, though still seen from a business perspective. In this sense, the workshop produces a collective vision based on knowledge from the community and business. This was also the case in workshop 2.

Workshop 2: Business Strategy

The theme of this workshop was *Future Rail Freight Transport 2008 – Development of Concepts.* EU transport policy states that efforts to change freight transport from truck to rail have the highest priority, however, the empirical evidence shows the opposite development. In a collaborative project between the Danish rail freight operator Railion Denmark, The Danish Technological Institute and Roskilde University it was decided to arrange a future workshop with the purpose of developing transport concepts for rail freight transport. The participants were a mix of employees from different departments in Railion, Railion's customer (actual and potential), the Ministry of Transport, public administration and research. At the workshop, Railion initially summarised their current situation in a highly competitive and turbulent market.

The criticism phase concentrated on four main problems concerning rail freight systems: The lack of focus on cost reduction, the lack of regularity and stability in quality, the lack of cooperation and intermodality and the lack of standards for transport quality.

As in other workshops, the utopian visions take the themes from the criticism phase into account in a creative way. Out of about 45 short utopian statements came utopian themes for 2030 like:

- An ILU (Intermodal Loading Unit – a container usable and practical for both road, rail and sea transport) will be developed
- A homogeneous European transport rail net including intermodal transport systems will be established
- Rail transport is profitable and reliable
- At least three European rail freight operators will compete on the market

These utopian visions focussed on a mix of external frame conditions for transport and internal evolution of the rail business concepts – somewhat to the surprise of the Railion participants, who had expected a discussion much more on present day-to-day problems. The result stresses that solutions in the transport sector under proper conditions can be developed on the basis of shared knowledge between industry and external interests in transport, and that the visions produced at the workshop represent such collaborative solutions among the actors.

The future workshop supported a strategic business process in the company of Railion and the collaborative work between Roskilde University, the Technological Institute and Railion has continued afterwards. From Railion's perspective, the future workshop made it possible to place daily problems of the company in a long-term perspective, which was evaluated as positive and inspiring. They were, however, a little sceptical of how the workshop's wilder utopian ideas could be used in the practical world after the workshop. Another effect of the workshop was that the collaboration during the workshop created new views and opinions about actors in Railion's logistical chains. Before the workshop, Railion had expected that they would be confronted with prejudices about rail transport, but distrust was less than assumed and an open-minded and positive orientation toward rail transport dominated throughout the workshop.

Workshop 3: Scenario Production

The theme of this workshop was: *Future Freight Transport in Europe in 2030 – with Focus on Environment, Economy and Regulation.* This workshop was arranged with the purpose of developing scenarios within freight transport, building upon the methodology of the *scenario workshop* of the Fleximodo project (Fleximodo 2004). The scenario workshop consists of two parts, qualitative scenarios and a workshop.

Qualitative scenarios and their function can be described as follows:

> "Scenarios try to describe some hypothetical series of occurrences. By using a relatively comprehensive scenario, the analyst is able to get in touch with occurrences and turning points demanding a critical choice. Afterwards these turning points can be examined more or less systematically. But the scenarios should not be used to 'prove' anything. They are literary and educational aids rather than tools for rigorous analysis. They should be used to stimulate, illustrate and learn, they should provide us with precision and richness in communication and to check details." (Our translation from Norwegian of Selstad, 1991)

The process of building scenarios begins with the search for driving forces, the forces that influence the outcome(s) of events:

Figure 5.4   Presentation of a vision of the European freight transport sector in 2030. This is the starting point for the phase of realisation

"Thus, in writing scenarios, we spin myths – old and new – that will be important in the future ... These myths in scenarios help us come to grips with forces and feelings that would not otherwise exist in concrete form. They help us describe them, envision them, bring them to life – in a way that helps us make use of them." (Schwartz, 1999)

The workshop was arranged with participants from the Danish transport sector: business, organisations, research and public administration. It was run in accordance with the principles of the futures workshop as described above, but with two exceptions. After the groups had presented their utopian visions and as an introduction with the phase of realisation, the participants were presented to two scenarios describing alternative frameworks for the development of the transport sector. One described a situation, were a continued high environmental awareness meant a high level of regulatory intervention in the transport sector, the other scenario that 'optimism' concerning the possibilities of solving environmental problems meant a decrease in public awareness and less regulation.

The other exception was that the realisation groups were asked to draw timelines from the present towards the utopia, and describe events necessary to make the utopia come real by the year 2030.

The main criticism of the current situation concerning transport was condensed into the following themes. There is a lack of standards in the transport sector, a poor integration of IT, and innovation is low. Given the deficit of knowledge, education, good image and innovation, it is a sector with lack of trust in other transport modes. A final criticism concerned the lack of regulation relating to transport in the inner cities.

This point of departure was the foundation for the utopias. Five groups discussing utopian visions for freight transport in Europe in the year 2030 were formed, and chose the following titles:

- For the benefit of all, the use of capacity should be optimal supported by IT
- All transport costs should be internalised in prices
- Common frame conditions for all transport modes over the whole Europe
- A trans-European rail freight system should be established
- City terminals for freight should be established in all cities over 100,000 inhabitants

In the realisation phase, the workshop asked the participants in the utopia groups to focus on events necessary to reach the utopia, events like changes in markets, changes in regulation, changes in infrastructure investments etc. The events should be marked on a timeline. After the workshop, a common picture of these events, across the utopia-groups, could be drawn. The events from the different groups were actually often similar, with a concentrated focus on: IT system integration, road tax based on the principles and technology of the German 'Maut' (road pricing scheme for trucks on motorways), fair and efficient pricing, EU standardisation of transport services, and EU systems of terminals, hubs and city terminals.

The five utopias and the corresponding realisations were closely related to the criticism phase signifying that some of the most important problems in the freight transport sector are intentionally solved through the direction selected for the utopia and through the actions chosen for the realisations. After analysing the final result of the workshop we can conclude the following:

The regulatory instruments to support the utopias are more convergent than divergent across the different working groups even though they worked with different aspects of future transport. This means that there is a degree of consensus among the experts about the main problems in the transport sector and the instruments needed for finding the solutions. Second, even though the utopias themselves are mainly unregulated (i.e. only regulated by the market forces) all roads towards the utopia include strong regulative actions through establishing transport systems and infrastructure investments in intermodal IT-driven transport systems, or through price regulation of the transport market reflecting the real transport prices including all external costs. Third, and against our expectations, the workshop showed a lack of focus on the driving forces behind transport demand or mobility management. The focus on factors like logistical decisions, production and distribution systems as generators of transport, regional development, lifestyle and demography, did not play a large

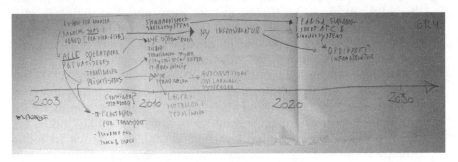

Figure 5.5   A timeline illustrating how rail transport can become competitive and obtain a large market share by 2030

role in the workshop. The focus was kept on the transport sector and not on the driving forces behind it.

The answers to the main questions were that it was possible through the workshop to establish inputs for scenarios. The workshop generated a variety of dimensions and dynamics to be used in future research concerning transport. Given the short time limit of one day, the different variables in the scenarios were kept to a more general level. From a scientific point of view, the material from the workshop needed more detailed work to be used in scenario building. It could have been fruitful if the participants had had the interest and time to work out more detailed scenario dimensions and events on the timeline in order to make the visions more 'socially robust'.

Future Workshops as *Mode 2 Knowledge Production*

In a field of research which, as yet, has little empirical input such as is the case with the freight transport sector, and in a field of research with high degree of different, often conflicting, actor interests,) workshops such as the scenario and future workshops described can be a fruitful tools. It can be regarded as an exponent of *Mode 2 Knowledge Production* (Gibbons et al., 1994).

This concept is a result of an analysis of how valid knowledge is created in present-day society and the shifting role of science and its norms. It is opposed to traditional (Mode 1) knowledge production by five main characteristics (Gibbons et al. 1994, Gibbons and Nowotny 2001):

- *Knowledge Is Produced in the Context of Application.* In mode 2, knowledge production is centred on problem solving organised around a particular application (as opposed to a particular discipline in mode 1). "Problems are formulated in dialogue with a large number of interests from the very beginning. The context is set by a process of communication between various stakeholders" (Gibbons and Nowotny 2001, p.69).
- *Transdisciplinarity*, as opposed not only to 'disciplinarity' but also to 'multidisciplinarity' or 'pluri-disciplinarity' is characterised by "a forum ... that provides a distinctive focus for intellectual endeavour" (Gibbons and Nowotny 2001, p.69), i.e. the problem as formulated by the stakeholders stays in focus but the framework to guide the problem solving efforts evolves in a dynamic process involving practitioners and researchers.
- *Heterogeneity and Organisational Diversity*, signifying that knowledge is produced by people of different skills and

experience, belonging to very different institutions of knowledge production, meaning not only universities and research centres, but also consultancies, government agencies, professional organisations etc.

- *Social Accountability and Reflexivity.* Knowledge is rarely produced for one single target group with specific values, but towards a broader spectrum of interests with a diverse set of values. Knowledge producers have to be accountable and ready to defend their results when confronted with these different values, and have to reflect this into the way the knowledge is produced and presented.
- *Quality Control* takes on a more complicated form in Mode 2 knowledge production. Traditional disciplinary values still apply within their own field, but have to be supplemented with criteria such as whether the knowledge produced fulfils its objects of e.g. cost effectiveness or market potential as well as being socially acceptable. The results have to be socially robust.

The future workshop can be seen as an organisational form to confront knowledge from a diverse group of people representing a diversity of institutions of knowledge production and also direct users of the knowledge. It can be regarded as a condensed and accelerated version of *Mode 2 Knowledge Production.* Whereas knowledge production mostly is spatially and temporarily dispersed, the future workshop seeks to concentrate the problem formulation by bringing together stakeholders and speed up the process through the phases of critique and utopian vision.

In the future workshops carried through, the process was too short to go beyond more than the initial steps of knowledge production. But even though some of the follow-up was done in a more traditional academic setting, the problem formulations and ideas of the future workshops prevailed and gave a broader foundation for the research.

Future Workshops in Strategic Studies – Concluding Remarks

In a field such as freight transport which is relatively poor in terms of academic understanding and conceptualisation, but has a lot of 'practical knowledge' the future workshop gives new possibilities for producing valid and robust knowledge. Summing up

- The methodology is able to produce new knowledge about the sector and requires far less demanding resources than other data producing methodologies such as qualitative interviews.

- The methodology is able to produce visions of business- and policy strategies as well as input to scenario building.
- The setting around the workshops creates 'free spaces' across actors and science and is a fruitful example of the development of science towards transgression across science and society.
- The workshops create processes of learning among the actors. They create common understandings of the borderlines between consensus and conflicts, but also common metaphors and languages for solving problems in the future. Metaphors like public freight transport (in city logistics) are such an example.
- The workshops create free spaces of 'communication', where participants can feel free to join the processes of creativity and are not bounded by the restrictions normally induced by relationships to the political and power structures.
- The methodology is very transparent – the rules are clear, the inputs and outputs are all documented, and the development of the process is determined by the participants.

The experiences gained from our workshops are that the borderlines between consensus and conflict are moved through the dialogue and the creative processes that take place within the workshop. The consciousness of more commonly shared utopian horizons might be a good platform for changing directions or orientations and overcoming present conflicts. Furthermore, the dialogue and activities during the workshop decreased the mistrust that was sometimes present before the workshop.

Workshops will often break down communicative barriers among different actors because the workshops aim to find common consensus and ignore potential conflicts. However, there is no intention to break fundamental differences in orientation and interest even after the workshop.

As is pointed out by Henscher and Brewer (2001), who used similar approaches to establish collaborative learning processes as an input for establishing a freight transport strategy for New South Wales, the aspects of resource limitations are not very well served by the approach presented. We see this as a limitation that might be overcome by modifications of the methodology, but at present we have no experience with this.

Scenario and future workshops are from our experience a rewarding tool in knowledge production and future studies about the transport sector. The workshops are tools that demand a high degree of concentrated preparation from the organisers, be it researchers, consultants or students. The relations between purpose, thematic headline, participants and workshop design demand deep reflection and specific preparation in advance to ensure results. It is a methodology among other data producing methodologies and can be evaluated as supplementary to other methodologies in social science.

One of the critical issues in the methodology is what is going to happen after the workshop. Some research strategies have excluded this phase and placed the responsibilities for the continuation of the realisation phase after the workshop to the participants. Other projects have clear designs where the workshop is an integrated part of a series of cumulative activities among actors and scientists in an action research setup. In both types of setups, the process from workshop to reality needs to be looked at with great attention.

Acknowledgements

The authors wish to thank Petri Tapio for comments on an earlier version of the paper.

References

Aagaard Nielsen, K. et al. (2001), 'Sustainability and industrial democracy', in Gowdy (ed) *Sustainability and Action*, Ashgate.

Drewes Nielsen, L., Jespersen, P.H., Petersen, T. and Hansen, L.G. (2003), 'Freight transport growth – a theoretical and methodological framework', *European Journal of Operational Research*, Volume 144, Number 2.

EU (2000), *Forecasting and Assessment of New Technologies and Transport Systems and their Impacts on the Environment* (FANTASIE), http://www.etsu.com/fantasie/fantasie.htm.

Fleximodo (2004), The Fleximodo Project www.cittadellascienza.it/-fleximodo/fleximodo.html.

Gibbons, M. et al. (1994), *The new production of knowledge. The dynamics of science and research in temporary societies*. Sage Publications Ltd.

Gibbons, M. and H. Nowotny (2001), 'The Potential of Transdisciplinarity', in Thompson-Klein, J. et al (eds) *Transdisciplinarity: Joint Problem Solving among Science, Technology, and Society*, Birkhäuser.

Henscher, D.A. and Brewer, A.M. (2001), 'Developing a freight strategy: the use of collaborative learning process to secure stakeholder input', *Transport Policy* 8 (2001) 1-10.

Jungk, R. and Müllert, N.R. (1984), *Håndbog i Fremtidsværksteder*, Politisk Revy, København (Translated from: *Zukunftswerkstatten, Wege zur Wiederbelebung der Demokratie* (1981)).

Nowotny, H., P. Scott and M. Gibbons (2001), *Re-Thinking Science – Knowledge and the Public in an Age of Uncertainty*, Polity Press, Cambridge.

OECD (2000), *EST! – Environmentally Sustainable Transport Guidelines*, http://www1.oecd.org/publications/e-book/9702191E.PDF.

Schwartz, P. (1999): *The Art of the Long View. Planning for the Future in an Uncertain World*, John Wiley & Sons, England.

Selstad, T. (1991): *Med krystallkule og computer. Prognoser og scenarier i samfunnsplanleggingen [With Cristal Ball and Computer. Forecasts and Scenarios in Societal Planning]*. Universitetsforlaget, Oslo.

TNO (1999): *TRILOG-Europe End Report*, TNO, EU Directorate-General Transport, TNO, Department of Logistics, TNO-report, Inro/Logistiek 2000-16.

PART III
MOBILITY AS A
POLICY THEME

Chapter 6

Mobility as a Policy Concept

Henrik Gudmundsson

Why Consider Mobility as a Policy Issue?

The capacity for people and goods to move around is a major concern in current socio-economic policies (CEC 2001; US DOT 2003). According to this view mobility provides unique benefits for both the economy and the individual. However the same movements are also acknowledged to be the cause of congestion and pollution, and the need for new road and rail links put increasing financial strains on public expenditure budgets. So, despite the benefits of mobility, *maximising* it is rarely defined as a policy objective, at least explicitly.

Instead, various expressions of a more 'correct' level of provision have been put forward. One of the predominant word constellations is 'Sustainable Mobility' being the stated overall aim of European transport policy.[1] By alluding to the general Sustainable Development agenda, this notion, while not clearly defined, does draw the attention to possible limits to (future) mobility. Another recent expression of this 'right' mobility is found in the Vision Statement of the Danish Ministry of Transport, which aims to provide "Mobility that creates real value."[2] This implies, by logical extension at least, that stimulating wasteful or pointless moving around should be avoided.

But can policies deliver what they so claim to intend? It is certainly fair to ask if they can deliver 'real value', considering the many failures and distortions that past transport policies have been marred by (Barde and Button 1990; Schmidt and Giorgi 2001; Winston 1999). It is also timely to ask if they can deliver sustainability, taking into account for instance the environmental implications of continued growth in physical movements of people and goods (Banister et al 2000, Tengström 1999; OECD 2000; OECD 1997).

---

[1] Since the first European transport policy White Paper (CEC 1992).
[2] Website of the Danish Ministry of Transport: URL http://www.trm.dk/-sw523.asp.

But even before that, it may be asked: Can policies, in fact, deliver mobility? The starting point for the present analysis is a sense that so far, this issue has not been sufficiently dealt with. Policy efforts have been devoted to regulating traffic, to supporting transport, to constructing networks, and even to promoting physical and economic access. While these notions are closely related, and in some respects may serve as surrogate measures for mobility, this chapter begins by making the claim that more efforts are needed to clarify what it would entail to deliver *mobility* rather than just physical movement of vehicles.[3]

The motivation for this enquiry springs from two sources:

The first source is the conviction that there is *more to mobility* than just traffic and transport, which brings both confusion and a ray of hope. Mobility is in many ways an ambiguous notion. It has a strong physical presence while it is also infused with meanings, aspirations and potentials. It is instrumental to serving other needs, but it has effectively transformed modern culture in its own image. It sustains the economy but to do so it requires substantial inputs of resources and time. Such ambiguities should be confronted squarely if 'mobility policy' is not to inherit them unnoticed. Meanwhile, the new perspectives that this notion may bring should also be laid open.

The second source springs from the view that the results of public policies should be monitored to check their ambitions. Monitoring of policy performance is a key instrument for state-of-the-art public management, but it is also potentially important to ensure wider public interests in policy outcomes through transparency of decision-making and accountability of policy makers (OECD 1995, Guerning 2001; Pickrell and Neumann 2001).[4] If the performance of policies is not monitored it is not only hard to adapt them to meet their ends, it may also be difficult for the public to exercise their democratic rights. So, if policies claim that they aim to deliver mobility then monitoring of them should be

---

3 This chapter considers *mobility* only in singular and with reference to physical movement of people, rather than in the plural, *mobilities*, as proposed by Urry (e.g. Urry 2000), who include in this notion also movements of objects, information, images etc.

4 "...the public will not pay more money, people do not vote, and our democratic institutions are threatened. Performance indicators and performance standards are the vehicle to help us translate, transfer, and use information for bureaucracies to evolve into what they are supposed to do." (Pisano, p 66 in Pickrell and Neumann 2001)

undertaken to clarify to what extent and to what avail this does actually happen.[5]

These motivations together points to a need for clarifying the concept of personal mobility and how it could be made operational so as to assess and monitor the results of policies that (cl)aim to provide it. For this purpose the chapter will put forward a concept of mobility, which arguably captures its key dimensions, and which also allows important policy aspects such as value and sustainability to be dealt with. As a tool for this conceptualisation a series of simple, heuristic diagrams will be employed.[6] This analysis will enable a first sketch of key elements to consider in a scheme for 'mobility policy' monitoring. The aim of the chapter is however *not* to define specific or technical indicators of mobility or to devise a practical monitoring program.[7] It will adopt a purely conceptual or 'idealist' approach, rather than looking for what is available in the measurement toolbox. Hopefully, by asking in this way *what* to monitor (rather than *how* to do it) the chapter can help stimulate thinking about what a mobility policy should be concerned with and what it should aim to deliver.

The Key Dimensions of Mobility

Mobility is a multidimensional concept, even if we have confined it here to physical mobility of persons. In this section we will attempt to clarify the following key aspects of mobility, in turn:

A. Mobility as potential as well as realised movement
B. Mobility as dependent on potency as well as tendency
C. Mobility as expressed in qualities and quantities
D. Mobility as externally and internally sustainable

A: Mobility as Potential and Realised Movement

Mobility refers to the ease of movement rather than just movement itself; it entails also *the potential* to move.[8] We have two basic aspects of mobility then, actual and potential movement. These are

---

5 For an overview of current practices in the field of transport and mobility policy monitoring in Europe see: van der Loop (2003).
6 The approach draws mainly from a Ph.D dissertation (Gudmundsson 2000).
7 There is a diverse literature on this subject, which we will not review (see e.g. Norwood and Casey 2002).
8 For similar understandings see e.g.: Kaufmann (2003) and Jones (1987).

not entirely separate but can be considered as a nested set, which is illustrated in Figure 1.

Actual movement is rather straightforward. It can basically be conceived in terms of distance and duration of the movement. In sequential terms one may count the frequency of trips etc. Actual movements of entities result is traffic flows; movement of people or goods in vehicles becomes transport. The arrow in Figure 6.1 may be thought of as an aggregate amount of actual travel undertaken, say, over a day by a person or over a year by population.

The *potential* movement derives from the transport systems' capacity to deliver movement. The infrastructure, vehicles, energy carriers, control systems and operators together enable a particular amount and type of movement to take place. This ability, or potential, is dependent upon the characteristics of each of the system components as well as their interaction enabled via the efforts of the operators. This potential varies in time and space, according to the local capacity of the transport system to deliver movement. It is typically much larger in a major city than in a remote rural area. This could be understood as a *systemic potential.*

Individuals can access or appropriate[9] a certain amount of the systemic potential that exists at a given location. This appropriated potential can be perceived as individual 'mobility resources'. Parts of these resources are technical means of movement whereas others are abilities of the individual (e.g. physical ability, driving skills, etc). Owning one or more cars in a household or having access to a road or rail network near the home represent mobility resources. The potential to deliver movement is dependent not only on the technical performance, but also of the systemic interaction among the elements. Congested roads or sharing the car in a family may reduce the individual potential (mobility resources) available in practice considerably.

When circumstances are in place (to be discussed in the next section) actual movement is realised as a specific manifestation of the potential that is offered by the system and available to the individuals. The difference in 'size' between realised and potential movement in Figure 6.1 illustrates a difference between how much travel would be possible compared to how much is actually done. For instance owning a car and parking it by the house means having a considerable potential available 24 hours a day, while it may be used only one hour. Private ownership typically restricts the car from being used more extensively by others that may need it, whereas alternatives with a similar potential (such as taxi) partly compensate for that, but at a high cost. In any case the

---

9 For developing the 'appropriation' concept, see Kaufmann (2003) p 37 ff.

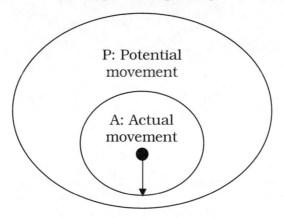

Figure 6.1   Mobility as actual and potential movement

potential to move does not match fully with the need to move (as will be addressed in the next section). Sometimes there is excess capacity, at other times there is too little. The available potential both enables *and* constrains the actual movement.

The relevance of the distinction between actual and potential movement can be made more evident if we introduce the objective of promoting the 'real value' of mobility. Both actual and potential movements have value to the individual and to society, but these values are not identical. The *actual* movement can produce net value through derived benefits from the activities it sustains (jobs, leisure at remote places, etc) plus a possible internal value of some movement in itself (enjoying a flight, for instance). The *potential* movement represents mobility resources and opportunities that hold additional values outside those derived from the activities sustained by the realised movement. These values have to do with advantages stemming from the ability to improvise in time and space, to escape quickly, to maintain flexibility etc. The distribution of this potential among the population is important in its own right, and a policy to promote mobility that creates 'real value' should consider both types of values. Meanwhile such a policy should of course also take into account the various *costs* associated with actual and potential movement. These costs include not only direct costs of transport, but also external costs. Often mentioned are external costs of actual movement due to congestion, pollution, accidents, etc. but some of the external costs are related to maintaining the systemic potential while not dependent on the level of actual movement (for instance costs due to effects of oil exploitation, fragmentation of nature etc.). Some of the external

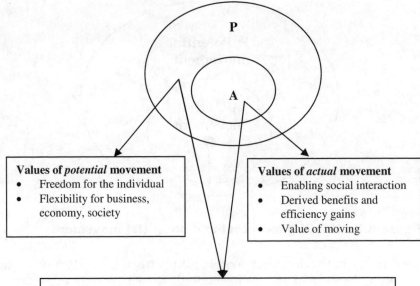

Figure 6.2   Positive and negative values associated with actual and potential movement

costs may be borne by other individuals than the ones who reap the benefits of actual movement, making it all the more necessary to factor them all into policy making. Figure 6.2 illustrates this range of 'value' and 'cost' elements (if not the full set).

The policy implication from this subsection is to stress the importance of changes in the level of potential movement in addition to ones associated with actual traffic. A mobility policy would need to address the potential, how it is produced, appropriated and distributed and also perhaps how it might be cultivated in valuable directions that would entail fewer external costs. *Monitoring of mobility policy would consequently need to cover potential as well as actual movement and the factors that control both of them.* This would again suggest two sets of indicators, one set for actual movement and another for the potential to move, with the latter set being distinctive to mobility policy, while also the more complex one.

B. Mobility as Dependent on Potency and Tendency

Now we will look at greater depth into the properties of the potential. To this end we divide the circle of potential movement into a *potency* (or *supply*) side and a *tendency* (or *demand*) side. When the two, potency and tendency overlap, actual movement may be produced, as illustrated in Figure 6.3.

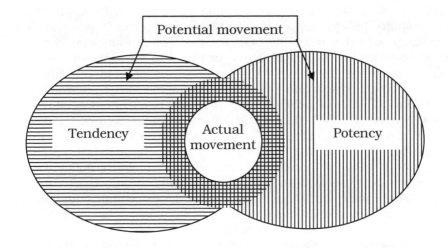

Figure 6.3   The potential movement as dependent upon tendency and potency

The *potency* side encompasses the properties identified in the previous section, namely the transport systems' potential capacity to deliver movement (at macro level) and the individual appropriation of resources to utilise the system (at micro level). The *tendency*, on the other hand, reflects the need or desire to move. This need is produced and conditioned by a range of socio-economic factors, which influence control the physical separation of activity spaces, and the preferences, roles, lifestyles and activity patterns of individuals. Together these factors create the pressure (tendency) to release the potential into movement.

Figure 6.3 illustrates these two main components of the potential. Jones (1987) defines them as two distinct dimensions of mobility, termed *potential action*, and *freedom of action* respectively. Potential action would refer to suppressed trips, that is, trips people would like to make but cannot due to technical or economic restrictions, while *freedom of action* means trips people could make with the available means, but may not need or want to.[10] This terminology suggests that a *mismatch* may exist between tendency and potency. On the right side needs not met, on the left side capacity not utilised (potentially excessive capacity). Both may even be present at the same time if the idle capacity cannot be employed to fulfil the needs due to technical mismatch (the empty rail car seats do not go in the desired direction) or due to appropriation mismatch (the empty car seats are not offered to non-car owners that may need them). Now what would these new distinctions imply for mobility policy? *Arguably, a mobility policy would need to deal explicitly with this mismatch.* On the one side suppressed demand may represent inefficient resource use and social exclusion; on the other, providing excessive capacity in terms of road building etc may be costly, risky, and potentially damaging to the environment. The aims of such a policy could therefore be either providing the most needed/least damaging capacity (as considered in conventional transport policy), *or* reducing the least needed/most damaging capacity, whatever would be most conducive to enhance the overall value of mobility offered. In short mobility policy would not necessarily seek to increase the capacity for movement in the traditional way but may also consider decommissioning or 'disarming' mobility capacities which could be considered underutilised or excessively destructive.

To illustrate the different options three broad strategy types are envisaged in Figure 6.4:

---

[10] We should make clear that the tendency side (Jones' potential action) is *not* mobility proper as defined here, but rather a representation of *accessibility* needs in demand for (potential) transport. Moreover Jones does not consider the 'overlap' suggested in Figure 6.3, where tendency and potency co-exist and match (meaning capacity is available for desired movements). And finally Mobility may not only be considered discretely, as in the concept of 'trips' used by Jones. Changes in mobility could also entail longer/shorter or faster/slower movements.

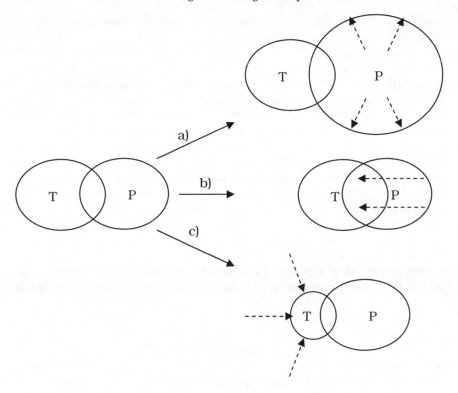

**Figure 6.4   Hypothetical strategies to address the 'mismatch'
problem**

a) The supply oriented *predict and provide* approach of
conventional transport policy has mainly extended the potency side
in the aim to cover 'more' of the tendency needs, without addressing
these directly (and perhaps missing them in part).[11]

b) A different way to address the mismatch could be to 'push' the
potency towards the tendency side in order to increase the overlap
rather than to expand the capacity. Car sharing policies could be an
example. Equipping public transport systems with facilities for
using wireless networks while onboard would be an example of the
opposite push.

c) A third approach may be to address the tendency side alone,
e.g. by employing land use measures to increase the density of
urban areas in the hope that it would reduce the need to travel. If
successful this approach may be the most effective in the long run,

---

[11] For critical discussions on the 'predict and provide' policy approach see
e.g. Terry (1999) and Vigar (2002).

but it is also highly vulnerable to more mobility intensive lifestyles.[12]

Whatever the specific policy approach, addressing the problem from the 'mismatch' perspective would, however, require monitoring on both sides to detect changes due to policies or other developments. This raises the problem of how to describe the mismatch including both the potency and the tendency side in an appropriate way. The *potency* can, at least in theory, be calculated in terms of the distance and speed that the transport systems can deliver at any given point in space and time (but see also the next section for additional qualities to be considered). A calculated breakdown of this systemic potential to individual locations is also conceivable even if the data requirements would be extensive. This holds the promise of mobility indicators that could be derived from observable characteristics. Measuring the *tendency* dimension would, on the other hand, have to establish the location of the relevant trip purposes and destinations for the specific population, which is a much more elusive task. For practical planning purposes some form of accessibility function for key urban destination types (housing, work, shopping etc) is often employed as an approximation to describe this tendency dimension (Tillema and van Wee 2003; Baradaran and Ramjerdi 2001). However, so far there have been few convincing attempts to develop aggregate policy indicators that could fully capture that side of the equation. No universally 'sound' way of solving this problem (identifying the travel needs of the population) has been found at the general level (Jones 1987).

The policy point to be made from this section is that measures of potential mobility proper (the potency side) would still be possible, even if there is no fully matching description available of the tendency (or accessibility needs) that would enable calculation of the 'mismatch'. The implied message is that mobility should not be approached only as a poor substitute for accessibility. Mobility and its variations across the population is important to monitor in its own right as a potency. Accessibility is an *additional* important concern, not the only one.

C. Mobility as Expressed in Qualities and Quantities

So far we have discussed mobility in terms of distance in time and space and the need to reach destinations. These are basic dimensions in which to describe mobility from the point of view of

---

[12] To this, see for instance Salomon and Mokhtarian (1998).

its *external* functions, while they do not fully capture the different qualities of movement in itself. Different modes of transport are often considered to service different 'symbolic-effective motives' of travellers (Kenyon and Lyons 2003): Cars may be thought to symbolise freedom and flexibility; trains offer safety and free hands to work; flights provide drinks, interesting views and a near-humiliating confinement of the body. These are of course stereotypes but the qualities such as safety, comfort, reliability, privacy, continuity, and even 'greenness' (Nilsson and Küller 2000) may be important choice parameters for various travellers in some relations. Such qualities are not separate from potential movement in time and space, they should rather be seen as important attributes of it.

Figure 6.5 illustrates roughly the potential mobility available at a hypothetical location taking into account different qualities of travel. The outer ring shows the fastest connection as the area that

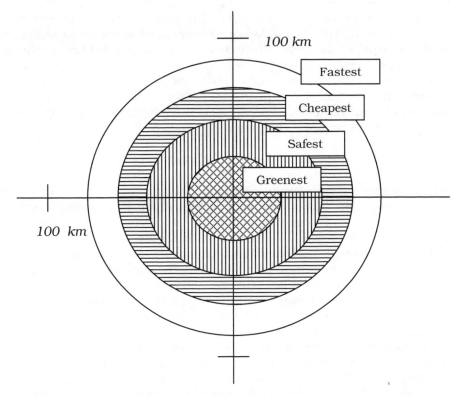

Figure 6.5   Illustration of qualitatively differentiated potential movement for four different mobility preferences, assuming different mode combinations in each case

could be covered within, say, one hour of movement from a particular point (e.g. a taxi). The second ring considers the cheapest link, while the two inner rings the most environmentally friendly and the safest alternatives, respectively. What emerges is a picture of a *qualitatively differentiated potential for movement*. This illustrates in a very simplified form how the mobility potential available to individuals with different qualitative preferences might be described and presented. If the objective of policy was to promote safe and green mobility it would be relevant to 'map' the potential reach of the various mode combinations at various locations in this way and possibly to minimise the gap between the potential reach of the green and safe alternatives compared to the faster or cheaper ones.

The qualitative dimensions of travel are of course difficult to capture fully. Some of these aspects are readily quantifiable (e.g. travel, time, emissions) while others are not (e.g. insecurity of female travellers; aesthetic qualities). For some travellers trade-offs are made on a daily basis, while for others choices of particular modes or routes are deeply entrenched (Jensen 1999). Importantly, travel often has to cross modes and involve interchanges and waiting at stops and terminals, which may weigh heavily in the overall appreciation of a trip. In any case an appropriate mapping and monitoring of mobility should seek to consider such qualities or be at risk of missing half the point.[13]

D. Mobility as Externally and Internally Sustainable

Sustainability is frequently cited as a major concern of recent transport policies. Much has been written about this subject (for a recent review see Gudmundsson 2004), but little clarity exists of what it actually means for mobility or transport to be sustainable. Hence monitoring schemes tend to reflect very broad overall definitions and objectives, often backed by sets of pragmatically selected transport indicators. This section aims to briefly reconsider sustainability and mobility in terms of the distinctions introduced in this chapter, not to resolve the issue but to suggest some directions for monitoring.

Sustainability literally means the ability to be maintained. Sustainable development refers to maintaining conditions for the well-being of both present and future generations. These conditions are often divided into environmental, social and economic

---

[13] The qualitative dimensions of mobility and how to conceptualise them will not be discussed further here.

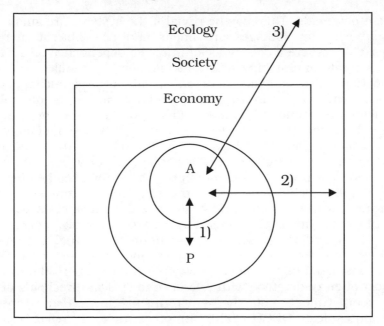

Figure 6.6   The roles of mobility in relation to sustainability

dimensions, mostly out of epistemic traditions. Mobility can be considered in several ways within this overall framework, as illustrated in Figure 6.6.

The distinction between actual and potential movement is again useful:

1) Basically actual movement is conditioned by the systemic potential. If this potential or capacity is exhausted, actual movement may come to a halt. Maintaining sufficient capacity to avoid breakdown may thus be defined as a criterion for 'internal' or local sustainability of the transport system. Controlling the 'gap' between critical capacities and actual movements of various kinds (road space, rolling stock, oil reserves, air quality, etc) is an obvious monitoring task at the system management level. Many such schemes are in place, even if they do not necessarily make explicit reference to sustainability.

2) Mobility sustains the wider economy and vice versa. Investments in the potential (e.g. transport infrastructure) are typically justified in terms of the expected socio-economic benefits from actual flows. Insufficient system investments may then in some cases slow down growth in wellbeing or even lead to breakdown. In other cases, however, the derived benefits of actual movements may be too small to justify maintaining extensive

system potentials. This may be trivial if the systems are small, and mobility-economy linkages are linear and reversible. It may be rather more severe if society locks-in to the dependence on systems that generate diminishing returns while becoming still more costly to sustain. Also conflicts between social fairness and economic efficiency may arise in this area. In any case it is difficult to establish the economic sustainability – or lack thereof – at the 'sector' level, due the many close interlinkages between mobility and the economy as a whole.[14] Monitoring of the 'economic sustainability' is therefore a major challenge, but at least it should aim to address the two-way relation that has been sketched here.

3) Finally, mobility draws on the physical environment, which sustains it with resources and absorptive capacities of its polluting outputs.[15] Providing the potential require materials, energy and land to expand the systems; in addition the actual movements produce emissions, noise, etc. Environmental sustainability has been considered in two different ways in the transport literature. It is most often understood with reference to critical thresholds of (all) the compartments of the environment to which transport contributes (e.g. OECD 2000). In other cases it refers only to environmental effects that are not conveniently included in standard Cost-Benefit analysis (Giorgi and Tandon 2000), which would be in particular long term systemic impacts on biodiversity, etc. In any case there would be a need to monitor the specific pressures compared with the distance to possible critical system levels.[16] However, since mobility is often only one among many contributors to each type of pressure on the environment (e.g. climate change) it is often not strictly possible to define environmental sustainability limits only for mobility, other than by some intermediate economic or political allocation.

All things considered a rigorous common definition of 'sustainable mobility' is hardly possible, since mobility does not take place in isolation from other activities and systems. Sustainability may however refer to system vulnerabilities at various levels and in different dimensions that would be useful to

---

[14] "Some authors have claimed that national programmes of public investment, including road construction, lead to high rates of social return measured in terms of economic growth and productivity improvement Other authors suggest (...) that, in general any contribution to the sustainable rate of economic growth of a mature economy, with well-developed transport systems, is likely to be modest. Our investigations support the latter assessment." (SACTRA 1999, p 3)

[15] See for example OECD (2000); Banister et al 2000; and Zietsman, J. and Rilett (2002).

[16] For a major, if not full-fledged attempt see EEA (2001; 2000).

monitor in any case. Key tasks for this monitoring would be to help ensure that,

- Potential mobility capacity it is 'big enough' to resist chocks, but
- It is not 'too big' compared with useful outputs, and
- Potential and actual mobility keeps within the environmental constraints allocated to it.

Summary and Discussion

The analysis in A-D above proposes a very 'rich' conceptual description of mobility. If this description was realised fully in practice it would cover the actual movement and the movement potentials available to (all) locations and ideally individuals in terms of parameters such as reach, speed, reliability, costs, comfort, environmental impact, and (partially at best) mobility supported access to desired destinations. The concept would describe potentials available at micro level at locations as well as aggregated to macro (regional, national) levels where it would show distribution and disparities in mobility, and enable comparison over time and with various capacity constraints of internal and external kind.

To realise this idea, extensive amounts of data would have to be collected, and importantly, many of the results to be monitored would have to be calculated. For instance the moving-around potential available to various socio-economic groups in a certain area or along a certain transport corridors would have to be computed from data on the availability and performance of all relevant transport systems in the particular setting (based on data on timetables, route networks, vehicle characteristics etc.). Table 6.1 summarises the broad types of information that would need to be compiled to make the concept operational, and it also indicates some of the more concrete measures that might have to be collected.

The 'Aspects' column of the scheme include measures of both actual and potential movement, the latter involving ideally both measures if a systemic potential and the mobility resources available to individuals.

The 'Dimensions' column exemplifies the types of information that would have to be collected in order to describe and calculate mobility in both aspects; that is, information on the capacities of all major transport system components and operator properties.

Table 6.1 Key dimensions for mobility policy monitoring

Aspect		Dimensions	Examples of measures	Input to
Actual movement		Volume, Quality, Impact Relevance of transport	Vehicle km Pass/tank Accident rates Travel speed Emissions Reliability Travel purposes	Measure/cal-culate negative impacts of mobility Illustrate needs Assess 'traditional' transport policy objectives
Potential movements	Micro	Mobility skills Mobility resources Mobility needs	Drivers licences/capita PT Card/capita Car ownership/capita Perceived sufficiency of mobility services	Calculate individual potential mobility Assess mismatch between needs and capacity
	Macro	System ser-vice/capacity System maintenance costs	Physical system size and character Number of seat km offered Service level of roads Destinations/areas available within X minutes System reinvestment needs	Calculate system potential mobility Assess mismatch between needs and capacity Assess sustainability

The 'Examples of measures' column suggests some of the data types that would be involved in making the dimension operational. Some of the proposed data are necessary to calculate potential mobility (e.g. car ownership, driver licenses, public transport seat kilometres, etc.), whereas others refer to negative externalities or sustainability issues (emissions).

The right hand column indicates the role of the content of each of the rows. The system would allow monitoring of system performance and output as well as mobility policy objectives.

Taken as a whole the task to define a monitoring program of this scope would seem monstrous, not least considering the recognised difficulties with just getting present, much more simple transport monitoring efforts to perform well.[17] It is clear that fulfilling such a program would require substantial amounts of data, and not least extensive calculations, since the potential mobility is a sort of speculative artefact with no direct observational reference. Most difficulties would likely be encountered if measures of accessibility to destinations (the tendency side) were to be incorporated in a meaningful way, but also areas like intermodal trip chains, and environmental impact are likely to cause trouble. An important point here is however that much of this information is already collected and in many cases just might need to be combined and compiled with the aid of tools like GIS, while in other cases simple examples based on selected data may serve to illustrate points just as clearly as huge compilations of data (see again Van der Loop 2002).

Exactly what kind of data and calculations would be needed to implement the concept and to produce an integrated message about mobility will not be explored here, but it would be a worthwhile task for further research, literature review and networking.

Conclusion

The chapter has addressed the concept of mobility from a 'realist' point of view – mobility as a dual entity that is real and have real implications, even if all of its capacities may not be observed directly. The claim is that mobility is an important policy issue, which deserves to be addressed and monitored as such. *Mobility should neither be reduced to 'transport' (or physical movement) as is often the case in existing 'mobility' policies, nor should it be reduced to only an inferior expression of 'accessibility', as is a tendency seen in some of the conceptual and critical literature.* Mobility has a role in itself, beyond (but not in opposition to) these two other important concepts.

If such a concept of mobility was to be made operational in terms of concrete measures, targets and indicators it would reflect very important elements of modern life and society, in a way that is not available today, and it could have several uses. First of all it might be used to inform the public directly about important aspects of their daily life situation and choice options. More importantly it

---

[17] Personal communications from members of the transport policy monitoring network and other monitoring officials.

could be used to assess the fulfilment of mobility policy objectives, and to confront and compare these with the already established objectives for e.g. environmental protection or traffic safety, to identify trade-offs and possible synergies. It could also be used to assess the effects of external changes (e.g. in oil prices) on mobility, and it could be drawn upon in the evaluation of the results of policies, not only transport policies, but also policies in other areas that influence mobility needs and opportunities (e.g. labour market, planning. housing, social services. etc). Finally it could contribute to the assessment of progress towards fulfilling Sustainable Development strategies and other overarching policy agendas.

Acknowledgements

I would like to thank Peter Jones, Jørgen Ole Bærenholdt, members of the European Transport Policy Monitoring network and colleagues at the FLUX Center for transport research at Roskilde University for helpful comments to earlier versions of this chapter. The former Danish Transport Council provided the funding to enable both research and network participation. The author carries the full responsibility for all propositions, remaining errors, etc. in this chapter.

References

Banister, D., Stead, D., Steen, P., Äkerman, J., Dreborg, K., Nijkamp and Schleisher-Tappeser, R. (2000), *European Transport Policy and Sustainable Mobility*, Spon Press, London and New York.

Baradaran, S. and Ramjerdi, F (2001), Performance of Accessibility Measures in Europe, *Journal of Transportation and Statistics*, Volume 4 Number 2/3, pp. 31-48.

Barde, Jean-Phillipe and Button, Kenneth (eds) (1990), *Transport Policy and the Environment. Six Case Studies*, Earthscan, 1990.

CEC (1992), *The Future Development of the Common Transport Policy – a global approach to the construction of a Community framework for sustainable mobility*, Commission of the European Communities, Brussels, 1992.

CEC (2001), *European transport policy for 2010: time to decide. White Paper*, COM(2001) 370, Commission of the European Communities, Brussels, Press 12/09/2001.

EEA (2000), *Are we moving in the right direction? Indicators on transport and environment integration in the EU*, TERM 2000, Environmental issues series No 12, European Environment Agency, Copenhagen.

EEA (2001), TERM 2001, *Indicators tracking transport and environment integration in the European Union*, European Environment Agency,

Copenhagen.

Gilbert, R; Irwin, N; Hollingworth, B and Blais, P, (2002), *Sustainable Transportation Performance Indicators (STPI)*, Project Report on Phase 3, The Centre for Sustainable Transportation, Toronto.

Gruening, G. (2001), 'Origin and theoretical basis of New Public Management', *International Public Management Journal* 4 (2001) pp. 1–25.

Gudmundsson, H. (2000), *Mobilitet og bæredygtighed – strategier, mål og institutioner i reguleringen af persontransport*, Ph.D-serie 8.2000, Handelshøjskolen i København, Økonomisk Fakultet, Samfundslitteratur, Frederiksberg, [*Mobility and Sustainability – Strategies, goals and institutions in the regulation of passenger transport*, Ph.D-series no. 8, 2000, Copenhagen Business School, Faculty of Economics, Copenhagen].

Gudmundsson, H. (2004), *Sustainable Transport and Performance Indicators*, Issues in Environmental Science and Technology No. 20.

Jensen, M. (1999), 'Passion and heart in transport — a sociological analysis on transport behaviour', *Transport Policy* 6, pp. 19–33.

Joint Expert Group on Transport and Environment (2000), *Recommendations for Actions for Sustainable Transport. A strategy Review*, Commission of the European Community Directorate-General Transport & Directorate-General Environment, Brussels, 26 September 2000.

Jones, P.M. (1987), 'Mobility and the Individual in Western Industrial Society', pp. 29-47 in Nijkamp, P. and Reichman, S. (eds), *Transportation Planning in a Changing World*, European Science Foundation, Gower, Aldershot.

Kaufmann, V. (2003), *Re-thinking Mobility. Contemporary Sociology*, Ashgate, Aldershot.

Nilsson, Maria and Küller, Rikard (2000), 'Travel behaviour and environmental concern', *Transportation Research Part D* 5 pp. 211-234.

Norwood, Janet and Casey, Jamie (eds) (2002), *Key Transportation Indicators: Summary of a Workshop*, Committee on National Statistics, National Research Council, National Academy Press, Washington, DC.

OECD (1995), *Governance in transition: public management reforms in OECD countries*, Organisation for Economic Co-operation and Development, Paris.

OECD (1997), *Towards Sustainable Transportation. The Vancouver Conference*, OECD Proceedings, Organisation for Economic Co-operation and Development, Paris.

OECD (2000), *EST! Synthesis Report of the OECD project on Environmentally Sustainable Transport EST*, Organisation for Economic Co-operation and Development and the Austrian Federal Ministry for Agriculture, Forestry, Environment and Water Management, Vienna.

Pisano, Mark (2000), 'Transforming Bureaucracies', pp. 66-68 in Neumann, L.A. et al (eds): *Performance Measures to Improve Transportation Systems and Agency Operations*, Report of a Conference, Transportation Research Board Conference Proceedings 26, National Academy Press, Washington, DC.

SACTRA (1999), *Transport and the economy*, Standing Advisory Committee on Trunk Road Appraisal (SACTRA), Department of the Environment, Transport and the Regions, London.

Salomon, Ilan and Mokhtarian, Patricia (1998), 'What Happens When Mobility-Inclined Market Segments Face Accessibility-Enhancing Policies?' *Transportation Research, D*, Vol. 3, No. 3, pp. 129-140.

Schmidt, Michael and Giorgi, Liana (2001), 'Successes, Failures and Prospects for the Common Transport Policy', *Innovation*, Vol. 14, No. 4, pp. 293-313.

Tengström, E. (1999), *Towards Environmental Sustainability? A Comparative study of Danish, Dutch and Swedish transport policies in a European context*, Ashgate, Aldershot, 1999.

Terry, F. (1999), 'The Impact of Evidence on Transport Policy Making: The Case of Road Construction', *Public Money and Management*, January-March, 1999 pp. 41-46.

Tillema, Taede and van Wee, Bert (2003), *Road pricing from a geographical perspective: a literature review and implications for research into accessibility*, Paper presented at the 43rd ERSA Congress August 27th-30th 2003, Jyväskylä.

Urry, John (2000), *Sociology beyond societies. Mobilities for the twenty-first century*, Routledge, London.

US DOT (2003), *DOT Performance Plan FY2004*, United States Department of Transportation, Washington DC.

Van der Loop, Han (ed.) (2002), *Transport Policy Monitoring in Europe*, Proceedings of the workshop held in Amsterdam, 17-18 October 2002, AVV Transport Research Centre, Den Haag, April 2003.

Vigar, Geoff (2002), *The Politics of Mobility. Transport, the environment and public policy*, Spon Press, London.

WBCSD (2001), *Mobility 21. World mobility at the end of the twentieth century and its sustainability*, World Business Council for Sustainable Development, Conches-Geneva.

Winston, Clifford (1999), *"You Can't Get There From Here" Government Failure in U.S. Transportation*, Brookings Institution, Washington DC.

Zietsman, J. and Rilett, L. R. (2002), *Sustainable Transportation: Conceptualization and Performance Measures*, Report No. SWUTC/02/167403-1, Texas Transportation Institute, The Texas A&M University System, College Station, Texas.

Chapter 7

The Institutionalisation of European Transport Policy from a Mobility Perspective

Anne Jensen

Introduction

> "What is indisputable, however, is that EU transport policy has always placed increasing mobility at its heart". (Jensen and Richardson, 2004 p. 76)

Driving on major European motorways or breathing the urban air of a European metropolis affects most humans, whether transport users or local citizens. In many respects, the European transport space appears overcrowded. The environmental hazards of an auto-mobilized Europe are becoming visible, affecting both human health and nature. However, the possibility of moving around adds a sense of freedom to the individual, and is articulated as 'the lifeblood' of the European Communities (CEC, 1993 sec. 3.1). Efficient transport systems are stressed as sustaining modern societies. The quality of life is thus affected in ambiguous ways by increased amounts of transport. At the same time, a European polity is taking form, accelerating the innovation of governance and changing the political landscape of Europe. Also within the transport area, the role of EU legislation and regulation is increasing.

Reflecting on such developments from an environmental perspective shows ambivalences between ostensible rational policies aimed at sustainable transport developments (CEC, 1992b; CEC, 2001b) and real world developments. One way to grasp these ambivalences is through an analysis of those conceptions of reality upon which the policy-making rests. The concept of mobility, it has been suggested, is significant for understanding developments in transport in late modernity (Urry, 2000; Nielsen and Oldrup, 2001; Kaufmann, 2002; Jensen and Richardson, 2004), also at European level.

At the European level, the Commission of the European Communities (the Commission) plays a significant role in policy-making (Richardson, 1996). This is partly due to its broad competences in initiating and formulating policies and setting the agenda (Wallace, 2000), and partly due to its status as "the central node through which most inter-organisational activities pass" (Héritier, 1999 p. 94). This turns the analytical focus to the Commission, and specifically to the Directorate-General (DG) for Transport and Energy.[1] Based on these reflections, the central research interest of this chapter has been to explore which influence the concept of mobility has had on the DG Transport and Energy's policy-making.

Backed by an institutional perspective, the chapter argues that the cognitive dimension of a transport policy institution has had a significant impact on the actual scope of transport policies. The main function of integrating a concept of mobility into European transport policy was to mediate a cognitive linkage to other policy areas, especially the internal market and cohesion policy. This had a triple effect. Firstly, in supporting the development of a comprehensive common transport policy, it contributed to the establishment of a legitimate transport policy area at Community level. Secondly, it supported the construction of a legitimate political identity for the DG Transport and Energy. Thirdly, from the perspective of European integration, it can be viewed as enhancing the constitution of the EU as a legitimate and natural political unit.

The next section briefly introduces the analytical framework. The analysis was conducted on the basis of an institutional analysis inspired by Foucauldian discourse analysis, and its background was an understanding of the European polity originating in theories of European integration. The third section provides the historical context by outlining the story of the emergence of a common European transport policy. In the fourth section, central policy documents from the most recent part of this process are analysed from the perspective of a concept of mobility. The fifth section addresses which role the concept of mobility has played in the development of a common transport policy. The sixth and concluding section sums up the findings.

---

[1] Though this focus is not intended to indicate that the Commission is the exclusive actor within European transport policies, neither that it necessarily is the most powerful.

Analysing Transport and Mobility in Europe

Institutional Perspectives

This chapter rests on the assumption that there are significant relations between the policy institutional framework and the development of (transport) policy. Institutions are understood as social constructs that in one way or another structure the actions of and interactions between social actors within a given field (March and Olsen, 1989; Aspinwall and Schneider, 2000; DiMaggio and Powell, 1991).[2] According to the new institutionalism,[3] institutions can be conceptualised as consisting of a regulative, a normative and a cognitive pillar (Scott, 1995; Laffan, 2001) or dimension (Jensen, 2003). The cognitive dimension is ascribed a content of symbolic systems and shared meanings (Scott, 1995), paradigms and ideas (Campbell, 1998; Hall and Taylor, 1996; Pedersen, 2003), cognitive frames (Campbell, 1998), cultural practices and cognitive patterns (Aspinwall and Schneider, 2000), or structures of meaning and interpretive order (March and Olsen, 1989). Hence, meaning and knowledge inhabit the cognitive dimension, and via this, institutions frame how politics and political problems are perceived and, also, how solutions and policies to handle these problems are developed.

This framing is dependent on an intimate relationship with the prevailing discourses within the institution (Jensen, 2003).[4] Central

---

[2] With this focus on framing and structuring of action, this chapter touches upon some of the same topics as Freudendal-Petersen in chapter 2.

[3] New institutionalism is a label covering a variety of theoretical and methodological approaches that address the above relation. Based on research agenda, theoretical roots, or epistemological and ontological stance, new institutionalism can be divided into three 'institutionalisms' – rational choice institutionalism, historical institutionalism and sociological institutionalism (Hall and Taylor, 1996, Aspinwall and Schneider, 2000, Pedersen, 2003). The latter has the most explicit focus on cognitive elements of institutional dynamics and has inspired the analytical approach of this chapter.

[4] Building on a Foucauldian concept of discourse (Foucault, 1970, 1979a, 1979b, 1999, Sharp and Richardson, 2001), it is assumed that the discourses of a policy area are intrinsically linked to the practises of this area, and equally to the potential policy institution. Whereas it is far from necessary in the case of discourses, policy institutions have sanctions and privileges attached to the rules, norms and forms of knowledge present in the institution (Andersen, 1994). Further, most often several discourses are at play in a given policy institution.

in the cognitive repertoire, which is embodied in the discourses, are stories of what the institution essentially is and its relation to the surrounding world, and these stories serve as tacit knowledge that helps interpret formal rules, norms and roles. In producing these stories, the institution itself emerges and changes (for example Berger and Luckmann, 1966). Thus, as a way of understanding institutional dynamics, the historical evolution of formal and informal rules, roles, etc. has increasingly attracted attention (Scott, 1995). The approach of political scientist Niels Åkerstrøm Andersen (Andersen, 1994) is based upon the historical emergence of institutions, and can aid in rectifying the precise interaction of the above elements of the cognitive dimension and their implications for framing actions.

Andersen analyses institutions in terms of three orders, namely a descriptive, a narrative and an argumentative order, each of which denotes a certain way of structuring and governing the actions and interactions of institutional agency. This approach of orders does not refer in particular to the cognitive dimension, but in the present context it serves to clarify significant cognitive elements.[5]

The *descriptive order* structures how objects are perceived. This includes which properties objects are assigned and in which relations objects are placed (Andersen, 1994). This implies a generation of facts by making observations and the articulation of social as well as natural phenomena within a specific policy area, for example transport, and placing these phenomena in causal relations that determine their possible causes and effects. This order is sustained by establishing criteria for how to represent phenomena as objects of investigation and of policy within the institutional setting, for example by pointing out that which is seen as a European transport policy problem, its perceived causes and effects, and the identified objectives of European transport policy.

The *narrative order* structures how action and agency are constructed and formed within the institution (Andersen, 1994). Thus, in contrast to rational choice institutionalism (Knight, 2001; Ostrom, 1991), agency, interests and intentions are perceived as constructs of the institutional setting rather than as given exogenously. This covers topics such as who is considered to be

---

However, it falls outside the scope of this chapter to further explore the distinction between institutions and discourses.

[5] Accordingly, the cognitive dimension of institutions was at the centre of the analysis, which pushed specific rules and roles and behavioural norms of the policy institution or in European transport policy-making to the perimeter of the analytical scope.

inside versus outside the institution, which (power) position the actor takes up, who is assigned the competence to exercise governance over whom, and how norms guide institutional action (March and Olsen, 1989; Finnemore, 1996). The narrative order concerns how political agency is constructed within the institution and how actors (roles) are endowed with legitimate claims to authority within the political field of the institution, for example who are considered to be legitimate policy makers of European transport policy.

The *argumentative order* structures how statements and arguments are perceived within the institution. This covers how reasons and justifications are included in order to add legitimacy and claims of truth to statements and arguments. This perception rests on a number of rules of acceptability, which are produced within the institution (Andersen, 1994), for example principles and norms of European transport policy. Rules of acceptance are 'last references'; those which are taken for granted and do not have to be argued further. As such, the argumentative order constitutes a way to select between different perceptions of political reality and different ways of handling the policy challenges faced by policy actors. The argumentative order thus expresses the sort of argument and reason which dominates the cognitive dimension of the institution. Put differently, it supplies the logical grounds for justifications and statements. The argumentative order indicates the knowledge systems, their hierarchies and references which are embedded in institutions. Legitimacy and acceptability of statements indicate the argumentative order of the institution, for example those figures of thought which serve to justify a specific transport policy initiative or which ideas are central to the strategies of the transport policy.

By including these three orders one arrives at an institutional analysis of European transport policy that centres on *what* transport was perceived to be, *whom or what* were considered as actual or potential legitimate transport policy actors, and *which criteria* were established for valid arguments, proposals and statements. Based on the intimate relationship between discourses and institutions, the method chosen was that of discourse analysis, to which I shall return below. For the analysis of European transport policy, the three orders were adapted to a European institutional setting which included a European integration approach.

Transport Policy in Europe – Integration and Diversity

Cooperation between the European states was founded on the objectives of security and economic restructuring in the aftermath of the Second World War (Castells, 1998; McCormick, 1999). These concerns created a need for policy institutions to support the cooperation and integration. European transport policy is initiated and developed in this wider setting of a European polity.

The *Treaty of Rome* of 1957 can thus fundamentally be seen as an initiative aimed at stabilizing the regional balance of power, while the security imperative was downplayed at later stages of European integration. Thus, the landmark signing of the *Single European Act* in 1986 and the ensuing creation of the internal market early in 1993 were driven more by the relative decline in competitive strength of European economies *vis à vis*, in particular, Japan and the USA. This development in combination with the sudden change of the geopolitical landscape of Europe after 1989 pushed the formal integration of the Community through the establishment of the European Union and the initiation of a common currency, the euro, with the signing of the *Treaty on the European Union* of 1992 (Castells, 1998). But other dynamics also had significant influence.

From the very start, the Community was founded on a split between conflicting visions of European cooperation, on the one hand hopes of a federal Europe, and on the other a looser cooperation between the nation states of Europe. This initial split is present throughout the history of integration, as a tension between intergovernmentalism and supranationalism (Cram, 1997; Castells, 1998). This tension has led to periods of deadlock and large uncertainty, but at the same time it has also stimulated innovation of governance, policies and institutional setups (Héritier, 1999; Wallace, 2000).

To cope with this unresolved tension, Community policy-making is based on a changing and highly complex system of governance (Castells, 1998). The EU polity is characterized by having decision-making and power dispersed between a range of centres, with policy-making taking place at and among multiple levels, in multiple ways, and with participation of a multiplicity of actors (Richardson, 1996; Cram, 1997; Wallace, 2000; Anderson, 2001). It is thus characteristic for Community policy-making that policy issues are anchored within multiple areas and at multiple levels, which is also the case for transport policy.

A Brief History of European Transport Policy

'European transport policy' refers to the transport policies which have the Community as their main frame of reference and jurisdiction. The main focus and overall aim of the policies change over time, as does the pace of development. A focus on these two tenets separated the history of European transport policy in three stages,[6] culminating with the ongoing formulation of the common transport policy. Following the general tendency of EU policy-making, the policy issues of the transport area are also anchored within a number of other Community as well as national policy areas.[7]

Stages One and Two – Preparing for a Common Transport Policy

The *first stage* coincided with the decades after the Second World War where motorized transport increasingly formed an integral part of modern society. The stage commenced with the signing of the *Treaty of Rome* in 1957 and lasted until the mid-1980s. A common transport policy as one of the four sector policies was established as a Community aim in *The Treaty of Rome* (EC, 1957; Wallace, 2000). During this stage, transport policies at European level were basically a "stated intention to facilitate international transport" (Schmidt and Giorgi, 2001 p. 294). The main Community initiatives were aimed at establishing Community standards, and at harmonising member-state regulations in the area of transport services in order to create common rules for transport to, from and crossing member states and for establishing the common conditions for transport services as laid down in articles 75 (a) and (b). In 1978, a Committee on Transport Infrastructure was created and a consultation procedure to enhance the co-ordination and development of infrastructure links in Europe was adopted. By 1982, this enabled a set of "modest ad hoc financial contributions to investments in projects of Community interest" (CEC, 1992b p. 51). The dominant view on transport in this stage was that of transport as a matter of spatial accessibility that referred to the

---

6   This is in accordance with those identified by Schmidt and Giorgi 2001.

7   The analysis focused on the policy-making taking place within the Commission, with primary focus on DG Transport and Energy. The interesting perspectives related to the influence of other actors and to the ongoing tension between supranationalism and intergovernmentalism, specifically those related to the influence and interests of the big member states and of the other Community institutions, are therefore not discussed in any detail.

(still international) region of the European Economic Community. The majority of specific transport policies were placed in the hands of the individual member states.

The *second stage* lasted from the middle of the 1980s to 1992. It took off with the revitalisation of the objective of an internal market in the early 1980s. Subsequently, the establishment of an internal and single European market gained momentum, leading to the signing of the *Single European Act* in 1986 (CEC, 1985; Young and Wallace, 2000). The main thrust of Community transport policies shifted from standardisation to liberalisation, and a number of transport sectors were targeted for liberalisation (CEC, 1992b) in order to create open markets with extensive competition. Transport policy at European level was thus incorporated in the efforts to achieve the internal market, and was seen as a precondition for an effective market; it was to provide links between the producers, markets and consumers. The principle of mutual recognition, i.e. that member states recognize each other's standards as valid for imported goods, resolved the policy deadlock stemming from the massive amount of legislation that had to be harmonized. Preceding this, the liberalisation of transport markets could be pushed forward even without widespread harmonisation, though harmonisation maintained a central position.[8]

Two rulings of The European Court of Justice pushed the process,[9] and qualified majority voting was introduced in the areas of shipping and of air transport. Especially the latter had been dominated by protectionist stands in the member states, leading to the halting of liberalisation reforms (CEC, 2001b; McCormick, 1999).

Lastly, a number of transport infrastructure projects were financed via the structural funds, especially the European Regional Development Fund. This source of financing became more accessible after a reform of the structural funds in 1988 changed the objectives for financing to be based on assessments of overall regional economic developments (CEC, 1992b), thus broadening the scope for community investments in trans-border infrastructure projects.

---

[8] See for instance CEC 2001b pp. 13-17.

[9] In 1985, the *Inactivity Verdict* determined that the Council of Ministers had not been active enough in promoting standardisation and harmonisation of transport services. Two years earlier, a ruling stated that harmonisation was not to be linked to liberalisation, i.e. 'full' harmonisation was not a precondition to start liberalisation, which made co-existence of the two approaches possible (Group Transport 2000 Plus, 1990; Héritier, 1999). This co-existence was part of a general Community trend to set the aim of an internal market in motion.

In the second stage, transport was thus still mainly perceived as spatial accessibility, and viewed as a matter of transport flows in the EU polity. No coherent transport policy was developed, but with the ideas behind the internal market gaining ground the groundwork was laid.

Stage Three – the Shift to a Common Transport Policy

In 1992, the *third stage* was launched with the publication of the first white paper addressing a common transport policy, *The Future Development of the Common Transport Policy – A Global Approach to the Construction of a Community Framework for Sustainable Mobility* (CEC, 1992b). From now on, transport policy became much more complex, and solidly integrated into other Community policy areas, especially regional policy and internal market policy. The 1992 white paper outlined the directions for the succeeding common transport policy.

First, the liberalisation of the transport markets was intensified. Consequently, at the end of the 1990s and in the beginning of the 2000s a number of member states opened up their rail transport to private operators. Further, the Single European Sky was launched, and the allocation of slots (landing units at airports) came to include a variety of private operators (CEC, 2001b). The effort to open up the markets also involved a reduction of state subsidies.

Second, the varied effects of transport on the natural and urban environment were addressed, reflected in the labelling of the approach to a common transport policy – *Sustainable Mobility*. From a focus on technical harmonisation and emission standards in the early stages, sustainable mobility expressed attempts to integrate environmental – and social – concerns into transport policy-making. At the turn of the century, this led to the objectives of a modal shift and of decoupling growth in transport from economic growth (CEC, 2001b). Furthermore, research into the environmental effects of transport was strengthened. A vast variety of research projects addressing sustainable mobility or specific environmental problems of transport were launched under the *Fourth, Fifth,* and *Sixth Framework Research Programmes* (CEC, 2001d; CEC DG TREN, 2004). Overall, the policy connected to a version of sustainability which conceptualized simultaneous gains for economic development and environmental protection, and the indispensable interdependence between these.[10]

---

[10] On a level beyond any specific policy area, this constitutes a societal and/or cultural meta-narrative – a storyline – of ecological modernization (Hajer, 1995).

Third, the Commission addressed the external costs of transport – or marginal social costs (CEC, 1998) – and placed on the agenda the internalisation of these in the price of transport. Not until after 2001 did this issue receive political attention, and still the Community regulation on how to price transport, how much to include, and where the revenue ought to be allocated was sparse (CEC, 1998; CEC, 2001b; CEC DG Press, 2003).

Fourth, during the 1990s, the problem of congestion increasingly became a major policy concern. From its classification as a minor environmental (!) problem early in the 1990s, congestion changed to a priority issue that was linked to a number of other topics, such as the capacity of infrastructure and urban development (CEC, 1992b; CEC, 2001b; CEC, 2003).

Fifth, safety, especially on the road, was a targeted area that led to several initiatives such as professional drivers' education and compulsory safety belts. Also, the technical safety requirements for vehicles increased during the 1990s (CEC DG Press, 2003). By 2001, road casualties had declined relatively, to approximately 40,000 a year at Community level (CEC, 2001b). Still, as the 2001 white paper remarks, this figure is equivalent to a minor plane crash a day, but receives far less attention (CEC, 2001b, p. 65). Further, following September 11th 2001, the security of ports, airports and major rail connections became an issue.

Sixth, trans-European transport networks – or the TEN-T – gradually developed. During the 1990s and as liberalisation of the transport sectors progressed, it became a dominant activity of transport policy (Jensen and Richardson, 2004). TEN-T is specified in the *Maastricht Treaty on the European Union* of 1992, and subsequently a 'TEN-T map of Europe' was drawn, which reached into all corners of the Community and included all modes of (motorized) transport.[11]

The point of the TEN-T projects is not only their magnitude. They must also benefit more than one of the member states, preferably by eliminating missing links in the networks. Lastly, projects at the edge of the EU, bordering to the candidate countries of Eastern

---

[11] In TEN-T projects of physical infrastructure, Community involvement is mainly financial, whereas in information projects, such as the Galileo satellite system, the Community also engages as initiators and managers. In 1994, the *Essen List* singled out 14 major infrastructure projects as priority projects. In 2003, a new list of priority projects was added, which included another six priority projects, with an extensive review scheduled for 2004 (CEC, 2001b). The Community share of financing was 10 per cent of total budget until June 2003, where it was doubled, to 20 per cent in an attempt to increase the rate of completion.

Europe are also permitted by the guidelines (EC, 1992; Jensen and Richardson, 2004).

Hence, in the third stage, a comprehensive Community strategy for influencing transport development has been emerging, and it has taken the form of the common transport policy, labelled *sustainable mobility*. Now, transport is perceived as more than accessibility, transport flows and movement. Transport is also the possible and future movement, and transport policy addresses a complex of problems associated with transport. The transport policies have thus developed into a multifarious policy area at EU level. This development has followed a course marked by moving in the three stages outlined in Table 7.1.

Table 7.1 European transport policy in three stages

	Main focus	Overall aim	Transport perception
Phase 1 1957 – mid 1980s	Technical standards	Creating accessibility	Access
Phase 2 Mid 1980s – 1992	Liberalisation Standards	Removing barriers for competition	Transport flows Access, movement
Phase 3 1992 – onwards	CTP Liberalisation Modal shift TEN-T	Addressing problems associated with transport	Mobility Transport flows Access, movement

A New Player – the Concept of Mobility Enters the European Transport Policy Stage

The story above indicates how the first and second stages of a European transport policy reflect the general development of the EU. During the third stage, however, things changed substantially. This is reflected in the way a concept of mobility entered the discourses of European transport policy and influenced the creation of a transport institution, by contributing to a descriptive, a narrative and an argumentative order.

In the early phases of this study, a concept of mobility appeared as an interesting perspective on the institutionalisation of European transport policies. In the subsequent analysis, application of the analytical optic of mobility made three issues of the emerging common transport policy appear significant, namely sustainable mobility, trans-European transport networks (TEN-T), and the free movement of goods and people. Furthermore, 'mobility' signified a certain perception of freedom, which constituted a fourth issue. Below, the descriptive, the narrative, and the argumentative institutional orders for all four issues are outlined.

For each issue, the inclusion of a concept of mobility, or closely related concepts, was evaluated according to the institutional approach introduced above. The institutional analysis was applied at an archive consisting of policy documents from the third stage of the transport policy,[12] and used discourse analysis as a tool. The discourse analysis focused on *what* transport was perceived to be, *whom or what* were considered as actual or potential legitimate transport policy actors, and *which criteria* were established for valid arguments, proposals and statements.[13]

Sustainable Mobility and Environmental Problems Related to Transport

It was the report *Transport in a Fast Changing Europe* (Group Transport 2000 Plus, 1990) that initially launched the concept of

---

[12] Starting in the archives of DG Transport and Energy with documents that were pointed out as central, such as the white papers addressing a common transport policy, it was noted each time that the documents referred to other documents. These latter were subsequently included in the analysis. They referred to yet more documents and so forth (so called snowballing). Eventually, this also included policy documents from other policy areas. This was supplemented with all white and green papers, and the action programmes issued in connection with the white papers, from the DG Transport and Energy. This process served two purposes: Firstly, the archive for the discourse analysis was constructed, and secondly, it pointed out which policy areas and policy issues that kept appearing. Among these, the ones relating to a concept of mobility were selected to be included in the institutional analysis.

[13] Specifically, it was noted each time the documents referred to transport policy problems and their relations; to an elaboration of the perception of transport; to actual or potential actors of the transport policy; to other policy areas, and to norms, ideals and principles. Lastly, it was noted each time a concept of mobility in some form was applied, for example accessibility, traffic flows, movement, sustainable mobility. The applied pre-understanding of the concept of mobility originates from Gudmundsson 2000 and from Kaufmann 2002, thus it entails two features worth stressing here: a tension between actual and potential mobility (in Kaufmann enraptured by the concept of motility), and a significant dimension of meaning, as also demonstrated by Gudmundsson in chapter 6.

sustainability, thus providing mobility – or sustainable mobility – with an entrance into the European transport policy area. Further, sustainability provided environmental problems with a platform from where they could be addressed. The most striking effect of this was in contributing to a descriptive order, where it supports the perception of transport and transports relations with society. Further, the environmental and social problems relating to transport could be articulated within the principle of sustainable development, without necessarily affecting the want for more mobility. Transport was thus connected to a wide range of problematic effects through the notion of sustainable mobility, and this further helped to highlight possible policy solutions.

Sustainable mobility represented two significant tenets of transport. Transport in this version of mobility was pointed to as a significant social activity in late modern societies. This led to the second and more interesting feature, namely the use of the notion as a way to address the ambiguities of late modern transport (CEC, 2001b p. 6). The linking of sustainability and mobility was presented as a way to address aims of an efficient transport system with a significant social and economic role, and of securing the freedom of choice for the user, in combination with addressing aims of a reduction of transports environmental effects. In the 1992 green paper, the notion of "sustainable mobility" was articulated in relation to "an overall pattern of sustainable development" (CEC, 1992a p. 43), and applied to a number of environmental degradations induced by activities in the transport sector (CEC, 1992a section V), a tendency also present in later documents (CEC, 2001a p. 4; CEC, 2001b pp. 9-10). Hence, sustainable mobility embodied a perception of transport, where transport is a necessity for late modern societies, but which simultaneously upholds ambiguous relations with society, including potentially highly problematic ones, thus contributing to establishing a descriptive order.

The issue of sustainable mobility has not had an equally strong bearing when it came to indicating legitimate actors, though it emphasised the trans-European character of the actions aimed at sustainability (CEC, 2001a p. 13). This was reflected in DG Transport and Energy's attempts to place the internalisation of the external costs of transport high on the agenda. Internalising costs was presented as a way to enhance the economic and social as well as the environmental performance of transport and thus prevent transport from remaining 'unsustainable' (CEC, 1995 pp. i, 50). Given the central position of the internal market in the EU, it was both legitimate and palpable to present the internalisation of costs as actions at Community level.

The start of a common transport policy coincided with both the Rio Summit and establishment of the internal market, the decision on the euro and the *Treaty on the European Union*. In this context, the notion of sustainable mobility appeared to satisfy all needs, as it included a ranking of environmental concerns alongside the social objectives inherent in cohesion and structural policy and along the aims of competitive and liberal markets inherent in the idea of the internal market. Further, when a modal shift was given a spearhead position in the sustainable transport strategy, the strategy included congestion and inefficiency, and stressed the importance of the TEN-T (CEC, 2001b). Hence, lack of accessibility, inefficiency and congestion were seen as obstacles to the integration of outlying regions and to the economic development which was expected to result from the creation of internal market and, whereas economic development was presented as a precondition for achieving sustainability. The approach of sustainable mobility must inevitably address these issues, and in doing so the issues contribute to the establishment of the rules of acceptability enclosed in the emerging argumentative order. In this way, the notion was full of promises from the start, especially by connecting to ecological modernism. Over the next decade the focus on sustainability became more diluted, and the significance of sustainability in the argumentative order faded.

Mobility and the Free Movement of Goods, Services, and Persons

With the issue of the free movement of goods, services and persons, the internal market and its ideological basis showed their force in contributing to the establishment of the argumentative and the narrative orders in particular. The ideas of competitiveness through an extended and liberal market, and of the economic development of the regions as well as of the Community resulting from increased access to central markets continued to have a strong influence as criteria for the acceptance of statements and proposals. From this perspective transport is assigned a crucial role in the completion of the internal market. The internal market is both the prime objective of the Community, enforced since the mid-1980s, and a project that involves all of the Community by definition, and with this status the internal market entailed an obvious option of asking for a European actor. Specifically with smooth and expanded access of European transport systems, the internal market and cohesion is made dependent upon such a European actor.

In the 1992 white paper on a common transport policy, the internal market is, on the basis of its core Community status, accentuated as an "area[s] of exclusive power", to invoke that "the

Community is obliged" to act within the field of transport policy, while "the necessity for action is established by the Treaty itself" (CEC, 1992b p. 20). The same thought reappeared throughout the third stage (see for example CEC 1992b p. 95, CEC 2001b, CEC DG Press 2003). The internal market was thereby made dependent on the actions of a legitimate European policy actor, who had a strong position in the emerging narrative order.

The evident strength of the idea of the internal market as a mover of economic development and as an agent of Community integration enforces the emerging argumentative order in this issue. This has the consequence that in relation to the internal market (increased) mobility itself is not put into question but seen as something which places certain demands on the common transport policy, i.e. something which is at the bottom line of the policy's objectives, for example in relation to enlargement: "...enlargement is set to trigger a veritable explosion in exchanges of goods and people between the countries of the Union...[...]...The lack of efficient infrastructure networks to cope with this anticipated growth in movements is still greatly underestimated. And yet that infrastructure is a key element of the strategy for economic development of the candidate countries and their integration into the internal market" (CEC, 2001b p. 91).

These figures of thought are present in numerous documents (for example CEC, 1992b p. 19; p. 95, CEC, 2001c p. 3). In the 1992 white paper, international or regional mobility is even articulated in terms of a "new European order" (CEC, 1992b p 95). As central ideas for no less than a new regional order, the basic ideas of the internal market – economic growth through an integrated and expanded liberal European market – stand as last references; as points of acceptance. This is accentuated by the employment of metaphors of the human body, as when European transport systems are termed "the lifeblood of the Community" and the "arteries of the internal market" (CEC, 1993 section 3.1, repeated in CEC, 2001b pp. 10, 19). Obviously, it is necessary to nourish one's lifeblood.

Mobility and the Trans-European Transport Networks

The most striking feature of the TEN-T is its contribution to creating a narrative order by identifying European infrastructure, including spatial planning, as an area where a European actor is both desirable and necessary. Further, it solidified the ideas supporting the free movement of goods, services and people, through the networks' evident position in the ongoing establishment of the internal market, in this way the issue of the TEN-T also contributed to an argumentative order. This pointed at transport infrastructure as a solution to policy problems instead of as causing problems.

Documents stressed that the TEN-T was a necessary condition for achieving the frictionless movement and vast access envisioned in the ideas of the free market. The networks are presented as an instrument that links the different parts and regions of Europe both by connecting outlying regions and new member-states to central markets and by efficiently connecting to corridors (CEC, 2001b p. 8, 91): "A unified European network is essential to guarantee genuine freedom of movement of goods and persons, to bring the outlying ... areas closer to the central regions and to create a bridge towards of the countries of Eastern Europe and the Mediterranean basin. If the infrastructure necessary is not completed and interlinked to enable trade to be conducted, the internal market and the territorial cohesion of the European Union will remain ideas that have failed to come to full fruition" (CEC, 2001c p. 3). This figure of thought is present throughout stage three (CEC, 1992b pp. 16, 51; CEC, 2001 p. 3; CEC, 2004 pp. 2, 17), also with the addition that TEN-T "is directly related to the objectives of sustainable development" (CEC, 2004 p. 3).

The foundation of the TEN-T is article 129 of the *Treaty on the European Union* which concerns projects of European importance (rather than those in the interest of individual member states). This represents the TEN-T as the issue, where the construction of a role for a European actor who can handle the challenges, is most evident. The role of creating an efficient European transport system is articulated as essential for both the objectives of cohesion policy, and for the internal market (CEC 2001c p. 3), and further for "the integration of the Community" (CEC, 1992b p. 16). The emphasis of the regional aspect (for example CEC, 2001b pp. 7, 10, 50; CEC, 2001c p. 3; CEC, 2004 p. 3)[14] transgresses the idea of a Europe of states and supports the constitution of 'a Europe of regions'. Hence, with reference to regions and cohesion, and to the internal market, the legitimate policy actor must represent Europe or the Community far more than it must represent a specific member state or industrial association. This linkage to the construction of Europe as a political unity is central for the emerging narrative order.

---

[14] For example TEN-T must be carried out with respect to the objectives of the structural funds. In the funding of regional development projects under these latter funds "accessibility considerations have played a major role" (CEC, 1992b p. 52). This is to be seen in the light of funding of TEN-T projects. They are only supported by the small TEN-T fund and they have historically relied heavily on investments via the structural funds (CEC, 2001b, Peters, 2003).

Mobility as the Embodiment of Freedom

The slightly surprising issue of mobility as the embodiment of a special version of freedom proved to be most forceful in its contribution to the establishment of an argumentative order. This relates to the way a concept of mobility is articulated in relation to the ideals of Western liberal democracy. In relation to freedom, the concept of mobility implies particularly the potential movement as well as frictionless options to move, at individual as well as Community level. Indirectly, this also supports the narrative order by pointing to the Community as the appropriate area for actions aimed at enhancing freedom.

In terms of the descriptive order, mobility is, on the one hand, simply seen as a symbol of freedom. On the other hand, an expanded option to move (in the version of auto-mobility) is seen a "cornerstone" of free societies, thus turned into a precondition of freedom (CEC DG Press, 2003): "The family car is often a symbol of a free society. This applies even more so in Eastern Europe where mobility is considered to be a cornerstone of emancipation" (Group Transport 2000 Plus, 1990 p. 10). This also applies in relation to free choice (CEC, 1992b p. 63).

It is in its contribution to the creation of an argumentative order that the articulation of mobility in relation to freedom demonstrates its powerfulness. Freedom is a fundamental norm embodied in ideas of Western liberal democracy, and integrating mobility in this perception evokes a new status for mobility. Not surprisingly, this normative linkage ties up with how the concept of mobility is connected to the internal market: "We Europeans take our mobility for granted...[...]...the single market rests on four basic freedoms: the free movement of goods, services, people and capital" (CEC DG Press, 2003 p. 3). Likewise, political actions at European level to manage the "problems that threaten our mobility" (CEC DG Press, 2003 p. 4) were justified with reference to this. This connection was stressed in several documents (Group Transport 2000 Plus, 1990 p. 29; CEC, 1992b pp. 19, 51; CEC, 2001c p. 3). Simultaneously, the ground was laid out for a reification of the change in patterns of mobility as a natural state of affairs: "Personal mobility...is now more or less seen as an acquired right" (CEC, 2001b pp. 6-7). This 'more or less acquired right' is not questioned or placed on an agenda for discussion or political action but is mentioned in the flow of "advance[s] of this policy" (CEC, 2001b p. 7), i.e. of the common transport policy.

Hence, by being articulated as a 'basic and essential right', mobility becomes untouchable. This is particularly evident when mobility is signified in relation to free flow, free choice, and accessibility. Pushed to the extreme: the more mobility, the more free a society. This interposes a reification of mobility as highly desirable as it draws on one of the founding ideas of Western democracy.

The Role of a Concept of Mobility in Creating a European Transport Policy Institution

In all of the four issues recurrent in the third stage, the establishment of the three institutional orders had commenced. The institutional orders also changed over the almost one and half decades which the policy documents cover. The findings of each of the four issues paired with the history of emergence of a European transport policy yield an understanding of how a concept of mobility influenced the policy-making of DG Transport and Energy.

A European Transport Policy in Creation

In the first and second stages of the emergence of a transport policy at European level, the overall aims and foci (see table 3.1) can be seen in the light of the general development of European integration, as presented in section 2. The harmonization of the customs union and the low level of political integration of the 1970s corresponded to the main focus of the transport policy as that of breaking down barriers to market access, i.e. harmonizing technical standards. Also the aim of removing barriers to competition within the transport area through market support, i.e. liberalisation and further harmonization of standards, is completely in line with, and laid down in, the project of creating a single European market. The lack of a comprehensive and self-contained transport policy in these stages reflects this, and the moving forces of the transport policy development appeared to be defined outside the transport policy area.

By the end of the second stage and even more so in the third, this changed. The main focus of the activities was to shape the common transport policy of the EU, symbolised by the 1992 white paper on *Sustainable Mobility* (CEC, 1992b), and the overall aim altered to one of addressing problems associated with transport. The policy development changed and achieved a measure of autonomy, though still intertwined in the European history of integration – a transport policy institution appeared to be emerging.

The Three Institutional Orders of the Emerging European Transport Policy Institution

The changes in the development of a transport policy took the form of the co-existence of different perceptions within the institutional orders, combined with no hard and fixed boundary between the dominant perceptions. In the third stage, the different institutional orders proved to have different statuses and prominence in the different issues.

The creation of a descriptive order was strongest within the issues of sustainable mobility and of the movement of goods, services and people. The former helped to pinpoint a wide range of environmental problems associated with the intensified patterns of transport in late modernity and to place them in a relation where causes could be identified and solutions envisioned. It furthermore enabled a legitimate inclusion of environmental as well as social and economic objectives in transport policy. The latter two provided a blueprint for the policy orientation. In arguing for the essential importance for the ongoing consolidation of an extensive European transport system and increased mobility, these objectives became impossible to oppose.

The establishment of the *narrative order* was most explicit within the issues concerning the movement of goods, services and people, and of the TEN-T. The project of the TEN-T is intimately connected to the backbone of the Community – the establishment and spread of a single European market, with its ideas of the free movement of goods, people, and services.[15] Indirectly, it also relates to the flipside of the Community *raison d'être*, the security concerns that contributed to the enlargement of the Community to the East. This renders evident a need for European actions and consequently a legitimate political actor capable of performing such actions. Also the issue of freedom contributes to this indispensable construction of a European policy actor.

An emerging *argumentative order* is most prominent within the issues of movement of goods, people and services, of freedom, and to a lesser extent of the TEN-T. For the issue of TEN-Ts, this concerns ideas of a necessary transport infrastructure – smooth and far-reaching accessibility – stretching to remote corners of the Community. By linking objectives and projects to the structural funds and to objectives of cohesion, the TEN-Ts integrate social as well as integrative figures of thought. For the internal market, the competitiveness of the regions and of the Community is made

---

[15] And capital, though this 'fourth fundamental freedom' does not figure significantly in relation to transport or mobility.

dependent on uninhibited and frictionless access to central markets which *per se* is seen as a mover of (economic) development. This connects strongly to the concept of mobility, and especially to the feature of potential transport. Lastly, the issue of freedom introduced ideas closely tied to Western democracy and human rights. These are also directly related to mobility, in the form of free choice and freedom to move, thus presuming this is possible anywhere at anytime – frictionless and boundless.

The argumentative order illustrates those basic ideas that proposals and statements cannot oppose. In the policy institution, specific rules of acceptance reflect these fundamental figures. This implies that when complying with the above noted rules of acceptance, it becomes increasingly difficult to contest the idea of enhanced mobility. Thus, to contest increased potential and anticipated as well as actual transport as an instrument in solving the main problems of transport – from environmental hazards to congestion and safety – also becomes difficult. At the same time, the rules of acceptance enable a policy to develop, as indicated by the vitality of the policy-making in stage three.

This strength and extension of the argumentative order in the third stage contrasts with the two earlier stages of a European transport policy. Though the institutional analysis does not cover the period until the end of the 1980s, the discourses of the third stage paired with the history of European transport policy indicate a specific feature. The argumentative order is not established until the third stage, hence the European transport policy did not establish a *raison d'être* of its own earlier; it was merely a reflection of the general development in European cooperation and integration whereby the development outside the transport area governed the development of the European transport policy. When an argumentative order was established during stage three, it was both symptomatic of, and contributed to, the development of an internal dynamic in European transport policy-making.

Conclusion

Scope of the Approach

This chapter has investigated the impact of a concept of mobility on the policy-making of DG Transport and Energy, in an attempt to understand the ambiguities of European transport policies. An institutional approach, developed within a social constructivist framework and building on a discourse analysis which was based on a number of policy documents, was applied. Examination of three institutional orders revealed some of the strong cognitive ideas present in European transport policy area that are taken for granted, and this to an extent where it becomes hard – and sometimes impossible – for specific transport policy initiatives to oppose those ideas. This applies specifically to the ideas which lay behind the project of creating the internal market and of creating the EU as a political as well as economic unity.

The design of the analysis was directed at the cognitive dimension of policy-making, with special emphasis on the evolution of meaning and of systems of thought viewed from the perspective of DG Transport and Energy. This produced a certain limitation since it only went some of the way to capturing the interplay between individual or organisational actors, or between policy institutions in the numerous specific decision making instances in the history of creating a transport policy at European level. This limitation also applies to the undoubtedly considerable influence of those actors, who yields considerable economic influence on the transport industries, including car manufactures and oil companies. Further, in spite of the Foucauldian fingerprints on the institutional approach, the chapter has addressed power relations indirectly, and thus does no justice to this significant topic of policy-making.

Creating a European Transport Policy and Integrating the Community

With these reservations in mind, it is time to conclude on the analysis. The cognitive dimension of institutions concerns the structuring of social behaviour that is associated with figures of thought, ideas and perceptions, and which in the present context included a concept of mobility. When the concept was integrated into the cognitive framework of transport policy-making, the most significant impact was its contribution to a change of the rationality of European transport policy. Hence, the approach indicated an understanding of the shifts in European transport polices through the evolution of the three institutional orders.

The *descriptive order* of the common transport policy evolved around the ambiguity captured by the notion of *sustainable mobility*. On the one hand, efficient transport systems and extensive mobility were articulated as necessary for achieving economic growth and regional development of the Community. On the other, this was acknowledged to produce a range of problems at Community level, for example increasing emissions of CO_2, congestion and road casualties. These problematic effects were also seen as hindrances for achieving the internal market and economic and social cohesion, leaving transport policy firmly anchored as a legitimate Community concern.

The *narrative order* showed how the TEN-T and the offshoots of the internal market produced a space for a legitimate and desirable actor not only at Community level but also with a significant Community orientation. With the DG Transport and Energy in an already central position, it is obvious for this Directorate-General to take on it this governing responsibility. In doing so, and in the context of a legitimate policy area at Community level, this brings together DG Transport and Energy as a unit. This further indicates that the political integration of the Community (also) takes place in numerous local places, such as with the development of a TEN-T or with the construction of legitimate governing capacity.

In the *argumentative order*, the influence of a concept of mobility showed to be significant. Through the long torpid start of the common transport policy, the influence of other policy areas had been crucial in overcoming deadlocks, especially the linkage to the ideas of the internal market, but also those of the cohesion policies and the perception of a win-win situation for environment and economic development inherent in the idea of sustainable development.[16] In stage three, the idea that far-reaching transport systems, frictionless access and open and liberal markets are essential in conditioning both the competitiveness and growth of the internal market and, in a wider perspective, freedom was present, and this idea justified policy initiatives. In placing this idea as crucial for the success of the internal market, the fundamental role of the internal market was not only consolidated; this idea also contributed to the ongoing integration of the Community as a political and economic unity, as did the linkage to freedom.

This central position of the internal market in the argumentative order proved to have far-reaching effects. The need for mobility became reified as a natural state of affairs which also implied the need for an extensive option to frictionless and far-reaching movement, access, transport systems – mobility. Moreover, certain directions for the transport policy were simply not accessible, blocked by those cognitive ideas originating in the policies of the internal market and objectives of integration of the Community. This is for instance the case with suggesting a reduction of motorized transport as a measure to mitigate congestion and CO_2 emissions, and with the internalisation of the full costs of transport in the price of transport. As it appears, such environmental initiatives are not allowed to defy the aim of integration of Europe or

---

[16] By linking up to a win-win relation, this perception of sustainability relates to the cultural narrative of ecological modernization.

of achieving the internal market, thus approaching a certain sustainability strategy. This indicates a hierarchy inherent in the ideas of the cognitive dimension of the European policy institution.

The three different orders each represent a distinct function of the policy institution – that is, they show co-existing ways of structuring institutional behaviour and interaction. From a bird's eye view, it thus appears that a transport policy institution has been established at European level, though in a far from mature form, and that the inclusion of a concept of mobility in its cognitive dimension has contributed significantly to the development of a common transport policy. Part of this is the policies that address the increase in transport in late modernity and the resulting environmental and social consequences. Hence, the analysed cognitive dimension has direct bearing on the future options for transport to contribute to a sustainable development – perhaps in the form of sustainable mobility.

Acknowledgement

I would like to thank Professor Ole B. Jensen, Aalborg University, Denmark, who spent energy and time on critically assessing the final draft, and Assistant Professor Jens Stærdahl at Roskilde University, Denmark, for inspiring critique at various stages of the chapter and for stimulating discussions. I am also grateful to the members of the FLUX research group for providing me with an always stirring, supportive and challenging research milieu. Of course, any statement made in this chapter is my sole responsibility.

References

Andersen, Niels Åkerstrøm (1994), *'Institutionel historie – en introduktion til diskurs- og institutionsanalyse' [Institutional History – An Introduction to Discourse and Institutional Analysis]*, COS forskningsrapport 10/94, Center for Offentlig Organisation og Styring, Copenhagen.
Andersen, Svein S. (2001), 'Institutional Approaches to the EU: Towards an Agenda', in Svein S. Andersen (ed.), *Institutional Approaches to the European Union. Proceedings from an ARENA workshop*, ARENA Report No. 3/2001, Oslo.
Aspinwall, Mark D. and Schneider, Gerald (2000), 'Same Menu, Separate Tables: The Institutionalist Turn in Political Science and the Study of European Integration', *European Journal of Political Research*, Vol. 38 No. 5 pp. 1-36.
Berger, Peter L. and Luckmann, Thomas (1966), *The Social Construction of*

    Reality. A Treatise in the Sociology of Knowledge, Penguin Books Ltd, London.
Campbell, John L. (1998), 'Institutional analysis and the role of ideas in political economy', in *Theory and Society*, Vol. 27, Issue 3 June pp. 377-409.
Castells, Manuel (1998), *The Information Age: Economy Society and Culture, Vol. III: End of the Millennium*, Blackwell Pbl., Malden and Oxford.
Commission of the European Communities (CEC) (1985), *Completing the Internal Market. White Paper from the Commission to the European Council* (Milan, 28-29 June 1985), COM(85) 310 final, June, Brussels.
Commission of the European Communities (CEC) (1992a), *Green Paper on the impact of transport on the environment – A Community strategy for "sustainable mobility"*, COM(92) 46 final, February, Brussels.
Commission of the European Communities (CEC) (1992b), *The Future Development of the Common Transport Policy – A Global Approach to the Construction of a Community Framework for Sustainable Mobility*, White Paper, COM(92)494, December, Brussels.
Commission of the European Communities (CEC) (1993), *Growth, Competitiveness, and Employment: The Challenges and ways Forward into the 21st Century*, COM(93) 700 final, December, Brussels (download from www.europa.eu.int/, pages numbered in succession).
Commission of the European Communities (CEC) (1995), *Towards Fair and Efficient Pricing in Transport. Policy Options for Internalising the External Costs of Transport in the European Union*, Directorate-General for Transport – DG VII, COM(95) 691, Brussels.
Commission of the European Communities (CEC) (1998), *White Paper – Fair Payment for Infrastructure Use: A phased approach to a common transport infrastructure charging framework in the EU*, COM(1998) 466 final, Brussels.
Commission of the European Communities (CEC) (2001a), *Communication from the Commission – A Sustainable Europe for a Better World: A European Union Strategy for Sustainable Development*, COM (2001) 264 final 15.5.2001, Brussels.
Commission of the European Communities (CEC) (2001b), *European transport policy for 2010: Time to decide*, White Paper, COM(2001)370, Brussels.
Commission of the European Communities (CEC) (2001c), *Proposal for a Decision of the European Parliament and of the Council amending Decision No 1692/96/EC on Community guidelines for the development of the trans-European transport network (presented by the Commission)*, COM(2001) yyy final, Brussels.
Commission of the European Communities (CEC) (2001d), *Sustainable Mobility. Results from the transport research programme*, DG Energy and Transport, July, Office for Official Publications of the European Communities, Luxembourg.
Commission of the European Communities (CEC) (2003), *Proposal for a Decision of the European Parliament and of the Council amending the amended proposal for a Decision of the European Parliament and of the Council amending Decision No 1692/96/EC on Community guidelines for the development of the trans-European transport network (presented by*

the Commission pursuant to Article 250(2) of the EC Treaty), COM(2003) 564 final 2001/0229 (COD), Brussels.

Commission of the European Communities (CEC) (2004), *Proposal for a Regulation of the European Parliament and of the Council laying down general rules for the granting of Community financial aid in the field of trans-European transport and energy networks and modifying Regulation (EC) no. 2236/95 of the Council*, COM(2004) yyy final, Brussels.

Commission of the European Communities DG Transport and Energy's Transport Research Knowledge Centre (CEC DG TREN) (2004), http://www.europa.eu.int/comm/transport/extra accessed 22.06.04.

Commission of the European Communities DG Press and Communication (CEC DG Press) (2003), *Europe at a Crossroad – The need for sustainable transport*, Luxembourg: office for Official Publications of the European Communities.

Cram, Laura (1997), *Policy-making in the European Union: Conceptual lenses and the integration process*, Routledge, London.

DiMaggio, Paul J. and Powell, Walter W. (1991), 'Introduction', in Walter W. Powell and Paul J. DiMaggio (eds), *The New Institutionalism in Organizational Analysis*, The University of Chicago Press, Chicago and London.

European Communities (EC) (1957), *Treaty establishing the European Community*.

European Communities (EC) (1992), *Treaty on the European Union*, Official Journal C 191, 29 July 1992.

Finnemore, Martha (1996), *National Interests in International Society*, Cornell University Press, Ithaca N.Y.

Foucault, Michel (1970), 'Diskurs og diskontinuitet', [Discource and Discontinuity], in P. Madsen (ed), *Strukturalisme*, Rhodos, Copenhagen, originally published as 'Réspons au cercle d'epistemologie', in *Cahiers pour l'analyse*, no. 9 (1968).

Foucault, Michel (1979a), *Discipline and Punish: The Birth of the Prison*, Vintage, New York.

Foucault, Michel (1979b), *The History of Sexuality. Volume 1: An introduction*, London: Allen Lane.

Foucault, Michel (1999), *Diskursens Orden, [The Order of Discourse]*, Spartacus Forlag, Oslo.

Group Transport 2000 Plus (1990), *Transport in a Fast Changing Europe. Vers un Reseau Europeen des Systemes de Transport*, Brussels.

Gudmundsson, Henrik (2000), *Mobilitet og bæredygtighed. Strategier, mål og institutioner i reguleringen af persontransport*, [*Mobility and sustainability*] Phd serie 8:2000, Copenhagen Business School, Samfundslitteratur, Copenhagen.

Hajer, Maarten A. (1995), *The Politics of Environmental Discourse. Ecological Modernization and the Policy Process*, Clarendon Press, Oxford.

Hall, Peter A. and Taylor, Rosemary C. R. (1996), 'Political Science and the Three New Insitutionalisms', *Political Studies*, XLIV, Vol. 44, No. 5 December, pp. 936-957, Blackwell Publishers.

Héritier, Adrienne (1999), *Policy-Making and Diversity in Europe. Escape from Deadlock*, Cambridge University Press, Cambridge.

Jensen, Anne (2003), *Institutionalisering af policy begreber.*

Diskursanalysens bidrag til at udvikle forståelsen af institutionelle kognitive forskrifter [The Institutionalisation of Policy Concepts. The Contribution of Discourse Analysis to Understanding Institutional Cognitive Scripts], Paper for 'Den 12. nasjonale fagkonferanse i statsvitenskap' 7. – 9. januar 2004 ['The 12th National Political Science Conference' January 7th – 9th 2004], University of Tromsö, Norway.

Jensen, Ole B. and Tim Richardson (2004), *Making European space: mobility, power and territorial identity*, Routledge, London.

Kaufmann, Vincent (2002), *Re-thinking mobility*, Ashgate, Aldershot.

Knight, Jack (2001), 'Explaining the Rise of Neo-liberalism', in John L. Campbell and Ove K. Pedersen (eds.), *The rise of neo-liberalism and institutional analysis*, Princeton University Press Princeton, N.J.

Laffan, Brigid (2001), 'The European Union polity: a union of regulative, normative and cognitivè pillars', *Journal of European Public Policy*, Vol. 8 No. 5 October, pp. 709-727, Taylor and Francis Ltd.

March, James G. and Olsen, Johan. P. (1989), *Rediscovering Institutions. The Organizational Basis of Politics*, The Free press, New York.

McCormick, John (1999), *The European Union. Politics and Policies*, Westview Press, Oxford.

Nielsen, Lise Drewes and Oldrup, Helene Hjort (eds.) (2001), *Mobility and Transport – An Anthology*, Note no. 01-03 August, The Danish Transport Council, Copenhagen.

Ostrom, Elinor (1991), 'Rational Choice Theory and Institutional Analysis: Towards Complementarity', *American Political Science Review*, Vol. 85, pp. 237-243.

Pedersen, Lene Holm (2003), *Miljøøkonomiske ideer i en politisk virkelighed [The Political Power of Environmental Economic Ideas]*, PhD Thesis, Department of Political Science, University of Copenhagen.

Peters, Deike (2003), 'Cohesion, Poly-centricity, Missing Links and Bottlenecks: Conflicting Spatial Storylines for Pan-European Transport Investments', *European Planning Studies*, Vol. 11 No. 3, 318-339, Taylor and Francis Ltd.

Richardson, Jeremy J. (1996), 'Policy-making in the EU: Interests, ideas and garbage cans of primeval soup', in Richardson, Jeremy J. (ed), *European Union – Power and Policy-making.* Routledge, London and New York.

Schmidt, Michael and Giorgi, Liana (2001), 'Successes, Failures and Prospects for the Common Transport Policy', *Innovation*, Vol. 14 No. 4, p. 293-313, Interdisciplinary Centre for Comparative Research in the Social Sciences.

Scott, Walter R. (1995), *Institutions and Organisations*, Sage, London.

Sharp, Liz and Richardson, Tim (2001), 'Reflections on Foucauldian discourse analysis in planning and environmental policy research', *Journal of Environmental Policy and Planning*, Vol. 3, No. 3, pp. 193-209.

Urry, John (2000), *Sociology beyond Society*, Routledge, London.

Wallace, Helen (2000), 'The Institutional Setting', in Helen Wallace and William Wallace, *Policy-making in the European Union*, Oxford University Press, New York.

Young, Alasdair R. and Wallace, Helen (2000), 'The Single Market. A New

Approach to Policy', in Helen Wallace and William Wallace, *Policy-making in the European Union*, New York: Oxford University Press.

Chapter 8

New Conditions for Decision-making and Coordination in Transport? Corporatisation and Division in the Danish Railway Sector

Claus Hedegaard Sørensen[1]

Introduction

During the last 15-20 years, reforms inspired by so-called New Public Management (NPM) have swept the public sector in large parts of the world. This is also the case in the transport sector. One can divide NPM reforms roughly into two groups, reforms regarding internal organisation, and reforms that are interorganisational and regard the organisation of the public service (Klausen and Ståhlberg, 1998: 11-12). This chapter deals with interorganisational reforms.

Since the mid-1980s what might look like an organisational revolution has taken place in the Danish transport sector. Previously, some important characteristics were the following:

- The Danish state railways (DSB) ran trains as well as buses and ferries.
- When the possibilities of building large bridges linking together different parts of Denmark and linking Denmark and Sweden were discussed, they were expected to be state bridges.
- 88 per cent of the buses in the Greater Copenhagen Area were produced in-house by a regionally run company.

---

[1] The main part of the research for this chapter was carried out at Roskilde University, and funded by the Transport Council/The Ministry of Transport in Denmark. A previous version of the chapter was presented at the World Conference on Transport Research in Istanbul, Turkey, 2004.

- The sole large airport in Denmark, Copenhagen Airport, was run by Copenhagen Airport Service, which was an administrative unit in the Ministry of Transport.

Today, this organisational set-up has been drastically changed:

- The former state railway has been split up into several corporations – some of which have private owners, while others are publicly owned.
- Two of the large bridges have been built (the third is subject to a decision-making process), and the owner of them is a limited company, however the Danish (and the Swedish) states are the only shareholders.
- Several private bus companies nowadays run the buses in the Greater Copenhagen Area and they are all subject to tendering.
- Copenhagen Airport is nowadays a limited company quoted on the stock exchange, the state owning 33.8 per cent of the shares.

Other changes have been seen, but these are probably the most important. The main argument for these reforms is the wish to improve efficiency, often stimulated by EU legislation. Investigating whether efficiency has improved is important and interesting, and it seems that efficiency gains have been obtained in some cases in Denmark. However, the focus in this chapter is not efficiency.

These reforms in the transport sector are equivalent to similar reforms in other societal sectors. At the level of the Danish state, the transport sector has, to a large extent, been subject to reforms. Some years ago, The Danish Ministry of Transport characterised the area as a sector, where "the development of new forms of organisation and management [...] have had a large impact", so that the transport area "today is the sector having the widest range of governance forms, [and] now is a kind of exploratorium" (Trafikministeriet, 1998: 49)[2]. This development is continuing.

The organisational revolution is reflected theoretically. In political science, a huge amount of literature written over the past few years argues that the nation state is taking a new shape, and many labels are used to characterise these changes. Several authors talk about 'governance' – a buzz word which is used in a multitude of ways – but often to describe a "structural change from one formal and authoritative centre of public decision and policy making [...] ('government') towards a multitude of more or less

---

[2] Throughout the chapter, I have – as in this case – translated Danish quotations into English.

autonomous entities, public as well as private institutions, associations and actors, networking within their respective domains of policy making ('governance')" (Hansen, 2001: 110). Rhodes stresses the same development when he defines governance, as "self-organizing, interorganizational networks characterized by interdependence, resource exchange, rules of the game and significant autonomy from the state" (Rhodes, 1997: 15 – see also Rhodes, 2000: 346). In Rhodes' view NPM reforms created networks: "[M]arketizing public services fragmented the institutional structure delivering those services. Because service users and their problems do not fit neatly into institutional boxes, organizations have to co-operate to deliver their services effectively. Such sets of organizations, or networks, do not work through competition but by co-operating with one another. So co-operation vies with competition as the organizing principle of service delivery" (Rhodes, 2000: 353). Hence, reforms to ensure market management ended up in cooperation, negotiations and network management, according to Rhodes.

The form of the state has changed, and conditions for decision-making have changed simultaneously. The hierarchical state has been reduced. The state form we experience now is a less powerful (but not necessarily smaller), more fragmented state. Policy networks are widespread, and the state, to some extent, participates with private organisations in these networks.

Aim and Scope of the Chapter

This chapter deals with reforms of the organisation of transport in Denmark. More specifically, I centre on corporatisation and division, although tendering and decentralisation to regions and municipalities are also important elements in a coherent picture of interorganisational NPM reforms in the sector. The term 'corporatisation' differs from privatisation because the new corporations are not necessarily private although they are to a varying extent regulated according to private law. 'Quangos' (quasi non government organisations) is a commonly used label for those corporations that are not totally privatised (Barker, 1982: 4). Corporatisation goes hand in hand with the division of large organisations into smaller ones.

Taking my point of departure in governance and network theories, the aim is to discuss the extent to which, and how, conditions for decision-making and coordination in the area of transport have changed.

Although taking a policy network approach, I limit the scope of the analysis to political and governmental authorities and those organisations and corporations which have experienced reforms. All other sorts of (private) organisations, which usually are part of a network analysis, are not included in the chapter.

I furthermore limit the chapter by analysing and discussing only one corporation, the largest railway operator in Denmark (DSB) and its environment. DSB is chosen because it is the corporation which has undergone the most comprehensive changes in terms of corporatisation and division in the sector. In the analysis I will discuss three questions:

- To what extent DSB is autonomous from the state?
- Whether or not DSB has changed its logic of action?
- How coordination is achieved in the new organisational setup?

In the conclusion I shall discuss how and to what extent conditions for decision-making and coordination have changed.

The empirical part of the chapter concerns changed conditions for decision-making and coordination seen from the point of view of persons of central importance in DSB and The Ministry of Transport. Thus, six persons have been interviewed for this chapter: A former permanent secretary of state in the Ministry of Transport, two former deputy permanent secretaries in the Ministry of Transport, of which one was also a member of the supervisory board in DSB, a former chairman of the supervisory board of DSB, a former chief executive officer in DSB, and finally a head of division in DSB. All interviewees have seen a draft of the chapter and confirmed their quotations. It might be relevant to mention that although five of the interviewees are chosen because of their former occupation or position, they all retired recently.

The interviews and the empirical analyses were carried out during spring 2003. In the meantime, a couple of legislative changes have occurred, and furthermore one organisation has disappeared while another has been formed. These changes will be mentioned throughout.

What has Happened to DSB?

In the mid-nineteenth century, the first railway tracks were opened in Denmark. The railways were organised as limited companies often with the state involved to some extent. However, the Danish state took over the main lines in Jutland and Funen, and in 1880 the railways in Zealand (Olsen, 2000: 805). In 1885 a directorate-general for railways was founded, and from 1915 this directorate functioned as a department, i.e. the director general referred directly to the Minister for Transport. Later shipping and buses became part of DSB's activities.

This organisational form means that running the railways was the responsibility of an organisation which was part of a politico-administrative system with the Minister for Transport as its head. The organisation remained until 1993 where several changes followed in rapid succession. It is the consequences of these changes which are the subject of analysis in this chapter.

Hence, DSB over a period of 10 years, developed from a directorate-general referring to the Minister for Transport, to several units owned in different ways and to different extent by the state: Three state agencies (The National Rail Authority, the Rail Net Denmark and the Accident Investigation Board, Denmark), an independent, public corporation (DSB), three limited companies with the Danish state owning respectively 100 per cent (DSB S-train Ltd), 50 per cent (Scandlines Ltd), and 2 per cent (Railion Group). The independent, public corporation (DSB) is owned 100 per cent by the state. Furthermore, two sections were sold off to private capital (DSB Buses to Arriva Ltd, and a section in the Freight Division to Danske Fragtmænd A.m.b.a.).

Freight transport in Denmark now works as a free market. Passenger transport in principle can also be free traffic but in practice contracts are made either after negotiations with the Ministry of Transport or after tender. By January 2003, a new train operator (Arriva), following a tender, took over part of the lines previously run by DSB. DSB and DSB S-train Ltd now run approximately 90 per cent of all passenger train traffic in Denmark.

The reformation of DSB is not finished yet. Probably, in future, DSB will be transformed from an independent, public corporation into a limited company (as has happened to the postal services), providing the possibility of selling shares. One also could expect that DSB S-train Ltd will be sold. As an interviewee said in connection to this research: "DSB S-train could be sold, the organisation is cut-and-dried for it".

Now, how have conditions for decision-making and coordination around DSB changed due to these reforms? I commence by discussing DSB's autonomy from the state.

CORPORATISATION AND DIVISION IN A PERIOD OF 10 YEARS
CAUSED THAT THE DANISH STATE RAILWAYS (DSB), WHICH
FORMERLY WAS A DIRECTORATE-GENERAL, TODAY IS DIVIDED
INTO A NUMBER OF ENTITIES OF WHICH SOME HAVE
AMALGATED INTO OR BEEN BOUGHT BY OTHER COMPANIES:

- THE NATIONAL RAIL AUTHORITY
- RAIL NET DENMARK
- ACCIDENT INVESTIGATION BOARD, DENMARK
- DSB – INDEPENDENT, PUBLIC CORPORATION
- DSB S-TRAIN LTD
- SCANDLINES DENMARK LTD
- RAILION DENMARK LTD
- ARRIVA DENMARK LTD
- DANSKE FRAGTMÆND A.M.B.A. (DANISH ROAD HAULIERS LTD)

Figure 8.1   Corporatisation and division of the Danish State Railways

To What Extent is DSB Autonomous from the State?

To answer the question as to what extent and how conditions for decision-making and coordination have changed in the area where DSB is involved, it is important to analyse whether or not DSB's autonomy from the state has changed – the subject in this section of the chapter. The state is seen as equivalent to the Ministry of Transport and the politicians in Parliament.

Increased autonomy is usually seen as a precondition for corporations behaving businesslike and working in a market like environment. Hence, one could expect DSB's autonomy to be increased.

I will proceed by describing the current conditions, and afterwards compare them to the previous conditions. Regarding the current conditions I will begin with the legal situation.

DSB came into existence as an independent, public corporation by a special Act. This Act stipulates that an independent, public corporation has similarities with a limited company. Hence, also the Danish Companies Act lays down conditions for DSB's autonomy. This Act stipulates that in limited companies – and in general it also applies to DSB (DSB Act, § 6) – the management and the supervisory board are not allowed to take steps that unduly benefit shareholders at the expense of the corporation (Companies Act, § 63). This section has been construed to mean that it would be "incorrect of the supervisory board – or for that matter of the management – in a corporation where the state has determinative influence to attempt to undertake an independent evaluation of what the minister or the majority of the Parliament would expect of the corporation and its supervisory board in a specific case". Rather "the supervisory board in any case both has the right and the duty to undertake an independent assessment of what will serve the interests of the corporation" (Werlauff, 1993: 196). Hence, DSB should behave independently, in decision-making, only safeguarding the interests of the corporation.

The DSB Act to some extent leaves the same impression of autonomy. Thus, it stipulates that DSB is a corporation, which "is to be run in a businesslike way" (DSB Act, § 2). In the comments to the Bill (which in Denmark are important contributions to the interpretation of a law), this specific section is related to the obligations of the supervisory board and the management to manage the corporation in line with "normal practice for the management of private corporations" (DSB Bill, comments to the Bill).

However, the legislative autonomy of DSB should not be exaggerated. The relation between the state and DSB is equivalent to the relation between a parent company and a subsidiary company (Werlauff, 1993: 22), and a subsidiary company to some extent has to accept being under the interest of the entire group if it does not harm the subsidiary company.

The DSB Act also stipulates limitations to the company's autonomy. Until recent changes in legislation, I saw four limitations:

- The minister's right to lay down the articles of DSB (DSB Act, § 5).
- The minister's right to appoint and – at any time – dismiss members of the supervisory board (DSB Act, § 4).
- The duty of information and a right of instruction regarding civil servants on the board of which there were two, one from the Ministry of Transport and one from the Ministry of Finance. These two principles, however, are disputed in the literature (Werlauff, 1993: 22, 277, 288-294; Christensen, 1995: 102-104, Heidmann, 2001: 448-451, Rigsrevisionen, 1998: 20).
- A number of other provisions in the DSB Act that ensure the Ministry and the Parliament all relevant information and impose

some restrictions on DSB's economic activities (DSB Act, §§ 4, 12, 20, Comments to the Bill).

How about practice? How do these rules work in practice? What autonomy does DSB possess?[3]

So far, The Minister for Transport has not dismissed members on the board of DSB in between the annual meetings.

The duty to provide information, and the right of instruction, however, seem to have had a large impact on practice. One division in the Ministry of Transport is responsible for railway policy. The deputy permanent secretary from another division represented the ministry on DSB's board. The responsible division, however, read all the material regarding the board and made a note to the board member commenting on each item on the agenda. "And depending on the subject matter he would comply with it [the note]", a former deputy permanent secretary said. A former permanent secretary of state similarly stressed that the civil servants on the board were obliged to follow instructions from the minister. He also said that the ministry's representative on the board informed him about discussions going on the board. Hence, the two principles, duty of information and right of instruction, although disputed in the literature, seem to have been employed in practice.

The literature often stresses that the right of instruction usually is not employed, either due to cautiousness because the right is disputed (Greve, 1999: 18), or because it is needless due to the representative's knowledge of the government's policy (Christensen, 1995: 104). My study renders another impression. The pure existence of the right of instruction seems to have been the underlying prerequisite for notes and discussions in the ministry.

The interviewees do not quite agree regarding the influence of the civil servants on the board. A former permanent secretary of state found that the civil servants from the ministries of transport and finance possessed a unique knowledge because "They were sitting at the foot of the throne". Thus, they possessed a particular position on the board, and the other board members listened to them with particular interest. A head of division in DSB similarly emphasised that the DSB board was an "Odd board, the members with the most influence on the board were the man from the Ministry of Transport and the man from the Ministry of Finance". However, a former deputy permanent secretary in the ministry found that the board members listened to those representing the ministries but "The

---

[3] Information and quotations in this and the following two sections stem form interviews unless otherwise stated.

board didn't always do what they said. They didn't have a majority on the board."

Following a change in legislation in spring 2004, the civil servants on the board have been withdrawn. Thus, today, there are no civil servants from the ministries on the board, and today, the only possibility for the minister to dismiss and appoint members of the board is at the annual meetings.

Other tools, however, also seem to be more important regarding the relations between DSB and the ministry. Of more importance are conversations and meetings between representatives from DSB and the ministry. Thus, a former permanent secretary of state stressed that telephone conversations and meetings are a typical way of communicating. He often called the chief executive officer in DSB, and sometimes the minister called the chairman of the board. Meetings are not held regularly but when there is a need. In some periods there might not be much communication while in other periods the contact is frequent. A deputy permanent secretary stressed that the meetings are rather dominated by briefings and discussions than by instructions and warnings. The impression is that the main purpose of these meetings is to establish a common understanding of different problems. An interviewee, who has been vice-chairman and chairman for three years in all, emphasised that during this period of time he has had about five meetings with the minister altogether. The minister never called him and he never called the minister. "That is not the way it works. It goes on a little further down in the system, and comes to me that way." Thus, he stressed that there is quite a lot of communication between civil servants in the ministry and employees in DSB, but usually not between the chairman of the board and the minister. More interviewees emphasise that the extent of contact and autonomy depends on whether or not DSB is in economic or political trouble.

Above, I have explained some of the tools the Ministry of Transport can utilise to influence DSB. Legally and in practice, the Ministry of Transport has considerable power over DSB. The former permanent secretary of state laughed when I referred to the stipulations in the Companies Act according to which DSB should behave independently, only safeguarding the interests of the corporation. He is convinced that in cases with one sole owner, any corporation whether owned by private or public capital is heavily influenced by the owner, and that the board in such situations does not behave independently. He furthermore found that Parliament forces the ministry to act that way. Hence, for the parliamentarians there is no limit to what they will direct the minister to do regarding corporations where the state is the sole shareholder[4]. He found that the National Auditors similarly expect that the ministry controls the corporations closely and makes its influence tell. And it is true that the National Auditors some years ago found that the ministry had neglected to safeguard the interests of the state in a specific case regarding a limited company (Magid, 2001: 5-6).

Two out of three interviewees from DSB argue along the same line. For example, a former chief executive officer in DSB said, "a board always agrees with its sole proprietor. If not it will be kicked out". He considered it would be wonderful if the supervisory board in between the annual meetings only served DSB's interests, "and it is clear that they try – part of the way – but when it comes to the crunch, they yield". However, a former chairman of the board stressed that he, in conversations with the ministry, several times emphasised that the role of the board was not to safeguard the interests of the ministry, but to safeguard the interests of DSB. That is the aim, but the board only go into battle when it is worthwhile, and he pointed out that the ministry can take revenge in many ways. Which brings us to the next paragraph.

All interviewees from DSB underlined that the Ministry of Transport has too many roles in relation to DSB: The ministry is the owner, the main contractor through Rail Net Denmark, the regulator through The National Rail Authority, the main customer through contracts. "Totally surrounded! No matter what you do, you will collide with the owner, the contractor, the regulator or the customer [...] So, that is the vice, that is what we call it", a former chief executive officer in DSB said.

During 2003, The National Rail Authority was established. The idea of this agency is to relieve the Ministry of Transport from some of these duties. Furthermore, in 2003, a supervisory board was established in Rail Net Denmark. These changes might loosen the vice, but it is more than likely that DSB still will find the corporation surrounded by the ministry.

Hence, in practice, DSB's autonomy from the ministry does not seem to be large. The autonomy of DSB stipulated by the Companies Act is legally restricted. Restrictions regarding the duty of information and the right of instruction have been disputed and the civil servants are now withdrawn from the board. Due to parliamentarian's expectations, the ministry using other tools, however, seems to control DSB closely and makes its influence tell. Interviewees from DSB feel 'surrounded' by the ministry. Meetings

---

[4] In Denmark, minority Governments are common, and this situation provides the Parliament with quite a lot of influence on governmental decisions.

and telephone conversations are held when considered relevant. Functional independency, i.e. the board's and management's authority to decide in specific situations seems to be challenged (Werlauff, 1993: 252).

Does this degree of autonomy constitute a change from the previous situation when DSB was a general-directorate? Five years before the change of DSB from a directorate-general to an agency in the Ministry of Transport, two researchers published a book about DSB. In this book, they also touched upon the autonomy of the Danish State Railways. Because DSB as a directorate-general referred directly to the Minister for Transport, the ministry did not influence DSB much. However, the minister and other parliamentarians to some extent did. Regarding the autonomy, the authors conclude, "one cannot say that the politicians do not rule the state corporations. But their direction is mainly implicit and reactive. They never provide the corporation with clear instructions for its activities [...] The system implies that the state corporation itself looks after strategic planning and 'translates' its consequences to the decision makers at the political level" (Arnfred and Olsen, 1988: 136-137). Their analysis leaves the impression that DSB had considerable autonomy previously. Today, DSB is subordinated to the Ministry of Transport, the control by the ministry does not seem just to be reactive, the ministry sometimes seems to provide DSB with very clear instructions, and the ministry sees itself as well as The National Rail Authority – and not DSB – as the unit responsible for strategic issues.

Thus, when comparing the autonomy of DSB today and before the reforms, my conclusions are that the autonomy today, contrary to the expectations, has not increased. Rather, for a period of time, which might have ended by the changes in spring 2004, the autonomy has been even more limited than before the reforms.

The former chairman of DSB board stressed that there is a growing awareness in the ministry that the entire corporatisation process does not make sense unless the ministry is ready to give the boards considerable independence. Probably, it is a result of this awareness we have seen in the legislative changes during spring 2004.

Autonomy is one thing, another is DSB's logic of action. One could expect it to be more market oriented due to reforms. That is the topic in the next section.

Has DSB Changed its Logic of Action?

Although DSB's autonomy from the Ministry of Transport is restricted, DSB's logic of action might have changed. As a directorate-general DSB was part of a politico-administrative system. Today the DSB Act stipulates that DSB 'is to be run in a businesslike way' (DSB Act, § 2), and also the Companies Act stresses that the board and the management should only serve the interests of the corporation (Companies Act, § 63). Similarly, a former permanent secretary of state found that representatives from these new corporations including DSB should explicitly act to the benefit of the corporation they represent. Thus, also the Ministry of Transport's influence on DSB might be used to push DSB towards a changed logic of action.

However, the legislation regarding DSB is ambiguous. Hence, the Comments to the DSB Bill stipulate that DSB takes care of among other things railway stations, "which is a common interest for all train operators and for the state". (DSB Bill, Comments to the Bill). The current contracts that exist between The Ministry of Transport and DSB similarly imply that DSB and DSB S-train Ltd should consider public interests, e.g. they should work actively for a consistent and coherent public transport system with good coordination between buses and trains. Hence, DSB should on the one hand behave businesslike, and on the other safeguard public interests.

Against this background, the question is whether or not DSB has changed its logic of action? To discuss the topic, I will distinguish between 'a logic of appropriateness' and 'a logic of consequentiality'. Logic of appropriateness refers to action based on identifying the normatively appropriate behaviour. Thus, the concept emphasises that individuals and organisations behave according to what they see as appropriate behaviour for people in their situation. While a logic of consequentiality is based on calculating the return expected from alternative choices. Hence, the concept stresses that we behave according to a utility maximising behaviour (March and Olsen, 1989: 21-26). A logic of appropriateness is what one could expect to dominate in the politico-administrative organisations, while a logic of consequentiality would be expected to dominate in the market (Sørensen, 2001: 45)[5].

---

[5] One might see the logic of appropriateness as a superior category under which logic of consequentiality is one among more possibilities. Hence, it is appropriate to pursue a utility maximizing behaviour at the market. That is the consequence of identifying the normatively appropriate behaviour. On the other hand, the logic of consequentiality might

Interviews with people from DSB leave the impression that in the previous situation DSB saw itself as an organisation that existed to the advantage of society, in DSB as in other public organisations a certain public service ethos existed. "We were not a company which had to sell anything. We were a public service you could buy", a head of division in DSB said. Literature suggests that a public service ethos, among other things, has to do with tolerance towards others' wishes and interests, a common discourse within which conflicts and contradictions are handled, and recognition of the need to work in partnership with others to contribute to the promotion of community well-being (Dalsgaard and Jørgensen, 1994: 36-37; Stoker, 2003: 9-10). My impression is that such an understanding was present in DSB as long as it was explicitly part of a politico-administrative system.

Several written sources as well as interviewees emphasise that DSB, especially in the 1970s and 1980s, acted politically in various ways. Consequently, a former Minister for Transport labelled DSB 'The 9th party of the Parliament' at a time when the Parliament consisted of eight political parties (Enemark and Lund, 1997: 125). However, in DSB's understanding these political activities, too, were in the interests of the passengers and society. This, however, is disputed, observers have stressed that the purpose of these activities was also to serve the interests of DSB (Sørensen, 1993: 115).

Now, it is safe to assume that some degree of public service ethos existed in the previous situation. DSB to some extent behaved according to a specific logic of appropriateness. Does this logic still exist, or has it disappeared due to reforms? A head of division in DSB stressed the difference between DSB and the new, private train operator, Arriva Denmark Ltd, "They behave differently from us because we still conceive of ourselves as a public service". Another example is the qualifications that members of the DSB supervisory board are expected to have. A former permanent secretary of state and a former chairman of the board both emphasised that the board members and especially the chairman should be capable of 'reading the political game', and have a certain 'sense' for the

---

alternatively be seen as the superior category via-à-vis a logic of appropriateness because an individual might behave appropriate at short sight and against his own interests, while this behaviour is utility maximizing in the long term. In this context, however, I use the concepts as two equal logic of actions, no one being superior to the other. Often both concepts are necessary to characterize the logic of action in an organisation at a specific moment. However, over time the relative strength between the two can change.

working of the political system. A situation where the Ministry of Transport disqualified a DSB-tender is also instructive. In that situation DSB considered the possibility of bringing the matter before the courts, but decided not to do so: "I do not find it appropriate that a supervisory board institutes legal proceedings against the owner. It would be highly unusual", the former chairman said. Thus, the interviewees from DSB leave the impression that the original logic of appropriateness still exists. DSB largely sees its function as contributing to the promotion of community well being, and not as contributing to a private company's profit. To considerable extent, DSB behaves according to what it sees as appropriate behaviour, and to a lesser extent according to a calculated self-interest.

However, this logic of action seems to be undergoing a change. Thus, a head of division talked about a 'cultural change' in DSB's marketing organisation. Another example is DSB's handling of a situation after the introduction of Arriva as a train operator in Denmark. At a specific railway station (Hinnerup) both operators, DSB and Arriva, were expected to stop at the station, and everybody agreed that passengers and society would benefit if DSB did stop. However, the contract between The Ministry of Transport and DSB does not give the latter any economic incentive to stop at that station, and hence it does not. The decision in DSB is due to 'a cold estimate', and a head of division in DSB admitted that "this is perhaps the best example of businesslike thinking" in DSB. If DSB did stop, it would benefit the competitor, Arriva. "There are limits to how stupid we want to be", an interviewee said.

How DSB should act in future situations of fragmentation and tendering has been considered. An interviewee quoted the present chief executive officer in DSB as saying that in the case of a future tendering of DSB's long-distance trains and regional trains separately, he "will abuse it". In that case he "really will run it [the traffic] as a contract, like Arriva does. Chase the money".

The question in this section is whether or not DSB has changed its logic of action. Previously, a logic of appropriateness and a public service ethos were present in DSB. Today, the same logic exists. Probably, the reasons are ambiguity in legislation and contracts, path dependency in the organisation, and a wish in DSB to keep political support in the Parliament. However, the wish to change DSB to be more businesslike is about to transform the organisation. Hence, if NPM reforms continue, in the future, we probably will experience an organisation acting to a large extent in accordance with a logic of consequentiality, safeguarding only the interests of DSB.

How is Coordination Achieved?

On the present railway scene, a lot of actors are on the cast list, while in the old days, DSB played the lead. In the introduction to this chapter I quoted Rhodes arguing that the marketising and division of public services in Great Britain created fragmentation, which again caused cooperation and network management. Hence, one could imagine that although DSB's autonomy from the Ministry of Transport is limited, both the fixing of these limitations and the space left for independent actions are influenced by negotiations in policy networks.

Before approaching the empirical data regarding networks, I will specify what a network is, and how it differs from other mechanisms of coordination. In a famous article published in 1990, Powell distinguishes between three concepts, namely market, hierarchy and network. Powell rejects the widespread conviction that all types of coordination can be usefully arrayed along a continuum where market is at the one end and hierarchy at the other. Rather, he finds it "meaningful to talk about networks as a distinctive form of coordinating" (Powell, 1990: 301). Inspired in particular by his article, some important characteristics of market, hierarchy and network respectively could look like this:

	MARKET	HIERARCHY	NETWORK
NORMATIVE BASIS	CONTRACT – PROPERTY RIGHTS	EMPLOYMENT RELATIONSHIP	COMPLEMENTARY STRENGTHS
MEANS OF COMMUNICATION	PRICES	ROUTINES	RELATIONAL
METHODS OF CONFLICT RESOLUTION	HAGGLING – RESORT TO COURTS	ADMINISTRATIVE FIAT – SUPERVISION	NORM OF RECIPROCITY – REPUTATIONAL CONCERN
KEY TO COORDINATION	THE INVISIBLE HAND	COMMANDS	TRUST
AMOUNT OF COMMITMENT	LOW	MEDIUM	HIGH
TONE OR CLIMATE	PRECISION AND/OR SUSPICION	FORMAL, BUREAUCRATIC	OPEN-ENDED, MUTUAL BENEFITS
ACTOR REFERENCES AND CHOICES	INDEPENDENT	DEPENDENT	INTERDEPENDENT

Figure 8.2   Market, hierarchy and network

Source: Lowndes and Skelcher 1998: 319, Peters 1998: 297-299, Powell 1990: 300, Rhodes 2000: 353.

My main contribution to Powell's characterisation is an addition of a new parameter, namely the 'key to coordination'. On the market, in a hierarchy and in a network, I see the keys to coordination as being the invisible hand, commands and trust, respectively. A few words about trust: Interdependency and cooperation in network engender trust, and trust is an important lubricant in network negotiations. Rhodes states: "Networks are a distinctive way of co-ordinating and, therefore, a separate governing structure from markets and hierarchies (or bureaucracies). Trust is their central co-ordinating mechanism in the same way that commands and price competition are the key mechanisms for hierarchies and markets respectively" (Rhodes, 2000: 353).

A complementary comment to the model concerns negotiations. I see negotiations as an important element in all three coordination mechanisms. Negotiations in hierarchy are influenced by the knowledge that a hierarchy exists. Thus, the coordination capacity of negotiations "can be enormously increased by virtue of the fact that they are embedded in the hierarchical structure". Scharpf talks about negotiations in the shadow of hierarchy (Scharpf, 1994, quotation p. 40). Negotiations in the market are characterised by contractual relationships over property rights, haggling, precision and suspicion. While the interdependency in networks implies a different tone or climate in negotiations, and some degree of a common understanding marks the negotiations. Thus, Powell stresses – a bit exaggeratedly – that "parties to a network agree to forego the right to pursue their own interests at the expense of others" (Powel, 1990: 303).

Now, market, hierarchy and network are analytical concepts, which in a modern welfare state hardly exist distinct from one another. The pure form does not exist. In everyday interactions elements of market, hierarchy and network will often be present. The question is whether a change has taken place, so that network characteristics nowadays are more widespread than in the previous situation.

Which occurrences in the last 10 years might contribute to a change? As explained earlier, DSB has been divided into several organisations. My interviews leave the impression that especially three are of importance in this respect. Hence, Rail Net Denmark, DSB S-train Ltd and the Ministry of Transport, which today attends to some of these duties which earlier DSB itself took care of. Other relevant stakeholders are Railion Denmark Ltd and Arriva Denmark Ltd, and probably the interviewees today would mention the National Rail Authority, too, which was not established when the interviews were carried out. Some degree of interdependence exist between on the one hand DSB and on the other hand these organisations.

More than any, DSB is dependent on Rail Net Denmark. This agency is DSB's most important contractor. A large contract regulates the relationship, a contract which has to be negotiated (Pfund, 2002: 88-89). One can imagine the extent of the negotiations necessary by watching how the responsibility of every single platform is divided: "Carrying out the split on the platform level was crucial. As a general rule, [Rail Net Denmark] was assigned technical equipment, service equipment, and platform infrastructure on its surface and below, whereas most equipment above the platform surface was assigned to DSB. For example, all the 'Do not cross tracks' signs belong to [Rail Net Denmark] since they fit into the order and safety signs category, whereas DSB owns the station name signs. [Rail Net Denmark] is responsible for cleaning the platforms, but DSB must empty the garbage bins. In turn, cleaning the railway station is DSB's responsibility. One can imagine the practical impact [...] Contrary to the general rule, passenger information equipment belongs to [Rail Net Denmark], including the station clock" (Pfund, 2002: 81).

Most interviewees find that the number of negotiations has increased. As expressed by a former chief executive officer in DSB: "All along you have to negotiate your way to solutions. You cannot command or make a resolve to do something and then carry it through, as you could if you were the sole actor". In connection with several examples he correspondingly said: "Now it is a situation of negotiations, where everybody has to get something". A head of division in DSB said that negotiations also took place previously, "But it makes a difference whether there is one at the head of the table who is in the same circle, or there are three different ones. We find the situation totally different".

Now, how can we understand this sort of negotiations, which seems to have increased? Does it exemplify a hierarchy, a market, or a network form of governance? To some extent we experience negotiations in the shadow of hierarchy. When I analysed the autonomy of DSB vis-à-vis the Ministry of Transport, telephone conversations, meetings, briefings, discussions and establishing of a common understanding were some of the tools which the ministry used to let their influence tell. The ministry sometimes issues an order, too. However, my impression is that fixing the autonomy of DSB takes place through negotiations in the shadow of hierarchy. Everybody knows that in many ways, and if not sooner then at the annual meeting, the ministry will let its influence tell. The hierarchy supplies the Ministry of Transport with strong power resources in negotiations with DSB.

But we also experience the market as a coordination mechanism. The characteristics are contracts, prices, haggling and suspicion. Interviewees articulated that a suspicious culture exist between DSB on the one hand, and Rail Net Denmark and the Ministry of Transport on the other. Similarly, a former permanent secretary of state in the Ministry of Transport talked about the new economics of contract where the corporations only safeguard their own interests.

Finally, negotiations and relations having the characteristics of networks are also experienced. A head of division in DSB said: "On the day to day work level, on the employee's side, people want things to work, and the conflicts there are between DSB and Rail Net Denmark have not been at that level [...]. Basically, people have had 30 years in the same company, and you cannot deprive them of the things they have had together [...] It would have fallen apart, in terms of traffic, if things had not worked at the bottom level". And a former chief executive officer in DSB said: "When things worked between DSB and Rail Net Denmark after the division and has done so for many years after [...] the reason is that the man below in the system, e.g. the one responsible for the timetable, knows who his counterpart in The Rail Net Denmark is, and calls him and talks with him. Many problems are solved at that level." Similarly, regarding the platforms, one author stresses that the cleaning teams from DSB and Rail Net Denmark help each other out (Pfund, 2002: 81). Hence, a common background, in this case a common history, is an important precondition for networks. That is also reflected theoretically. Thus, Powell stresses that "[n]etworks should be most common in work settings in which participants have some kind of common background – be it ethnic, geographic, ideological, or professional. The more homogeneous the group, the greater the trust, hence the easier it is to sustain network-like arrangements" (Powell, 1990: 326).

Hence, many relations are characterised by complementary strengths, trust, a high degree of commitment and interdependency. It seems, however, that a vertical distinction exists. It is the employees at lower levels in the organisations which are able to negotiate in a network-like manner, while at the top level of the organisations market-like and hierarchical forms of negotiations prevail. A head of division in DSB put it this way, "It is more the bosses who are allowed to romp about and are allowed to destroy things when they are set free. There have never been so many director jobs as there are today." However, the vertical distinction is not total. Conflicts and tough bargaining at the top of the organisations influence interactions at lower levels of the organisations: "It is obvious that this management infects down through the system. When it is negative up there, it will end up by being negative down here, too."

The interviews furthermore give the impression that coordination today is more difficult and more time-consuming. A former chief executive officer said: "By accomplishing these divisions, you add fuel to the fire, and people's understanding of their independence increases, and then they try to behave as such, and it makes the task of coordinating and managing more difficult. Thus, no doubt that the separation of DSB S-train into a special limited company made the task of managing considerably more difficult and more complicated. It raised some expectations by the employees [...] which created a good deal of friction that otherwise would not have arisen." And regarding the vertical split into track (Rail Net Denmark) and trains (DSB) a head of division in DSB said: "It is like this that in all the initiatives we take there is always something regarding the tracks, and there is always something regarding the trains. You cannot make a train without seeing to it that the infrastructure matches it. And it is obvious that it creates an enormous amount of coordination. It is a strain that coordination work."

A former deputy permanent secretary from the Ministry of Transport emphasised that the vertical division in rail and trains has been a necessary method of making more effective the system. However, he expressed the problem of coordination by saying that the ministry lacks competence, tools, information and the resources to be capable of steering sufficiently well. The general expectation was that the founding of the National Rail Authority in summer 2003 would contribute to resolve these problems.

The quotations stress that today the *process* of coordinating is more difficult. However, some interviewees also found that the *output* of the processes is poor compared to earlier. The specific examples either concern coordination of timetables across modes (ferry/train) and across operators (DSB/Arriva), or regarding infrastructure investment.

Above, I quoted Rhodes saying that marketisation corrodes trust, cooperation and shared professional values, and thus, coordination and steering through networks. That is a view which was confirmed in some of the interviews. For example, a former chief executive officer talked about the special relationship that 'cement' the different organisations because of their history. He characterised the current situation as a process of 'weathering' of the cement. He expected that "all these mechanisms [which make the system function] will gradually dry up or disappear, and then the system will gradually function worse and worse". The understanding is along the lines of my conclusions regarding a changed logic of action in DSB. Thus, in the future I would expect to see an organisation acting to a larger extent in accordance with a logic of consequentiality, safeguarding only the interests of DSB[6].

In such a case, the share of coordination that takes place by network will have to be substituted by either coordination by hierarchy or by market mechanisms. In continuation of this, a former deputy permanent secretary in the ministry talked about the need for more regulation.

Against this background, my conclusion is the following: The number of negotiations has increased, and these negotiations reflect all three types of coordination mechanisms: hierarchy, market and network. Thus, to some extent, I can confirm the hypothesis one could advance, following Rhodes, that the reforms have created fragmentation which again causes cooperation, negotiations and network steering. The network steering, however, might not only as Rhodes suggests, be a product of the organisational fragmentation. To some extent network management might be a mechanism of coordination which was also used before the reforms, and thus it is carried with from the previous situation.

Hierarchy and market dominate at the top levels of the organisations, and thus the more strategic decisions, while network dominates at lower levels of the organisations. Coordination is more difficult at all levels, and the share of coordination taking place through network is threatened. Above, the conclusion was that hierarchy and market dominates in the strategic decisions. If that is true, a future weathering away of network coordination should not threaten the strategic decisions. However, coordination among employees at lower levels of the organisations might in the future be threatened. Future reforms in the railway sector probably will advance the market as a mechanism of coordination at the expense of hierarchy and network. Thus, an important question for future

---

6 Such a development seems to have taken place in the British Railway sector. Hence, an inquiry after one of the railway accidents in Great Britain stated in a report: "Privatisation has created a big cultural change. There is now little inter-linking of culture from one company to another. There has been a loss of comradeship between drivers, signalmen, cleaners etc. There is no longer a sense of working together. Questions of delays and attribution of blame strengthen the divide. This has led to a lack of confidence in others. No one is encouraged to discuss someone else's problem, or volunteers, or shares information" (Landbroke Grove Inquiry, seminar on employee perspectives on safety, 18 October 2000, here quoted from Wolmar 2001: 182). Now, it is important to remember that the British reforms in the railway sector are considerably more radical than the Danish. Hence, one cannot directly transfer the experiences to Danish conditions.

research is, if market mechanisms will be able to handle coordination satisfactorily.

Conclusions

The aim of this chapter was to answer the question as to what extent and how conditions for decision-making and coordination in the area of transport have changed due to NPM reforms. I answer the question only in relation to DSB and its environment.

According to my empirical research, some conditions for decision-making and coordination have changed, while others have not. The number of negotiations has increased, and these negotiations reflect all three types of coordination mechanisms: hierarchy, market and network. Thus, also network as a mechanism of coordination has increased. The increased number of negotiations is a consequence of the division of DSB into several units. Hierarchy and market seem to be dominating at the top levels of the organisations, while network is dominating at the lower levels of the organisations. The process of coordination is more difficult and complicated than earlier.

However, DSB's autonomy, contrary to the expectations, so far has not increased. Regarding the logic of action in DSB, a logic of appropriateness and a public service ethos exist today as they did earlier. Probably, due to ambiguity in legislation and contracts and due to path dependency in the organisation.

The reforms have started a process. The chapter indicates that a growing awareness exists in the Ministry of Transport which might in the future cause more autonomy for DSB. The continuation of NPM reforms probably will change DSB's logic of action to be more in accordance with a logic of consequentiality, safeguarding only the interests of DSB. Such a change seems to be under way. And finally, I expect in the future a weathering away of network coordination which can threaten coordination among employees at lower levels of the organisations.

More than any, Rhodes studying the British situation has provided inspiration for this chapter. Some of his observations in Britain are also experienced in the Danish railway sector. Hence, it seems that a fragmented DSB due to NPM reforms creates some degree of network coordination. However, network coordination might also to some extent be inherited from the time before the organisational changes. As in Britain, we also experience that cooperation vies with competition as the organising principle. That is the (future) strengthening of a logic of consequentiality at the expense of a logic of appropriateness and a public service ethos, and the weathering away of trust. The chapter also confirms that the reforms have created a greater need for coordination and so far the Ministry of Transport is not sufficiently capable of accomplishing the task. Thus, similarities exist between Rhodes' analyses in Britain, and the Danish railway sector.

However, there are also deviations. The autonomy of DSB has not been increased, which one should expect to be the case. So far, DSB has not really changed its logic of action. The network as a coordination mechanism is present at lower levels of the organisations but does not seem to have great importance at the top levels of the organisations.

Now, can these conclusions be generalised to other parts of the transport sector in Denmark which have experienced reforms of the same kind?

Due to the formal conditions we can divide quangos as well as privatised corporations into four categories depending on whether the state owns shares and if the Act that establishes the corporation stipulates special conditions:

- The Controlled: State sole shareholder. Stipulations in law.
- The Connected: State shareholder among others. Stipulations in law.
- The Affected: State owns shares. No stipulations in law.
- The Autonomous: State does not own shares. No specific law.

In this categorisation DSB belongs to The Controlled. The state is the sole shareholder and the DSB Act leaves the state with considerable possibilities to control DSB. E.g. the corporations formed to build the large bridges belong to the same category. One could expect to get similar findings investigating other corporations belonging to The Controlled, while one could expect different findings studying corporations belonging to some of the other categories. However, the categorisation is only based upon the formal conditions, and a broader study of these corporations might leave us with other categories.

Acknowledgements

I have received valuable comments to a draft of this chapter from Professor Erik Werlauff, Aalborg University, Senior Research Political Scientist Inger-Anne Ravlum, Institute of Transport Economics as well as student Katrine Munk, Ph.D. Student Anne Jensen, Associate Professor Per Homann Jespersen, Post Doc

Researcher Henrik Gudmundsson, Professor Ole Jess Olsen, English consultant Andrew Crabtree, all from Roskilde University, and from three interviewees. Katrine Munk has also transcribed the interviews.

References

Arnfred, N. and Olsen, O.J. (1988), *DSB skifter spor. Ledelse i en offentlig erhvervsvirksomhed [DSB changes tracks. Management in a public company]*, Blytmanns Forlag, Copenhagen.

Barker, A. (1982), 'Governmental bodies and the networks of mutual accountability', in A. Barker (ed), *Quangos in Britain. Government and the Networks of Public Policy-Making*, MacMillan Press Ltd., London, Baskingstoke, pp. 3-33.

Christensen, P. (1995), 'Når staten driver forretning' ['When the state runs a business'], in L. Adrian, P. Blume, A.W. Bentzon, P. Christensen, L. Goldschmidt, J.V . Hansen, M. Hartlev, K. Ketscher, U. Kjellerup, V. Vindeløv (eds), *Ret & privatisering [Justice and privatisation]*, GadJura, Copenhagen, pp. 85-110.

Companies Act, lovbekendtgørelse no. 324, the 7th of May 2000.

Dalsgaard, L. and Jørgensen, H. (1994), *Det offentlige. Sektorens og de ansattes værdier og værdighed [The public sector and the employees' values and dignity]*, DJØF, Overenskomstforeningen, Copenhagen.

DSB Act [Lov om den selvstændige offentlige virksomhed DSB og om DSB S-tog A/S], no. 485, the 1st of July 1998.

DSB Act, changes [Lov om ændring af lov om den selvstændige offentlige virksomhed DSB og om DSB S-tog A/S], no. 265, the 20th of April 2004.

DSB Bill [Forslag til Lov om den selvstændige offentlige virksomhed DSB og om DSB S-tog A/S], no L 85, the 6th of May 1998.

Enemark, R. and Lund, J.M. (1997), 'Hvem styrede DSB og P&T?' ['Who governed DSB and the Post?'], in C. Greve (ed), *Privatisering, selskabsdannelser og udlicitering. Et politologisk perspektiv på udviklingen i Danmark [Privatising, corporatisation and tendering. A political science perpective on these development in Denmark]*, Systime, Århus, pp. 105-135.

Finansministeriet, Justitsministeriet, Statsministeriet and Trafikministeriet (2003), *Statslige aktieselskaber – tilsyn, ansvar og styring [State limited companies – inspection, responsibility and management]*, Finansministeriet, Copenhagen.

Greve, C. (1999), *Offentlige selskaber, demokrati and reform [Public limited companies, democracy and reform]*, Enkefru Plums Støttefond, Copenhagen.

Hansen, K. (2001), 'Local councillors: Between local "government" and local "governance"', *Public Administration*, Vol. 79 (1), pp. 105-123.

Heidman, P. (2001), *Advokatundersøgelse om statens varetagelse af ejerskabet til Combus A/S [Lawyer's inquiry into the state's conduct of the ownership of Combus Ltd]*, Trafikministeriet, Copenhagen.

Klausen, K.K. and Ståhlberg, K. (1998), *New Public Management i Norden.*

178   Social Perspectives on Mobility

Nye organisations- og ledelsesformer i den decentrale velfærdsstat [*New Public Management in the North. New forms of organisation and management in the decentralised welfare state*], Odense Universitetssforlag, Odense.

Lowndes, V. and Skelcher, C. (1998), 'The Dynamics of Multi-organizational partnerships: An Analysis of changing Models of Governance', *Public Administration*, Vol. 76 (2), pp. 313-333.

Magid, P. (2001), *Beretning om granskningen af Combus A/S* [*Account concerning the scrutiny of Combus Ltd*], Trafikministeriet, Copenhagen.

March, J.G. and Olsen, J.P. (1989), *Rediscovering institutions. The Organizational Basis of Politics*, The Free Press, New York, Toronto, Oxford, Singapore, Sydney.

Olsen, O.J. (2000), 'Offentlige virksomheder' ['Public industries'], in T. Knudsen (ed), *Dansk Forvaltningshistorie II. Stat, forvaltning og samfund. Folkestyrets forvaltning fra 1901 til 1953* [*The history of Danish public administration II. State, administration and society. The administration 1901-1953*], Jurist- og Økonomforbundets Forlag, Copenhagen, pp. 799-826.

Peters, B.G. (1998), 'Managing horizontal government: the politics of co-ordination', *Public Administration*, Vol. 76 (2), pp. 295-311.

Pfund, C. (2002), *Separation Philosophy of the European Union – Blessing or Curse? A contribution to the theme of separation of infrastructure from operations*, LITRA, Bern.

Powell, W.W. (1990), 'Neither Market nor Hierarchy. Network Forms of Organization', in *Research in organizational behavior*, Vol. 12 (2), pp. 295-336.

Rhodes, R.A.W. (1997), *Understanding Governance. Policy Networks, Governance, Reflexivity and Accountability*, Open University Press, Buckingham, Philadelphia.

Rhodes, R.A.W. (2000), 'The Governance narrative: Key findings and lessons from the ESCR's Whitehall Programme', *Public Administration*, Vol. 78 (2), pp. 345-363.

Rigsrevisionen (1998), *Notat til statsrevisorerne. Om ministerens beføjelser og forpligtelser i forbindelse med visse selskaber og virksomheder m.v.* [*Information note to the auditors of public accounts. About the minister's rights and obligations in connection to some corporations, etc*], Rigsrevisionen, Copenhagen.

Scharpf, F.W. (1994), 'Games Real Actors Could Play. Positive and Negative Coordination in Embedded Negotiations', *Journal of Theoretical Politics*, Vol. 6 (1), pp. 27-53.

Stoker, G. (2003), 'Pursing Public Value through Networks of Deliberation and Delivery: Can an emerging management paradigm meet the challenge of efficiency and democracy?' in *Conference on Democratic Network Governance*, Copenhagen, Denmark, May 22-23, 2003. Downloadable from website: http://www.demnetgov.ruc.dk/conference/papers.

Sørensen, C.H. (1993), *Slår bro fra kyst til kyst? En analyse af Socialdemokratiet og Øresundsforbindelsen* [*Building a bridge from coast to coast. An analysis of the Social Democratic Party and the Oresund connection*], Hovedland, Højbjerg.

Sørensen, C.H. (2001), *Kan Trafikministeriet klare miljøet? Om integration af miljøhensyn i trafikpolitik og institutionelle potentialer og barrierer* [Can the Ministry of Transport manage the environment? About integration of environmental concerns into transport policy and institutional potentials and barriers], Jurist- og Økonomforbundets Forlag, Copenhagen.

Trafikministeriet (1998), *Trafikredegørelse 1997* [*Traffic Account 1997*], Trafikministeriet, Copenhagen.

Werlauff, E. (1993), *Statsselskaber. Redegørelse til Erhvervs- and Selskabsstyrelsen, Industriministeriet, om statslige aktieselskaber* [*State corporations. Account on state limited companies to the Ministry of Industry*], Erhvervs- og Selskabsstyrelsen, Industriministeriet, Copenhagen.

Wolmar, C. (2001), *Broken Rails*, Aurum Press, London.

Chapter 9

Democracy, Civil Society and Automobility: Understanding Battles against Motorways

Maria Figueroa

Introduction

Civil society has been protesting motorways that go through their own communities since attempts to build automobile infrastructure began in the 1930s. Despite their frequency and ubiquity on the global scene, battles against motorways have been ignored as a direct subject of research[1]. They have received attention, indirectly, as part of complex decision making processes in studies of urban planning and urban politics (Altshuler, 1965; Altshuler and Luberoff, 2003; Falkemark, 1999; Townsend, 2003), as contributors to the creation of social movements (Jamison et al., 1990) and as part of the demands people present in public discussion of the risks set by mega-projects (Flyvbjerg et al., 2003). More conventionally, battles against motorways have been understood as part of individual or neighbourhood/communities' demands based on both self-interest and on genuine concern for the public good, expressing dissent on different grounds to public infrastructure projects in their surrounding area. The main goal of this chapter is to present some propositions to help us to begin understand battles against motorways as arenas for political contestation and deliberation of the civil society that can influence both transport policy and the political culture of automobility.

Civil society is here understood as a "sphere of social interaction between the economy and state, composed above all of the intimate sphere (especially the family), the sphere of associations (especially

---

[1] The author with the assistance of Eric Britton from 'The Commons: Open Society Sustainability Initiative' (http://www.ecoplan.org), Paris, has initiated an international survey of 'world road battles' (October 2004). Further information can be obtained or given at 'The New Mobility Agenda' webpage: http://newmobility.org/.

voluntary associations), social movements, and forms of communication" (Cohen and Arato, 1995). Civil society organizations exist outside direct control of the market and the state and are based in communicative action (Habermas, 1992). This independence from market and state forms the key to the capacity of civil society to serve as a site for the generation of democratic action. This chapter will further consider civil society as inseparable from the spatial and functional context of infrastructural and technological mobility systems in which it is imbedded. I will use the term civil society of automobility accepting the claim that automobility has contributed greatly to the mobilization of modern civil societies becoming a relevant factor in the decline of citizenship and the public sphere (Putnam, 2000; Sheller and Urry, 2003).

The understanding of battles against motorways as practices of the civil society of automobility provides two points of departure that set a reference for the focus of this chapter's analysis: firstly, civil society protesting against motorways will be understood as collective action that accepts mobility as a public good and does not seek to impose a regression to a fixed or relatively immobile society. Secondly, the understanding of battles against motorways will be based on a conception of power struggle since the practices of the protesting actors, their argumentation and discourses do not seek to gain control, conquer or endanger the systems that support automobilism. The focus of the analysis presented here is given to the political role of the protest against motorways meaning to their possibilities to generate *influence* through the life of democratic associations and through unconstrained discussion about the cultural significance of automobilism.

Analytical Framework

The theoretical perspectives used in the analysis are rooted in the field of democracy, planning and urban sociology. The democracy and planning perspectives which influence this analysis mostly maintain that an argumentative or deliberative approach to democracy and planning constitute basic elements in the resolution of societal and environmental conflicts. These perspectives place a strong emphasis on the role that an active, diverse and multidimensional public sphere has for revitalizing democracy. My concern for the public sphere derives from the work of Jürgen Habermas, but the specific focus has been shaped by a range of authors whose work dwells on the idea of what constitutes a meaningful political life, especially those that have contributed to the areas of democracy, planning and environmental politics (Dryzek, 2000; Fischer, 2003; Hajer and Wagenaar, 2003; Torgerson, 1999; Healey, 1993; Elling, 2003). Based on these theoretical perspectives to concentrate my analysis in processes initiated by the civil society to protest motorways.

The urban sociology perspective that informs the present analysis derives from the work of Manuel Castells who has described the changing reality that a 'network society' of mobility flows (autos, people, information) has created for civil society (2002). It also takes account of the work of Mimi Sheller and John Urry (2003), who maintain that automobility has generated a new *theme* and *style* of political contestation. I accept their definition of automobility as the "complex amalgam of interlocking machines, social practices and ways of dwelling, ...in a mobile, semi-privatised and hugely dangerous capsule" (Sheller and Urry, 2003).

Automobility facilitates 'freedom of movement' and contributes to promoting this freedom as an important objective of modern society. Automobility generates a theme for political contestation because not everybody can achieve this 'freedom of movement' by car, at least not at the same time or without imposing a cost on someone else's freedom (e.g. congestion). In Sheller and Urry's view, this makes automobility a *theme* for potential conflict between what they called 'urban civility and democratized mobility' (2003). One interpretation of this 'potential conflict' places transport itself at the centre of the conflict between those promoting continued economic growth and those wishing to contain it. It gets manifested in reactions or protest that urban dwellers may possibly initiate against decisions that contribute to facilitating unlimited automobility, or democratized automobility, such as in protest against new motorways. This interpretation sees the protest against motorways as conflicts between pro-mobility and anti-mobility constituencies in society. I shall argue here that another possible interpretation of the protest relates them to a growing sense of *ambivalence* towards the currently experienced levels of democratized mobility. Ambivalence can be a relatively important factor that helps explain the extent to which this protest can be seen as practices where people accept mobility but seek to negotiate how much 'more or less' of it is acceptable. This explanation is given to contrast the conventional understanding of such protest as representing either conflicts of the radicals or narrowly focused interest group of the civil society typified as 'not in my backyard'[2].

---

[2] The concept 'not in my backyard' or 'NIMBY' was first used in the United States in connection with the discovery of toxic waste sites and the community-based politics that emerged to confront it (Fischer, 2000).

Analysing the practices of the civil society of automobility entails giving attention to the inseparability of human subjects from the transformed public spaces, the flows of traffic, the ubiquitous presence of technological devices and systems supporting mobility (Sheller and Urry, 2003). The character of the civil society has been remoulded by its mere inception and interplay with the systems that facilitate mobility and connectivity around the world in real time and at zero distance (Castells, 2002). For example, the physical fragmentation of our daily lives has had a visible dampening effect on community involvement, collective civic engagement, and the public sphere[3] (Putnam, 2000). In Denmark, while civic engagement has remained high over the years, public participation has shifted from collective to individualistic forms seeking to influence public administrators more than decision-makers. This influence is exercised via media and professional interventions and in the process, "an important two-way dialogue between the general public and the politicians has been weakened" (Togeby et al. 2003). This framework considers the changes in communication linked to the spatiality of the urban environment, for example the shift of civil society's political communication from real spaces to virtual spaces. Thus, a second element of this framework focus on the *style* of the protest in an attempt to provide answers to the question '*How* the protest might help create new arenas for political communication and contestation? Accepting that civil society cannot be detached from the mobility conditions in which it is immersed, this analysis discusses to what extent civil society, when protesting against motorways, exemplifies a form of the renegotiation of public space for political communication and action and, what kind of political significance actions of civil disobedience, non-violent demonstrations and politics of comics may have influencing the larger culture of automobilism.

Finally, to undertake the analysis of the political *influence* that battles against motorways attain, the question "*What* might protest against motorways be accomplishing?" is answered with the proposition that they might achieve a certain level of political influence that signals modest advances for democratization in

---

[3] A decline on trends in civic engagement (political and civic participation, religious participation, formal and informal connections, altruism, volunteering, reciprocity, etc) has been documented thoroughly in the USA (Putnam, 2000). In Putnam's study, 'mobility and sprawl' is only one of four factors (the others being pressure of time and money, technology and mass media, generational differences) that explain this decline. For Sheller and Urry (2003), factors such as pressure of time, technology and mass media are included in the more comprehensive concept of mobility they use.

transport decision-making. I use three criteria suggested by John Dryzek (1996) to identify positive advances towards democratization: *Franchise*: refers to the number of individuals participating in any setting, *scope*: concerns the range of issues which are subject to popular control, and *authenticity* refers to the degree to which this control is substantive as opposed to symbolic (Dryzek, 1996).

Presentation of the Empirical Case Study

The battle against the motorway cutting through the cities of Århus-Silkeborg-Herning, in Jutland, Denmark serves as empirical case study for this analysis. The battle in question has been over the decision to build a high-class road whose middle section (38 Kilometres out of a total length of 75 Kilometres) will have to cut through one of Denmark's most beautiful landscapes and nature reserves: the valley of the Gudenå[4] river, which is located in and around Silkeborg (Vejdirektoratet, 2002). In January 1993, a proposal for a construction act [*anlægslov*] was sent to the Danish Parliament [*Folketinget*], to authorize and finance the project. Later that month, a newly elected government coalition (Centre-Left) took the position that 'no roads would be built through a protected area' (Stærdahl et al., 2003). As a consequence, the Parliamentary decision adopted [*anlægslov*] approved only the construction of the two outer stretches of the motorway and recommended further investigations for the middle stretch around Silkeborg. Today, the two outer sections of the motorway are already built and functional (Figure 9.1).

---

4   Gudenå area is included as part of reserved areas in a legislative act called '*Sminge-og Gødvadfredningen*' that affects 1400 hectares in Denmark since 1975. In total, Gudenå, Gjern Bakker and the forest of Silkeborg are amount 250 appointed 'EU habitat areas' for they provide life support to special kinds of valuable birds, animals and plants. Technically a new motorway cannot be placed at the interception of two appointed 'EU habitat areas' unless there are not other possible alternatives and the motorway is considered of important value to society in which case provisions have to be made to minimize the potential pervasive consequences for the animals, birds and plants for which the area was appointed in the first place (Vejdirektoratet, 2002).

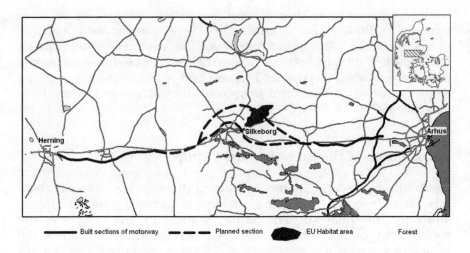

Built sections of motorway   — — — Planned section   EU Habitat area   Forest

**Figure 9.1   The Århus-Silkeborg-Herning motorway. The
location of this area within Denmark is indicated
in the insert**

Methodology

The focus of the analysis is on civil society's response to the
decision to build the Århus-Silkeborg-Herning motorway. The
analysis attempts to gain an articulated understanding of the
practices of some of the civil society groups participating in the
protest. The practices are "the ways in which people negotiate in a
structured and meaningful manner the challenges they encounter
in life's course[5]" (Wagenaar and Cook, 2003). This case offers
special features of interest to the analysis of the practices of civil
society protesting against motorways, a phenomenon of evolving
sophistication in developed western societies[6]. Firstly, the battle in

---

[5] According to Wagenaar and Cook (2003), *practice* entails: action,
community, situatedness, criteria, standards, warrants, knowing,
dialectic, discourse, emotions and values. This analysis looks at
practices as a combination of only four of these elements e.g.: actions
(people negotiate the world by acting upon it); emotions (action requires
engagement, certain situations must be sufficiently important to merit
the risk and effort of active involvement); values (the search for problems
and solutions, reasons for what we do what we do in concrete situation);
and discourse (vehicle by which the practical active negotiating of reality
takes place e.g. telling stories).

[6] For example, in USA battles against highways have lead to sophisticated
claims of environmental justice groups. In the UK, by 1994 the scale of

Silkeborg has developed over the course of the last ten years; this offered a good number of practices, official records and publications that were helpful for developing the background for this analysis. Secondly, the actors have changed very little, both in the oppositional groups of civil society and in technical positions of the administration during the years covered by this chapter. The nationally, regionally and locally elected authorities have changed, but have not altered the decision that further investigation should be allowed so as to find a solution. This continuity of actors and positions proved very useful for gaining insights into the evolution of the practices and for gaining access to direct information, through a number of personal interviews with different participants and institutions. This opportunity is rare given the impermanent character of social activism and organizations today, particularly in transport politics.

In what follows, I complete the description of the case through the presentation of the actions of the actors working in favour of the road and of the actors working against the road. These seemingly fixed categories are not intended to describe actor's deeply held positions. The distinction is only valuable for gaining a closer look into the evolution of activities, discourses and means of action of the groups of the organized civil society acting in this case. Table 9.1 provides a brief overview of the main actors, what they represented, their roles and specific duties in the case. Figure 9.2 presents a time line of the decision-making process that illustrates when these particular actors have been more active in the process.

Actions of Actors in Favour of the Motorway

The initiative for building a motorway[7] between Århus and Herning was originally proposed to the Transport Committee[8] by members of

---

    grassroots protest against the construction of new roads had risen to such a level that it was described as "the most vigorous new form in British environmentalism" (Lean, 1994 cited in Sheller and Urry, 2003).

[7] Public roads are classified as main national roads, county roads and communal roads. Main national roads that have relevance for the national traffic are administered by the state. (Bekendtgørelse af Lov om offentlige veje af d.21/7 1993;§1 og §2)

[8] In Denmark, the decision to build a high-class road infrastructure, such as a motorway or a bridge has to be taken in the Danish Parliament [Folketinget]. This process takes the form of two laws, the initial project law [projekteringslov] gives authorization to the administration to proceed with the investigations that define the project and the second law [anlægslov] contemplates the full characteristics of the planned

Table 9.1   Main actors in favour/against Århus-Silkeborg-Herning motorway

Name	Description, Examples	Role in this case
Danish Parliament (*Folketinget*)	Organ empowered to legislate. Has 179 members, has 24 permanent committees.	Passes two laws to a) initiate planning process b) authorize project.
Transport Committee	17 members, workshop of the Parliament. Decisions are prepared in the committees.	Examines bills and proposals for parliamentary resolution. Calls/Puts questions to Ministry.
Ministry of Transport	Coordinates Road, Rail, Air, Sea administrations.	Instructs the Road Directorate.
Road Directorate (*Vejdirektoratet*)	Technical road administration.	Planning of the road, prepares laws, in charge of EIA, decides routing, supervises the construction.
Forest and Nature Agency	Under Ministry of Environment.	Revises and gives consent to proposal.
Regional/Local Authority (County: *Amt*/ Municipality: *Byråd*)	Amt: Århus, Ringkøbing; Byråd: Herning, Ikast, Silkeborg, Gjern, Galten, Ry, Them, Århus.	Initiate idea, meet with Transport Committee, Participate with Road Directorate in initial technical committee.
Private Consultants	COWI: contract for parts of environmental impact assessment (EIA).	EIA: fauna, flora, nature protection, traffic accidents, barrier effects.
	Møller og Grøn.	EIA: landscape aesthetic.
Private Associations – Road Lobby	Federation of Danish Motorist Car Importers Association.	Produces report in support of motorway, delivers it to Transport Committee.
DN (Local Silkeborg)	Danish Society for Nature Preservation.	Environmental Organization.
JmOM	People of Jutland against Superflous Motorways.	Civil Society Group.
SF	Socialist People's Party.	Political Party.

project and its financial implications. Within Parliament, a Transport Committee reviews most of the evidence for the project, (e.g. that the project has been reviewed by other authorities and the results from the environmental impact assessment). The Transport Committee maintains direct connections with the Ministry of Transport and is open, during certain periods, for the submission of oral or written inquires by actors that wish to have a say regarding a project or present specific proposals. The Committee passes most of the inquires/proposals it receives to the Ministry of Transport.

some of the regional and local authorities in the area: Århus and Ringkøbing regional authority [*Amt*] and, Herning, Ikast, Silkeborg, and Århus municipalities [*Byrådet*], which were interested in seeing their region prepared to take part in the expected economic benefits that two projected mega-projects: 'the Great Belt Bridge' connecting East and West Denmark and the 'Øresund Bridge', connecting Sweden and Denmark would potentially bring. They were equally giving voice to a number of constituencies in the region that expected a sort of compensatory investment in the form of transport infrastructure to the region of mid-Jutland after the plans for the mentioned two mega-projects had been laid out.

Road lobby groups such as the Federation of Danish Motorists, the Car Importers Association, and others, supported this initiative through written reports submitted to the Transport Committee.

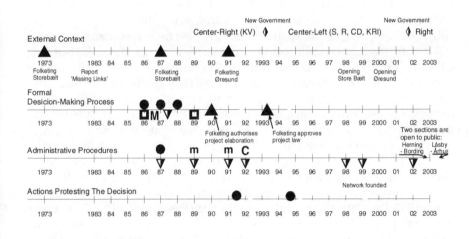

Symbol	Actor
▲	Parliament: Folketing
M	Ministry of Transport
▼	Road Directorate
m	Forest & Landscape, Ministry of Environment
●	Regional / Local Authorities
C	Consultants
◻	Private Associations
◆	Civil Society Group: "JmOM"

Figure 9.2   Timeline of the decision-making process of the Århus-Silkeborg-Herning motorway

Thus by 1987, the Transport Committee recommended the initiation of a process to consider this initiative to the Ministry of Transport. The Ministry instructed the Road Directorate to establish and preside over a technical committee that included representatives from the localities and regions, which had been actively involved in the initiative. A report from this committee was due to define the transport problem and the appropriate solution for meeting the demands of the communities concerned.

Figure 9.2 shows the intense activity of actors favouring a motorway, which took place around 1987. It is interesting to observe that none of the civil society actors had any knowledge of this ongoing process until 1991 when the actual decision-making process was already significantly advanced. Not surprisingly, the first report submitted by the Road Directorate in 1988, recommended a high-class road between Århus-Silkeborg-Herning as the solution. From the beginning, the active involvement of politicians in the parliamentary Transport Committee, the road lobby groups, regional authorities and private associations were decisive to the contemplation of a motorway as the most favourable decision. For example, the actual traffic demands within the region played only a secondary role supporting this decision (Nielsen and Anderson, 1994). When asking one of the decision makers about the not so convincing argument concerning transport needs and economic development supporting the decision, the answer given was that there is a "psychological need for a city like Silkeborg to have a highway" (interview with Jørn Würtz, former mayor of Silkeborg, presently vice-mayor, cited in Stærdahl et al., 2003).

The proposal for the routing of the different sections had to be subjected to environmental impact assessment[9]. In this more technical phase, the Road Directorate contracted out parts of the analysis. Two consultancy companies were given the task of investigating central topics for the environmental impact assessment procedure such as: the consequences for flora, fauna and nature, traffic accidents, barrier effects, air pollution, and, landscape and aesthetic consequences. The Ministry of Environment, through the Danish Forest and Nature agency, reviews and gives the approval of all big infrastructure projects in open areas. Based on this evidence the Road Directorate makes its final recommendation for one best solution from the technical, economic, environmental point of view to the Ministry of Transport.

---

[9] To comply with Council Directive 85/337/EEC of 27 June 1985 on the assessment of the effects of certain public and private projects on the environment, OJ 1985, L175/40, amended by Council Directive 97/11/EC, OJ 1997, L73/5. (EIA Directive)

The Ministry passes this recommendation to the Transport Committee for a last discussion and when the decision reaches the plenum in Parliament it is already in the form of a project law [*anlægslov*] that includes details of the routing and financial means to execute the projected road.

The years 1990 to 1992 were of intense activity for the Road Directorate regarding the culmination of the studies for the planned motorway[10]. By 1991, civil society groups had begun their involvement raising their voices in alarm especially in the towns of Silkeborg and Gjern where the protected area is located. Beginning that year, a large number of claims in opposition to the road (letters, signature, visits to politicians, letters to the media) started to inundate all levels of government. The new Centre-Left coalition government that came into power in early 1993, favoured a reconsideration of the case in relation to the protected area. The decision was then passed in Parliament to build only the two outer sections of the projected motorway leaving the middle stretch to further investigations.

Actions of Actors against the Motorway

The actors protesting against the motorway include a number of 'not in my backyard' groups that took their names from the area they were defending: 'Group against Motorway from the North of Silkeborg'; 'Ringvej Group against the Motorway'; 'Funder-North Group against the Motorway'. Their argument against the motorway is simple, they accepted the motorway but did not accept its routing through their particular surroundings. The evolution of practices of only one of these groups: the 'Group against Motorway from the North of Silkeborg' will be studied in detail. This is due do the relevance of the practices of this particular group in connection with the analytical framework selected. This group later became the

---

[10] The Directorate had produced two environmental impact assessment reports for Silkeborg, one in 1992 and a second one in 2002. Throughout these processes a number of public hearings have been conducted, and citizens have had opportunities to object. Many of the objections are related to very specific problems since the public debate during the hearings is restricted to the alignment question. In general the NGOs participating regard this public hearings important to obtain information on the details of the project but, object that the decision to build the highway had never been discussed in public and, solid evidence for the need of the highway have never been made public (Stærdahl et al., 2003).

'People of Jutland against Superfluous Motorways', which in Danish is '*Jyder mod Overflødige Motorveje*' (JmOM).

The actions, values and discourses of two other relevant actors in the fight against the motorway will structure this analysis: First, the Danish Society for Nature Preservation (DN) which represents the largest and oldest environmental organization in Denmark[11]. Second, a political party[12] the '*Socialistisk Folkeparti*'[13] 'the Socialist People's Party' (SF) will be included in the analysis mostly in connection with the actions of the two other actors. SF has been consequent in opposing the motorway on the basis that the investment could have been used for improvements in public transport or to modernize the railway connection between the affected communities. SF is considered part of the political society[14] that can act as a mediating sphere through which civil society can gain influence over the political-administrative process (Cohen and Arato, 1995).

The Danish Society for Nature Conservation's (DN) involvement in the opposition to the Århus-Herning motorway started in the spring of 1991. Before that, DN has had little experience in confronting political issues related to transport, and it was only two years later, in 1993, that it created its own transport section (Nielsen and Anderson, 1994). DN's main argument against the Århus-Herning motorway was to oppose the planned motorway on the basis of the inevitable damage to the environment of the protected area that it would bring. Also, DN's initial stand was to question the need for this motorway directly criticizing the Regional authority in Århus for the lack of information on this big infrastructure project in the 1989 Regional plan.

---

[11] I will refer mostly to the actions of its local committees in Silkeborg/Them, Gjern, Galten and Århus that have been directly involved in the opposition against this motorway.

[12] A political party belongs to what Cohen and Arato have defined as the 'political society' (1995) distinguishing civil society from both a 'political society' of parties, political organizations, and political publics (in particular, parliaments) and an 'economic society' composed of organizations of production and distribution, usually firms, cooperatives, partnerships, and so on.

[13] Parties in Denmark play an important role in political life. They are represented in Parliament, Council and Municipality levels, and also can act as pressure groups outside elected bodies by e.g. making interventions in newspapers, holding meetings or bringing their points of view to the fore in other ways. Socialistic People's Party is one of the small parties in Denmark (six to nine per cent of voter representation). It claims to run on a red and green platform (www.sf.dk).

[14] See note 12.

JmOM is a grassroots organization founded in 1993; it has around 140 members of which only half are active in direct actions. Originally the group was founded in 1991 as the 'Group against the Motorway from the North of Silkeborg', as one of the 'not in my backyard' groups. However, after two years of activism against the motorway and many internal disagreements over what alternative they should support instead of a motorway, they decided to review their stance and redefine themselves giving way to a rebirth of the group in the spring of 1993 resulting in the present JmOM. As JmOM, they opted for a clear focus on fighting against 'superfluous motorways' in general and in favour of alternative modes of transport such as trains. They started by attempting to fight the Århus-Herning motorway and have attempted to make their presence felt against other big infrastructure and motorway projects such as the Great Belt Bridge and the last section of the motorway that connects the cities of Århus and Aalborg in the north of Jutland.

In the protest groups' initial phase, DN, JmOM and the 'not in my backyard' groups cooperated in taking formal steps to try and change the decision-maker's minds via: letters, visits, public talks, signature collection, articles in local newspapers, sometimes in conjunction with SF. This initial phase lasted two years. By 1993, after the decision was taken to start building the two outer sections of the motorway, JmOM felt that a change of strategy was necessary and a second phase of direct actions begun. Initially, they organized marches and sits-in at the construction site, later in their process they changed the style of their direct actions to non-violent demonstrations and a new number of thought-provoking actions ensued. Two of their most visible actions have been the painting of a bridge with art work in 2000, and 137 days living on top of a tree in front of one of the motorway building sites in Snåstrup Mølle. These two actions gave the group media attention and diverse forms of recognition within Denmark, from 'brave and creative citizens' to 'unserious and rebellious group' (interview with Leif Thomsen, DN Silkeborg). Many other smaller actions had been taken before and after these events. In 1999, JmOM together with other environmental groups and anti-motorways groups in Denmark founded the 'Network against Superfluous Motorways' that has a website (www.overflod.hjem.wanadoo.dk) and meets once a year.

DN and SF have changed, over the years, their stance against the motorway and are concentrating on providing inputs to negotiate a possible routing of the road. DN's change of stance came as a result of what they perceived as pressure from their constituencies (members) towards finding a conciliatory position. DN believes that their members are not against motorways per se and would not be happy if this was the stance DN took (interview with Birgitte Ingrisch, DN Copenhagen). SF party's position is that after the two outer sections of the road have been built, new traffic problems for Silkeborg have arisen, so although still opposing the motorway, they see it as a necessary, fair discussion to try to find a solution to this problem. They have been very active in the Danish Parliament negotiating a thorough analysis of the alternative routes for the motorway (interview with Morten Homann, member of Parliament, SF).

JmOM have not changed their stance in opposing the road. They are not constrained by their members to make compromises, however their local support has dwindled. At the same time, their national support has increased together with their cooperation with other environmental groups and anti-motorways groups around the country. What JmOM sees as their next step regarding the Silkeborg motorway is to make an attempt to bring a complaint to the European Union Court of Justice for violation of the European Habitat Directive[15]. This will not be simple, however it will prove that civil society can be a source of pressure on the state (Dryzek, 1996). In the meantime, keeping up the pressure through direct actions seems to have worked, so far, in delaying the motorway through Silkeborg (interview with Bente Fuglsbjerg, JmOM).

The Analysis: Insights into Battles against Motorways

To begin to understand battles against motorways, this analysis seeks to gain insights from the Silkeborg case and the theoretical framework to illustrate possible interpretations as to *why* battles against motorways occur, *how* the practices of the protest group might provide important arenas for political contestation and ultimately, *what* the battles might accomplish in practice.

Why Battles against Motorways?

The conventional understanding of civil society protesting against motorways has not changed much since its beginnings, largely linking these protests to narrow self-interested groups that may be directly affected by the routing of the road and simply do not want

---

[15] Council Directive 92/43/EEC of 21 May 1992 on the conservation of natural habitats and of wild fauna and flora, OJ 1992, L 206/7, as amended by OJ 1997, L 305/42, in force from July 1994.

to see the road going through their backyards[16]. However, many things have changed since the beginning of road infrastructure provision, particularly in rich western nations that have by now consolidated the development of complex systems of roads supporting automobility. Civil society has also changed and cannot be understood in separation from the mobility systems within which it operates. Is it possible that the protest against motorways may have gained a different connotation or meaning beyond 'not in my backyard' groups?

To a certain degree, democratized automobility, or unlimited automobility is closer to being realized in advanced economies. One indication of this is the level of car ownership. There is, for example, a narrowing of the gap of car ownership between the United States and other rich nations in Europe and Asia. The average car ownership in the European Union was 488 cars per 1000 inhabitants in 2001 (European Commission and Directorate-General for Energy and Transport, 2003). Civil society now largely lives in urban spaces with high levels of automobility. I shall claim that beyond the overall consensus on the benefits of mobility in modern life, there is a certain uneasiness with the environmental and social consequences of unlimited automobility. Automobility is a theme of political contestation because of the growing *ambivalence* that society seems to experience towards it, both at the individual and at the societal levels. I would like to suggest that the frequency and ubiquity of actions of civil society against motorways might express this ambivalence and the need to resolve it.

Three facts explain what I mean by *ambivalence* towards automobilism: Firstly, for better or worse the historical shift in infrastructure, technology and consciousness that supports a highly mobile generation of people and facilitates connectivity of peoples across distance and time cannot be reversed (Castells, 2002). Secondly, most people enjoy one form or another of the options for consumerism and gain from the opportunities for emancipation and new identities that contemporary forms of travel,

---

[16] At least this would be the case in Scandinavia. In the USA, the community politics of 'not in my backyard' has been reinterpreted by a radical environmental populist movement, the environmental justice movement pointing, among other things, to the disproportionate incidence of motorways cutting through low-income and working class communities particularly those of African Americans, Latinos, Asian Americans and other ethnic groups. The environmental justice movement has not achieved the same echo in Scandinavia where a more homogeneous population in terms of race and income make the basic claims of environmental justice groups less appropriate to explain the location of motorways.

communication and trade can bring (Root, 2003; Sheller and Urry, 2003). Thirdly, many people feel uneasy or affected individually by the environmental and social consequences of living in highly mobile environments. The sense of ambivalence refers to the practices through which people attempt to both enjoy automobility and find something they can do to tame it, without abandoning or rejecting it.

People care about their freedom to move by car but dislike congestion; have learned to tolerate higher levels of noise and pollution in exchange for unlimited use of their cars but wish to retreat to cleaner environments at home where they can forget about noise and pollution. There are limits to unlimited automobility and most contemporary urban dwellers have a good sense of what these limits are (Hagman, 2002; Anderson et al., 1998). Most people choose not to act individually upon this knowledge, as they perceive their contribution would be minimal in solving a big problem while it will create greater personal annoyances for having to accept restrictions to their private automobility[17].

Other possibilities in relation to action become, then, more desirable and practical for the internally ambivalent civil society of automobility. For instance, many more people are interested in trying to affect public decisions concerning urban and transport development and many are directly protesting the politics of automobility (Whitelegg, 1997; Sheller and Urry, 2003). I shall argue that the consolidation of groups of civil society protesting against motorways beyond 'not in my backyard' interests, towards more sophisticated forms of political contestation can be partially explained by the ambivalence that civil society experiences towards automobility.

Arguing against the system that supports automobility makes it easier to direct difficult questions concerning responsibility away from the self, e.g. avoiding the need to have to confront or accept restrictions to personal automobility – and it makes it easier to oppose and restrict conditions that are perceived as allowing the excesses of automobility and its environmental and social consequences.

---

[17] Acting individually according to known existing limits in transport is very difficult (Hagman, 2002; Jensen, 1999; Witherspoon, 2004), so for many a form of denial is prevalent (my contribution would be so minimal; the problem – pollution, congestion – is not so bad here, it is worst in developing countries or another city). Many others declare feelings of being caught or trapped in circumstances (bad connections, family conditions, etc.) (Hagman, 2002; Jensen, 1999).

Reviewing the case of the actors in Silkeborg protesting the motorway, DN, the environmental organization, changed its initial stance of opposing the road to one of negotiating about the road not to upset its members, nation-wide, whom DN conceives as people who do not wish to see DN challenging motorways in their name. They are ambivalent, worrying about the environment while caring for their personal automobility. Similarly, JmOM's more radical stance against the road seems to illustrate, at some level, the same ambivalence, as a group they:

- Focus their attention on motorways and not on cars, or car use.
- Critique the expansion of the system supporting automobilism but not the system per se.
- Accept that a certain provision of motorways is necessary, critique what they perceive as 'superfluous motorways' so there is a base line that is acceptable and perhaps also that some of its consequences seem acceptable.
- Focus on building alternative modes of transport, and also ways to minimize, not prohibit or condemn car use, so its stance is not against automobility or mobility in general.
- Even when their critique includes lifestyle issues they avoid a critical focus on the citizens themselves as users of the system.

The theme of automobility can be seen to create both a desirable goal for modern life and concerns for its effects on society and environment, generating a sense of ambivalence in civil society. This ambivalence can be a relatively important factor for understanding protests against motorways beyond self-interested practices or conflicts from the radicals into practices that seek to tame the conditions that favour unlimited automobilism. The protests are arenas for political contestation where some of the civil society actors find opportunities to express and try to resolve this ambivalence. I will now turn to the issue of *how* these practices are carried out.

How the Protest Might Create New Arenas for Political Contestation

The urban public space has been de-politicized and transformed into flows of autos and information in modern cities (Castells, 2002; Sheller and Urry, 2003). This section proposes that protests against motorways may contribute to re-politicizing public space and generate styles of political contestation capable of influencing decision-making and the political culture of transport politics. The style of political contestation that gives expression to the politics of the comic and to non-violent forms of demonstrations illustrates this proposition. This section considers some of the practices of the organized groups protesting motorways in Silkeborg.

Road battles offer an opportunity for civil society to regain public spaces for political debate. To the extent that political debate in public spaces has lost its importance and given way to virtual forms of communication (Sheller and Urry, 2003), road battles offer a reason and a place for public debate. People are highly attached to particular spaces, the threatened destruction of which is often bitterly resisted. The politics of defending a space stems from the fact that 'space' comprises a set of physical forms that convey signs and meanings to the observers (Urry, 1991). Those meanings are important in their effects, in the case of Silkeborg, the politics of defending an unspoilt landscape with signs and a variety of possible meanings to the neighbourhood is one important reason for the protest. In Silkeborg, a motorway would have the effect of defacing and mutilating the spatial features that have made the valley of the Gudenå stand out as a special place, features that make in a sense *the* place in Silkeborg and have helped to construct what people feel and think about it. To build a motorway through the protected area would be, symbolically to demolish the whole place.

JmOM protests in Silkeborg have attempted to take on the existing public space before the road in different types of demonstrations. Some protests have taken place in the forest, the lake, and the trees that need to be felled before the road is built. The way to fight for the space is by using it to forward open debates and political deliberation. The number of participants on such demonstrations is often larger than the JmOM group itself. Among the reasons that explain the long life of JmOM is, in part, the emotions and new sense of purpose achieved through these actions, reclaiming common public spaces and finding a conviction that they are on a worthy mission. The downside of this style of action is the risk of exclusion from the political arena by other actors who may disqualify them as 'unserious', 'rebellious' or simply too radical. JmOM have confronted this reality which has come to affect their local support.

The opportunity of unconstrained discussion time has often also been the result of the actions to regain public space for political action and debate in Silkeborg. Both, the extra time for deliberations and the unconstrained discussion are features that help restore community, sparking the civic imagination to invent new ways of connecting socially. Both are difficult to replicate in decision-making processes, in public hearings in transport planning and environmental assessment procedures constricted by impending decisions and time limits. The scope and time for deliberation during such public meetings offer few opportunities for the expression of honest uncertainties, to play with ideas and possibilities including different considerations and other elements of lifeworld rationality such as aesthetics and values (Elling, 2003).

A second aspect of re-politicization explored here is the role of the comic in transport politics. JmOM has taken the decision to carry out direct actions of non-violent forms inspired originally by Mahatma Ghandi in India that have been re-interpreted reflecting new circumstances. Non-violent demonstrations have become a resource for JmOM (Vestergaard and Mattesen, 2003). Through non-violent demonstrations, JmOM has attempted to give expression to the politics of comics. The politics of comics have been interpreted as a way to separate political actions from the story line of tragedy and atmosphere of crisis that green politics and politics in general seems to offer, taking instead ironic stances that can focus on deflating pretences and mocking excesses (Torgerson, 1999). According to Torgerson, comedy is irreverent, disintegrative, exposing and disrupting settled patterns of conduct, belief, power and authority (1999).

JmOM's have been successful at using comedy as their strategy for direct action seeking no other goal than to renew comic tension, to keep the story alive. Among many such actions, they have made a swimming demonstration in the Gudenå river, delivered a giant cake decorated with a motorway cutting through a marzipan-nature area to a conference of European Ministries of Environment that took place in the city of Århus in 1993, and they have painted a motorway bridge with art work in 2000. The goal is to focus on carnivalesque images exposing and ridiculing the sombre spectre of the administrative mind (Torgerson, 1999). In this analysis, these forms of demonstration are interpreted as an arena of political dissent and action that can begin to pose serious criticism to decision-making procedures favouring motorways over other transport modes and challenging the state and administrative procedures in transport decision-making. I will now turn to the question of *what* all these actions have accomplished.

What Might Protest against Motorways Be Accomplishing?

Beyond directly affecting the decision to construct a motorway the possible outcome that concerns this analysis the most, has to do with the battle's contribution to influence policy and improve democratic practices in transport.

To discuss this in connection to Silkeborg, I use the criteria of *scope, franchise* and *authenticity* developed by Dryzek (1996). Beginning with scope I made a distinction between two possible ways of analyzing improvements in *scope* as: a) range of issues subject to public control within the administrative procedures for decision-making and b) a range of issues put forward for consideration by the organized civil society as part of the debate. The analytical difference between the two forms of scope is important. Considering only the first form, it is possible to conclude that a reduced scope limits democratic debate, as it has been in the case of Silkeborg. Considering, the second form, scope helps reveal the contributions to the debate that organized civil society protesting motorways may have in fact made in addition or beyond self-interested 'not in my backyard' objectives.

Regarding the analysis of scope as being a range of issues subject to public control given within the administrative procedures, the process in Silkeborg, was from the start defined by a reduced scope in both the formulation of the problem and its solution. As was stated above, the regional and local authorities were highly motivated to find that a high-class road infrastructure was the necessary solution to the transport problems of their region. The Ministry of Transport could have involved the rail authorities in the initial technical work but, in this case, the task was given to the Road Directorate. The regional and local authorities did not open a debate about the necessity of this motorway with their local constituencies and the project did not exist in previous plans.

Between 1987 and 1993, none of the regional or local authorities organized public meetings regarding the motorway project (Nielsen and Anderson, 1994); public involvement thus was postponed to the public hearing phases of the environmental impact assessment procedure where the scope was limited to a discussion of the alignment of the motorway. Examination of the second form of scope is necessary for b) the range of issues being put forward by organized civil society to the authorities, irrespective of the administrative procedures and real bargaining possibilities deserves consideration:

From issues of limited scope 'not in my backyard' to a critique of motorways as problematic transport politics: The case of motorways as problematic transport politics for the environment was reinforced by the claims of the 'not in my backyard' groups in Silkeborg. The mounting concerns of some of these groups for the planned project over specific sections of the preserved area helped to bring pressure for greater consideration of the environmental values of the area as a matter of *scope* that needed attention from the authorities.

Motorways as problematic transport policy that disregards other viable alternatives to transport problems was brought up by JmOM, and SF, who claimed the need for setting a different agenda in transport policy. Both JmOM and SF, while rejecting the road wanted also to open a discussion of alternatives to the motorway that could be viable. They sharpened their arguments against the motorway by placing it in the context of a critique of the regional and local transport politics that generally favours road transport solutions over integration with other modes (interview with M. Homann, SF).

From a critique of motorways based in environmental tragedy to attempts for inclusion of other elements against motorways such as aesthetics and life style considerations: Comparing DN and JmOM interpretations of what they conceived as the problem with motorways can illustrate a progression in the scope of the critique beyond environmental concerns. DN initially opposed the motorway on environmental grounds. However, experience taught them that a critique founded on environmental grounds was both difficult to sustain, particularly to their own members, and weak as an argument to stop the motorway (interview with Leif Thomsen, DN Silkeborg). For example, disrupting the habitats of animals, birds and plants could be alleviated through special designs for the roads, barriers, animal passages, and reforestation schemes and so on. In short, a critique of the motorway on the basis of the environmental tragedy that will unfold did not provide substantial ammunition to make the motorway proposal crumble (interview with Leif Thomsen, DN Silkeborg). DN then shifted its position to accepting the motorway and to negotiating only where and how.

Conversely, JmOM maintained its initial stance attempting to organize its critique around a number of issues that included the environment but were not limited to it. For example, a list on their webpage presents the following reasons against motorways: "they pollute, damage nature, produce noise, damage the landscape, create more traffic, destroys community, centralize the economy, create longer distances to work, create unemployment, do not reduce traffic accidents but displace them to adjacent roads, reduces consideration of alternative transport choices, and are unnecessary to resolve transport problems" (www.overflod.hjem.-wanadoo.dk).

Beside this list of arguments against motorways, members of the group are making attempts to broaden the discussion to debate in real and virtual forums, books, and pamphlets about automobilism and related issues such as "the need to reduce speed in people lives not to increase it" (Vestergaard, 1999). Among the issues they are considering in order for them to make the case against motorways they ask questions such as "what does it mean for a society to be entangled in a comprehensive system of motorways" (Vestergaard and Mattesen, 2003). They present themselves as "fighting against the increasing automobilism and its unavoidable consequences: more motorways, because they find that the consequences for people and the environment are all too high" (Vestergaard and Mattesen, 2003).

Similarly, in their written statements JmOM introduced a critique of automobilism and the system of motorways that supports it; they propose that a new agenda is necessary to move transport politics to become a discussion of the "type of society that we wish to have" (Vestergaard and Mattesen, 2003). This type of rhetoric in their discourse reflects a more general critique of modern society, which radical environmental groups in Denmark were already embracing in the early seventies (Jamison et al., 1990). JmOM is running the risk of receiving the same kind of critic that the early radical environmental groups received for presenting a 'closed' and 'untenable' position against automobilism. However, a combination of factors, such as those described earlier, contributing to a sense of ambivalence, may assist such rhetoric in gaining a different connotation today that may carry on beyond the lifetime of JmOM and influence similar groups, environmental organizations, interest group and the larger political culture of automobilism.

Presenting concrete demands to the administrative system: A final consideration as a matter of increased scope, the case of protest in Silkeborg shows that a number of concrete political demands to the administrative apparatus have been posed for:

- improving democracy in the decision-making process,
- improving planning and investment of alternative transport solutions and,
- complying with environmental regulations or directives.

It is not simple to fulfil these demands, and they would require significant changes in some administrative procedures. However, what such demands clearly signal is that civil society can be a source of pressure on the state. In this particular case, a number of procedural weaknesses might exist that cannot be simply neglected by the administration.

Two promising moves signalling how the administrative apparatus may be encouraged to make changes in transport decision-making procedures are the European Directive for Strategic Environmental Assessment[18] (SEA Directive), applicable to all projects, plans and programs that are required by national law in European member states and, the Århus Convention on Access

---

[18] EU Directive 2001/42/EC on the assessment of the effects of certain plans and programs on the environment.

to information, Public Participation in Decision-Making, and Access to Justice in Environmental Matters[19].

The SEA Directive establishes, for example that all plans, programs and projects will need to be given an early opportunity for consultation to the public, environmental authorities and other members affected by the plan, they will need to consider alternative options, evaluate cumulative environmental impacts, and show how those considerations have influenced the final decision. Although promising, one of the potential weaknesses with the SEA Directive's implementation is that it leaves the form the consultation process should take open to interpretation. In Denmark, for instance, it is still unclear as to the extent to which this directive is applicable to the transport sector since the Danish planning law does not institute a system of transport plans. Overall, implementation of this new directive is expected to be a step in the right direction towards democratization in decision-making.

In the case of the Århus Convention, parties have committed themselves to the adoption of its provisions into their national legal systems (De Lange, 2004). The provisions of the Århus Convention list the specific rights of access to information, public participation and access to justice in environmental matters that can 'contribute to the protection of the right of every person of present and future generations to live in an environment adequate to his or her health and well being' (article 1 of this Convention). In general these two legal instruments are important steps towards facilitating democratic practices and environmental protection in the European urban planning and transport systems.

As second criteria in the analysis of whether civil society protesting motorways improve democratic practices, *authenticity* refers to the substantive rather than symbolic control over issues the public has. In Silkeborg, despite the reduced scope of the debate informing the decision-making process, I have argued before that a second type of scope could be analyzed that has a potentially larger significance. In practice, civil society has not substantive control over issues that conform the debate yet, as the case of Silkeborg illustrates, there is a real possibility that the voices and arguments created in the collective actions may have been successful in penetrating the authorities mind, if the delay in taking a final decision about the motorway is attributed to the extent of the civil society protest. Additionally, other initiatives by the regional administration to take into account improvements in the rail connection as part of the regional plan for development of the Århus

---

[19] UN/ECE Århus Convention, (Denmark), 25 June 1988 (entered into force 30 Oct. 2001), (1999).

region and municipality can be attributed to advances in authenticity achieved by the organized, protesting groups of civil society. However, gains in authenticity may be more the exemption than the rule in protests against motorways. Most roads do get built despite the protests. Silkeborg is a rather unusual case for a road battle, and the issue of having achieved substantive control over 'the decision to build the road' is intended here more as a hypothesis than as a fact.

Improvements in *franchise* or the number of individuals participating have occurred, even when the character of the supporters may have changed significantly. Taking again the case of JmOM, what started as a 'not in my backyard' group in 1991, became in 1993 the 'People of Jutland against superfluous motorway' JmOM, which for a number of years received extensive local support. Later JmOM joined efforts with other similar groups and environmental organizations in Denmark to give way in 1999 to the national association or 'Network against superfluous motorways' that links similar groups in Århus, Vendel in North of Jutland, Alssund, Fyn, North Sealand, Copenhagen and Nykøbing F, in short in many cities all over Denmark. However, after the opening of the two outer stretches of the Århus-Herning motorway, local support for JmOM has almost disappeared (interview with Bente Fuglsbjerg, JmOM). In response to this, JmOM has gone from locally based discussions to organize far-reaching efforts through a number of publications, a bi-annual newsletter, a webpage, participation in publicly organized debates, annual meetings, forums in internet and an electronic mail list, making a good part of this outreach effort 'virtual'. As discussed earlier the group have also taken every opportunity to take direct actions reclaiming public space. Gains in franchise has shifted over time, from a large initial local base to a more widely located, virtually organized constituency.

From the point of view of franchise, scope and authenticity, it could be said that what civil society protesting against motorways in Silkeborg has accomplished so far is modest but significant contributions to improve democratic practices in transport decision-making.

Concluding Remarks

The main concern of this chapter has been to provide some propositions to be debated drawn from contemporary policy and urban sociology analysis to help rethink battles against motorways. The analysis has provided elements that help understand *why* civil society protests against motorways can be understood beyond 'not in my backyard' aims, *how* these practices might create new arenas for political contestation and *what* they might be accomplishing.

The analysis has made the proposition that a sense of *ambivalence* towards increasing automobility might be a relatively important factor to explain *why* protest against motorways can be explained beyond conflicts of 'the anti-mobility radicals' or practices of 'not in my backyard' groups toward organized efforts from the civil society seeking to 'tame' not to devolve or contest automobilism. People enjoy automobility but are concerned about its social and environmental consequences. For many, increasing levels of automobility generate ambivalent feelings. Motorways become easy targets to oppose through collective actions that do not confront the system as a whole or target directly individual auto ownership and use.

The protests are a sign of positive collective engagement with politics within a time of delusion, rejection of politics and decline of civil society collective engagement. Questions related to aesthetic and lifestyle issues are modestly brought for consideration into the general transport debate in Silkeborg, for example: "what does it mean for a society to be entangled in a comprehensive system of motorways" or "to discuss transport politics is to discuss what kind of society we wish to have[20]" (Vestergaard and Mattesen, 2003). Also, a modest effort to re-politicize the public space, offer the participant community instances of unlimited and unconstrained communication that may favour authentic communication. Non-violent demonstrations and actions styled in the politics of the comic have become resources for *how* to express the protests groups' arguments. As a result, elements of aesthetics and lifestyle considerations form an important component of their critique to motorways indicating both a progression in discourse from self-interested 'not in my backyard' and a departure from a discourse based exclusively on environmental considerations. However, the consolidation of a solid critique against unlimited automobilism have also become a difficult exercise for the oppositional groups, who are always risking 'exclusion' from the political debate if they are perceived as being simply too radical or can be easily identified with 'closed' positions against modern society and automobility.

The insights from the case analyzed reveal some aspects of *what* the protests against motorways might accomplish. Overall they can begin to be considered an evolving form of political dissent of the civil society that brings modest improvements in transport sector

---

[20] My own translation of '*at diskutere trafikpolitik er også at diskutere, hvilket samfund vi ønsker*'.

democratic practices. These improvements are perceived in connection with the *influence* generated through an opening of the scope of debate and through placement of concrete demands to the administrative apparatus for improving procedures e.g. democracy in decision-making, integration of transport policy making towards consideration of mixed modal solutions, compliance with environmental planning procedures and European directives. The administrative apparatus needs to be responsive to these demands as it also receives pressure from above, through initiatives such as the European Directive on Strategic Environmental Assessment[21] and the Århus Convention[22]. The significance of civil society protesting against motorways as an evolving practice of political dissent on the theme of automobility has been thus highlighted in this chapter.

Acknowledgements

I would like to thank Per Homann Jespersen and Anne Jensen from FLUX – Centre for Transport Research at Roskilde University, Claus Hedegaard from The Institute of Transport Economics, and Henrik Gudmundsson from National Environmental Research Institute for their reviews of earlier drafts of this chapter. Also, I would like to give a special thanks to Craig Townsend from Concordia University, Canada, Bo Elling from Roskilde University, and Jeppe Læssøe from the Technical University of Denmark for their constructive criticisms of the final version. Thanks too to Matthias Ketzel and Ritta Juel Bitsch for helpful assistance with the figures.

References

Altshuler, A. (1965), *The City Planning Process: A Political Analysis*, Cornell University Press, Ithaca, New York.

Altshuler, A. and Luberoff, D. (2003), *Mega-Projects The Changing Politics of Urban Public Investment*, The Brookings Institutions, Washington, DC.

Anderson, M., Meaton, J., Potter, C. and Rogers, A. (1998), 'Greener Transport Towns: Publicly Acceptable, Privately Resisted?', in Banister (ed), *Transport Policy and The Environment*, pp 267-297, Routledge, London.

Castells, M. (2002), 'The Space of Flows' in Susse (ed), *The Castells Reader on Cities and Social Theory*, pp 314-366, Blackwell, Oxford.

---

[21] See note 18.
[22] See note 19.

Cohen, J. and Arato, A. (1995), *Civil Society and Political Theory*, The MIT Press, Cambridge, Massachusetts.

De Lange, F. (2004), 'Beyond Greenpeace, Courtesy of the Århus Convention', in Somsen, H., et al (eds), *The Yearbook of European Environmental Law*, pp. 227-248, Oxford University Press, Oxford.

Dryzek, J. S. (1996), 'Strategies of Ecological Democratization', in Lafferty, W. and Meadowcroft, J. (eds), *Democracy and The Environment Problems and Prospects*, pp. 108-123, Edward Elgar Publishing Limited, Cheltenham.

Dryzek, J. S. (2000), *Deliberative Democracy and Beyond: Liberals, Critics, Constellations*, Oxford University Press, Oxford.

Elling, B. (2003), *Modernitetens Miljøpolitik [Environmental Politics in Modern Times]*, Frydenlund grafisk, Copenhagen.

European Commission and Directorate-General for Energy and Transport (2003), *Energy & Transport in Figures 2003*, Brussels.

Falkemark, G. (1999), *Politik, Lobbyism och Manipulation: Svensk Trafikpolitik i Verkligheten [Politics, Lobbyism and Manipulation: Swedish Traffic Politics in Reality]*, Bokförlaget Nya Doxa, Nora.

Fischer, F. (2000), *Citizens, Experts and the Environment: The politics of Local Knowledge*, Duke University Press, Durham.

Fischer, F. (2003), *Discursive Spaces for Participatory Governance: From Design Properties to Communicative Practices*, Working Draft, Presented at the Conference on Democratic Network Governance, Roskilde University, May 22-23, Denmark.

Flyvbjerg, B., Bruzelius, N. and Rothengatter, W. (2003), *Megaprojects and Risk: An Anatomy of Ambition*, Cambridge University Press, Cambridge.

Habermas, J. (1992), 'Further Reflections on the Public Sphere', in Calhoun, C. (ed), *Habermas and the Public Sphere*, MIT Press, Cambridge, Massachusetts.

Hagman, O. (2002), *Bilisten och miljön: Bilanvändare i stad och land om bilismens goda och dåliga sidor [Car Drivers and Environment: On the good and bad sides of car driving in cities and rural areas]*, Göteborgs Universitet.

Hajer, M. and Wagenaar, H. (eds) (2003), *Deliberative Policy Analysis: Understanding Governance in the Network Society*, Cambridge University Press, Cambridge.

Healey, P. (1993), 'Planning Through Debate: The Communicative Turn in Planning Theory' in Fischer, F. and Forester, J. (eds), *The Argumentative Turn in Policy Analysis and Planning*, pp 233-253, Duke University Press, Durham.

Jamison, A., Eyerman, R., Cramer, J. and Læssøe, J. (1990), *The Making of the New Environmental Consciousness. A Comparative Study Of The Environmental Movements in Sweden, Denmark and The Netherlands*, Edinburgh University Press, Edinburgh.

Jensen, M. (1999), 'Passion and heart in transport – a sociological analysis on transport behaviour', *Transport Policy*, 6. [1], pp 19-33.

Nielsen, J. and Anderson, M. (1994), *Transport og Miljø et studie af magtens rationalitet i infrastrukturplanlægningen med Århus-Herning motorvejen som case. [Transport and environment a study of rationality of powering infrastructure planning with Århus-Herning motorway as case]*, Master

Thesis, Department of Environment, Technology and Social Studies, Roskilde University.

Putnam, R. (2000), *Bowling Alone: The Collapse and Revival of American Community*, Simon & Schuster, New York.

Root, A. (ed.) (2003), *Delivering Sustainable Transport A Social Science Perspective*, Elsevier Science, Amsterdam.

Sheller, M. and Urry, J. (2003), 'The City and the Car', in Root, A. (ed), *Delivering Sustainable Transport a Social Science Perspective*, pp 171-190, Pergamon, Amsterdam.

Stærdahl, J., Schroll, H., Zakaria, Z., Abdullah, M., Dewar, N., and Panich, N. (2003), *Environmental Impact Assessment in Thailand, South Africa, Malaysia and Denmark*, Working report prepared within the Research network 'Critical Comparative Environmental Impact Assessment (EIA) in 4 countries', DANCED, Roskilde University.

Togeby, L., Andersen, J. G., Chistiansen, P. M., Jørgensen, T. B. and Vallgårda, S. (2003), *Magt og demokrati i Danmark: Hovedresultater fra magtudredningen*, Århus Universitetsforlag, Århus.

Torgerson, D. (1999), *The Promise of Green Politics Environmentalism and the Public Sphere*, Duke University Press, Durham.

Townsend, C. (2003), *In Whose Interest? A Critical Approach to Southeast Asia's Urban Transport Dynamics*, PhD Dissertation, Murdoch University.

Urry, J. (1991), 'Time and space in Gidden's social theory', in Bryant, C. and Jary, D. (eds), *Gidden's theory of structuration, A critical appreciation*, pp 160-175, Routledge, London.

Vejdirektoratet (2002), *Motorvej Herning – Århus ved Silkeborg. VVM-redegørelse Hovedrapport [Motorway Herning-Århus through Silkeborg, Environmental Impact Assessment Main Report]*, Rapport nr. 254.

Vestergaard, J.S. (1999), *At skynde sig langsomt, om bilisme [To hurry up slowly, on automobilism]*, Forlaget Klim, Århus.

Vestergaard, J. S. and Mattesen, F. (2003), *Ti år med Jyderne. Jyder mod Overflødige Motorvejes historie, idegrundlag og resultater [Ten years with People of Jutland Against Superflous Motorways, history, ideas and results]*, Klim, Århus.

Wagenaar, H. and Cook, N. (2003), 'Understanding Policy Practices: action, dialectic and deliberation in policy analysis', in Hajer, M. and Wagenaar, H. (eds), *Deliberative Policy Analysis*, pp 139-171, Cambridge University Press, Cambridge.

Whitelegg, J. (1997), *Critical Mass*, Pluto Press, London.

Witherspoon, S. (2004), 'Democracy, The Environment and Public Opinion in Western Europe', in Lafferty, W. and Meadowcroft, J. (eds), *Democracy and The Environment Problems and Prospects*, pp 39-70, Edward Elgar Publishing Limited, Cheltenham.

Epilogue

Mobility, Sustainability and Beyond

Henrik Gudmundsson, Thyra Uth Thomsen and
Lise Drewes Nielsen

Mobility, of course, cannot stand unquestioned. And surely, it doesn't. In these modern times most people – individuals, policy makers, researchers – are somehow aware that unlimited movement is but a dream, and a dangerous one at that. This dream is constantly being reproduced in a multitude of scenarios, from the grand narratives of policy designs to the 'civil society of auto-mobility', from the outputs of commercial image industries, to the 'compressed time-space' of everyday life. But the idea of a frictionless world does not feel quite as comfortable as it appears.

In the last decade or so *sustainability* has served as one of the key metaphors for framing this unease. Sustainability basically refers to concerns for the welfare of future as well as present generations considering the limited pressures that can safely be put on the life-support systems of Planet Earth. Mobility is an obvious target here because of its sheer physical volume, ubiquity and growth. Sustainability has therefore been added to other, longer-standing concerns over socio-economic side effects of transport developments, not least its immense toll in human lives, and the uneven social distribution of its benefits. Hence, notions such as 'sustainable mobility' have been coined as rhetorical constructions in an attempt to epitomize the need to contain the growth of physical transport within certain environmental, social and economic limits. Many official (and unofficial) bodies at local, national and global levels have pledged allegiance to this notion, while few, however, have dared to claim they actually deliver it.

The authors behind this volume are frustrated with some of the 'lived world' mobility developments, and share the unease embodied in the notion of sustainability. In fact, many of our efforts over the last decade – individually and as a group – have been devoted to addressing precisely this challenge and to bringing it to the forefront of our work. As evidenced in the book, this has led us deep into various aspects of transport, mobility and policy, some of them in close connection with sustainability, others seemingly more remote from it. We have all felt a need to explore what the 'lived world' of mobility looks like and how it works, not least to be better equipped to understand possible interventions in it. As should be evident from the contributions, we do not see this 'real world', only as physical infrastructures, traffic flows and supply chains, but fully as much of concepts, institutions, story lines and other social constructions that serve to frame, guide and sometimes confuse human actions. We have each in our own way sought a better understanding of the roles of mobility – and its concepts and institutions – in daily life, in the performance of companies, in research and in the development of policies – and counter policies. We hope to have contributed in this way to elevating mobility from being considered as merely a 'technical' tool for which demands are entirely driven from other, more 'fundamental', needs to standing as an issue of social interrogation in its own right. In short, we have been looking for its formative *and* restraining powers *vis-a-vis* modern society and contemporary policy, and this search has only just begun.

Now, however, after having reported our findings in this ongoing quest, we again have felt a need to reflect over the challenge of sustainability and our concerns for it. This may, after all, still be one of the most important 'social perspectives on mobility' that needs considering. The aim of the reflection was not directly to review the contributions of each chapter in the book, but rather to reconsider our own 'habitus' as mobility researchers. The key question we asked ourselves was therefore not only: How can our research contribute answers to the question of sustainability, but also: what does it mean to us now? We also felt compelled to share the results of this discussion with others at this point, not only to pay our tributes to a critical research agenda but hopefully also to inspire colleagues in a similar position. This final section of the book is therefore an attempt to reflect on our subsequent discussions of sustainability, rather than a 'backward' review of the previous chapters.

Our discussion quickly revealed two potential dangers to the very idea of sharing sustainability as a critical research perspective on mobility:

The first danger is to subscribe fully, as researchers, to notions like 'sustainable mobility' that have been defined in a political context. In fact there are many ambiguities in the attempts to wed sustainability and mobility directly. How much mobility can the planet sustain? How much mobility do modern societies need? Who should decide the one or the other? Questions like that cannot be answered simply if we recognise the many different shapes and forms mobility assumes, and the many dimensions and scales to sustainability. In fact 'sustainable mobility' means quite different things to different people, and this could weaken its role for both research and practice. In short it is imprecise, sensitive to strategic interpretation, and somewhat bound to a particular context in time, space and discourse. This does not mean that we want to give up sustainability again. However, these risks suggest that we need to be rather *precise* about what this 'link' between mobility and sustainability means to each of us, we need to be *specific* as to how it should be approached analytically, and we must be *modest* in terms of what detailed insights in the 'lived world' we can expect it to deliver.

The second danger is to let normative confusion over sustainability scare us into our own little ivory towers. The understanding of mobility that would emerge from such a fragmented and disinterested research approach may well be that mobility is deeply embedded in modernity; that it is highly complex and that reformative policies therefore are bound to produce ineptitude, irrationality, inertia etc. Such insights may be critical to understanding the conditions for achieving sustainability, but they also need to be challenged. Otherwise the very elevation of mobility to a core defining tenet of contemporary society may lead to *reification.* A paraphrase of this position could read: "Without mobility (as we know it) modern society could not exist; and therefore we must accept it as a given fact". If such a view were taken too far we would close the door to possible changes in modern society of which we are only vaguely aware (or mobility, as we *don't* know it yet). Mobility would hardly have emerged as a research topic at all if no one had felt intrigued by its massive social and environmental interruptions, and if no one, indeed, had wanted to challenge the shortcomings of conventional, piecemeal research in dealing with them. This does not mean that we would abandon again in-depth research of the mobility/modernity nexus, but these risks suggest a need to be *reflexive* in our own accounts of mobility, to keep in contact with the *consciousness* that led us into the study of it, and to continue be *open* to insights that can be gained from other views.

Upon further reflection we found that producing this volume together has demonstrated our potential to balance between those dangers and still share a common view: We can study the drivers of mobility in detail, and still be aware of its negative implications. We can acknowledge the key roles mobility plays in the lives of people and organisations, without reducing it to essentially one indifferent choice (e.g. car or not; bridge or not; road or nature). We can scrutinize mobility policies and their formation without taking their rationales for granted, we can even turn them against themselves and ask: whose values, what effectiveness, which sustainability?

We also found, however, that our roles as researchers in this respect can not always be the same: There may be a time to sharpen the knife of sustainability as a critical norm; there may be a time to analyse the systemic barriers that would block the realisation of it, and there may be a time to explore the strategic terrain of discourse where battles over norms and realities are fought (or at least reflected). We may even divide the tasks between us according to capacity, interest and external obligations. But to maintain a meaningful dialogue among us (avoid the first danger) and still keep our critical horizons open (evade the second one), we need first to recognise the value of each contribution and each approach, and secondly also to be prepared to discuss their limitations and blind spots within some broader scheme, in which sustainability would be one, if not necessarily the only, critical question to be asked. Such a scheme could perhaps be called *reflexive mobility research.*

In the following, we have identified not one but six different ways to approach the sustainability/mobility nexus as researchers. Each of them has its merits, but also its shortcomings that we also need to take note of. Each of them has echoes in the various chapters of the book, but as already said, the reflections aim to go beyond them. After briefly describing each approach, a few summary remarks pointing beyond sustainability are added as a conclusion.

a) Sustainability as Systemic Reflexivity

From a realist point of view, sustainability can be made operational with criteria like ecosystem limits, resource constraints, and economic savings rules. Such criteria can be built into societal planning frameworks; sets of targets and performance indicators to measure them can be identified, and procedures for adjustments in policies based on feedback can be set up. In this way sustainability (or at least some aspects of it) may be integrated as 'systemic reflexivity' for learning in societal sub-systems (local, national, global). Planning frameworks of this kind have in fact been used to problematise critical transport/mobility trends, from the emissions of Carbon Dioxide, to the unfavourable developments in transport prices. However this 'policy planning' approach often rests on very contestable assumptions about rationality, and the actual impact of these systems on societal learning towards sustainability has yet to be demonstrated. Research tasks in this dimension would therefore not only involve the definition of fuller sets of sustainability/mobility indicators, but also explore the cognitive, institutional and political contexts in which 'reflexive' monitoring systems are or could become embedded.

b) Sustainability as Individual Reflexivity

Sustainability is not a concern that is only confined to a systemic level. As should be clear, individual actions have implications not only for immediate mobility but also long term effects (e.g. sustainability). In order to make a difference in practice, these effects also need to be reflected at the level of the individual social actors that have to adapt their behaviour. In fact, we now know that most people (car drivers, operators, forwarders, etc), are well aware of the environmental and social effects of mobility and the resulting dilemmas and paradoxes, and this may nurture some optimism on behalf of sustainability. But strong mechanisms often seem to keep these concerns from influencing individual practice, 'structural stories' being but one of them. There is a need for further research to explore the conditions for 'disturbing' the unfavourable links between perceptions and actions in order to enable a sustainability-oriented practice. Meanwhile, it is necessary to keep in mind that reflexivity-driven changes in behaviour at the individual level in the long run are also dependent upon changes also in systemic conditions (policies, market structures, norm systems etc).

c) Sustainability as a Front of Contestation

The wide scope of sustainability, with its many dimensions and possible interpretations, means that it appeals to actors throughout all sectors of society and across the globe from north to south. While this wide scope may itself sometimes confuse interaction, it also bears the potential to unite individual or 'private' protests in a wider front against critical trends in mobility. In fact sustainability serves as a shared reference point for many critical interventions, including debates about urban car traffic, predict-and-provide-policies, specific transport investments etc. The integrative, holistic qualities of the sustainability concept may thereby in fact help to bring together different voices that would otherwise not hear one another, and it could thus potentially help to condense a framework for a general contestation of current mobility patterns and policies. There are, however, likely to be crucial conditions for these different voices to sing in harmony, and for them to be listened to. Research would be needed to try to understand the common denominators of these various mobility contestations and the role that concepts like sustainability and mobility could play in uniting (but potentially also in frustrating or even diverting) them.

d) Sustainability as a Strategic Construction

Sustainability is frequently used in political discourse not only by 'protesters' against automobilism, but also by its staunchest advocates. Such use of the term should not necessarily be assumed to signify political capacity and/or will to adapt practices according to 'realist' notions of limits let alone 'radicalist' calls for change. But what does it then signify? The prominent strategic use of sustainability concepts calls for analyses of interests and powers that are operative in policy documents and political discourses. To that effect, an analysis of strategic language use in order to interpret and possibly even deconstruct sustainability needs to be added as another research perspective. The main risk here could be the one of relativism. If any sense of a meaning of sustainability *beyond the texts* is lost then its critical potential may disappear in the countless definitions and interpretations – but even that may be an important lesson in its own right.

e) Sustainability as a Limited Notion

Whatever way sustainability may be defined, perceived or constructed, its realisation in practice is bound to meet obstacles of many kinds. To achieve sustainability, the mechanisms that produce (potential) unsustainability should certainly catch our attention. These mechanism are at play everywhere in the policies, practices and perceptions of mobility, and not least in the socio-political frameworks that surround them: From the travel habits of an individual to the systemic reforms of public transport systems; from the organisational practices of a transport company to the restructuring of global supply chains. Already these few examples demonstrate that it may be hard to draw a limit as to what is an important barrier to sustainability and what is not. Rather than trying to make this impossible distinction here, we would instead stipulate that sustainability in order to remain a productive critical notion may need research to clarify how it connects to a range of other, more 'established' concerns, from safety and security on the one side to efficiency and democracy at the other. This could potentially help a sustainability agenda to draw systematically from a wide range of critical research – but this could also lead to diminishing its role as necessarily 'the' overarching approach to question mobility.

f) Sustainability as an Interdisciplinary Invitation

Finally, sustainability represents – taking into account the broad range of issues drawn up in the above – not least a challenge to 'methodological myopia' (as in Denmark and elsewhere presently a tendency to frame all policy issues within a narrow cost-benefit or exchange value perspective). Sustainability strongly suggests recognising economic assets and concerns as well, yes, but it does not necessarily imply epistemological closure to deal with them. This multi-disciplinary implication of sustainability, drawing from an integrated system view, reinforces the general approach to mobility explored in this book, and this is perhaps our most widely shared commitment beyond the basic critical horizon: We need sustainability to keep talking to one another....

Beyond Sustainability

All in all we do see sustainability as a notion that still carries substantial and needed critical potentials. It evokes responsibilities for environmental and social protection that are constantly at risk of erosion from myopic decision-making, perceived structural necessities and strategic actions, and these responsibilities are in need of conceptual support as well as institutional safeguarding.

But we are also concerned that sustainability has been applied so widely and with so little genuine action for change ensuing that we see a serious risk for it to lose its abilities to *both unite and bite*. Sustainability represents a normative inspiration and guideline, but it may not necessarily exhaust, let alone aggregate, the full list of normative concerns that should be taken into account in critical analysis of mobility and its policies. It helps to pose important analytical questions to our understanding of mobility and its limits, but it does not by itself define or fully convey the analytical tools by which to explore and understand its constitutive factors. It enjoys a prominent strategic position, but this position is vulnerable to both 'capture' by various political interests and to 'cacophonia' in the wider debates. While these weaknesses do not make us reject it, we are perhaps now altogether more cautions about it than we were before.

All in all this means that not only mobility but also sustainability needs a reflective dimension to it, and we hope that by staging this debate in public we may have contributed in a small measure to achieving just that.

Index